AROUND THE WORLD IN

80GAMES

THE EARTH SHAPED BALL

AROUND THE WORLD IN

80 GAMES

THE EARTH SHAPED BALL

STEVE McCLUSKIE

ISBNs:
Paperback: 978-1-80541-483-4
eBook: 978-1-80541-482-7

for Tash
forever young, forever loved

CONTENTS

INTRODUCTION

It's funny what goes through your mind when you're wired up to a machine in intensive care. It was January 24th 2015, the day after my 46th birthday. That morning I'd had the worst asthma attack of my life. I'd been rushed to hospital a few times before, but this was on another level. Blacking out in the ambulance, I eventually opened my eyes to find myself in a hospital bed soaked in sweat. I'd been fighting for my life and the doctors were amazed I'd pulled through. Things had to change and quickly.

I was born and raised high up in the Rossendale Valley, East Lancashire, where dinner is tea, the men are men and the sheep are worried. Growing up, I loved those films like The Great Race, Those Magnificent Men in their Flying Machines and Around the World in 80 Days. Everything seemed so unrestricted, colourful and exotic, and above all so totally different to my quiet, cobbled street and whippet existence (Yes, I had both. How northern can you get?) I'd always seen myself as an adventurer, but apart from a few short forays into the unknown, I'd hardly been intrepid. With my son Danny all grown up and ready to fly the nest, this felt like my last chance to fulfil my globetrotting dreams, before my lungs packed in altogether. I knew my travels had to somehow involve my love of the beautiful game......

It had taken me a while to admit it, but I was against modern football. I love my club and have supported them from the terraces since I was 12 years old. What I couldn't escape though was the overwhelming feeling that I, like millions of others, was being had. Our game had been taken off us, re-packaged and sold back to us as if we should be grateful. The great grandchildren of the millions of working-class people, who had been the lifeblood of the game for over a century, were now at the mercy of ravenous commercial interests, preying on club loyalties passed down through the generations. I was tired of the billionaires, the Blatters and the boardroom behemoths, and it was a crime against football that those legions of loyal traveling fans were being completely overlooked when the suits were arranging daft kick-off times to fit TV schedules. Add to that the growing disconnect between players and fans at the top level, and the picture was looking grim.

However, in amongst the saturating media coverage, Ronaldo's garish goal celebration and the full-sleeve designer tattoos stands the one simple truth: nobody, not even you Sheikh Mansour, can ever *own* the game. As long as there are banana leaves in Uganda and tin cans in Lancashire, football will always belong to the people.

As a kid I'd been obsessed. Every evening and weekend I'd take my ball to the local field to see if I could get a game going; jumpers for goalposts and all that. We'd play on until the night swallowed the ball, returning home muddy, exhausted and exhilarated; replaying goals, missed chances, finger-tip saves, great passes and last gasp tackles over and over in our minds. Stories were written and heroes were made. The game was simple. The game was everything. In exactly the same way, far from the voracious commercialism of the modern game, I decided there and then, gasping for breath in my hospital bed, that I was going to try and go around the world in 80 games. Armed with just four jumpers and a ball, I'd invite people in villages, towns and cities to come and join in the unadulterated magic of a game of footy.

What happened next was beyond my wildest dreams.

KICK OFF

GAMES 1-15

AUSTRALIA-NEW ZEALAND-THAILAND-CAMBODIA-
VIETNAM-CHINA-JAPAN-SOUTH KOREA

GAME 1: AUSTRALIA

Date: March 6th 2016, 12.45pm
Ground: Murray Park Oval, Adelaide

TONY DORIGO'S DAD

Breathless and bog-eyed I boarded my plane for Adelaide, Australia, 10,000 miles from home.

The first leg of the journey was on a deluxe A380 airbus from Manchester to Dubai. There I sat in spacious economy comfort, watching films with loosened top button and belt, happily sending silent little farts out into the cabin's beigeness. At no point did I feel like I was flying. This was in total contrast to the eleven hours I then spent sardined on a 747 down to Adelaide.

The best bit about cramped flying is when you're jammed in the middle of two other passengers and you need a pee, especially when you've just had your meal and the trays have yet to be collected. I was like a horse let loose in a lamp shop. Within seconds of standing, I'd managed to stick my thumb in a chicken dinner, whack my head on an overhead locker, then trip over a flailing headphone wire, which sent me lunging across the aisle to come face to face with a startled portly woman shoveling in a sherbet lemon.

My travelling companions were the very lovely Helen to my right and Graham to my left. Helen was a young trainee nurse from Kenya. Her vibrancy and beautiful black shining skin made me feel about as attractive as a bleached and wrinkled big toe. Graham was an earthy, gravelly voiced chap from Huddersfield who had been born old. We all got along famously on this mammoth journey.

My mate Christian Wilson picked me up from Adelaide airport. We'd been to college together in Burnley, Lancashire many moons ago, when The Housemartins' "London 0 Hull 4" album was never off the turntable. Chris, a proud Yorkshireman, is funny, off-beat and generous to a fault, though his habit of striding around in just his skin-tight underpants would compromise even the most affable wombat. I stayed for a week with him and his wife Robbie in tranquil Magill, Campbelltown. Their young children, Archie and Charlie, plus Ziggy the darting, collapsing sheepdog were also in residence, as were four barking frogs.

I spent the first few days adjusting to the jet-lag and being shown around this sedate capital city of the state of South Australia. Under stunning evening skies, and to the sound of lunatic, screaming cockatoos bringing daylight to a close, Chris and I watched some great games of local football, including the team he coached, St. Peter's. I also caught up with an old mate from home whom I used to play football with. Gavin Park was a great striker back in the day. Faster than a toupee in a hurricane, you could play any sort of decent through ball to him and we were virtually guaranteed a goal. As for my mission, I must admit I didn't have a clue where to start. With only three days to go before my departure for New Zealand, it was time to move my hairy bum.

THE GAME.......

"I made the run so why didn't you pass you greedy bastard?" "Don't call me a greedy bastard you greedy bastard!"

Chris mentioned that a group of older men had a kick-about in the nearby Murray Park Oval every Sunday. On a steaming hot late Sunday morning, we wandered up there to find to find a 7 v 8 in full flow. The swearing was terrific. These greying and balding men were playing as if their lives depended on it - bollocking and badgering each other with all the intensity of their younger selves. It was a colourful and wonderful spectacle. There were Aussies, Italians, Croats and Greeks; azzurri blue shirts mixed with crimson bibs, Aussie gold and a wide assortment of different coloured ankle strappings and knee supports. Chris donned his boots to even up the numbers.

Although a captive audience, if ever there was a perfect way to start my journey then this was it. A group of blokes in their senior years, still playing for playing's sake and loving every minute of it. Chris and I chatted to them during their half-time break, and some agreed to join us for a kick-about at the end of their match. In the two minutes it took me to plonk my jumpers down on the grass in readiness, I was drenched with sweat. I will never know how those chaps carried on to complete another 45 minutes in that cauldron.

Shattered, but driven on by the spirit of the game, eight of these fellows eventually came over to play with us. They spoke of how they remembered playing in parks and streets like this as children, and how important it had been for them, not only in terms of enjoyment, but in learning about courage and camaraderie. Watching them play at close quarters was magical. Although exhausted, they were all still hungry for the ball, looking for space, trying clever one-twos and flicks and tricks, and forensically dissecting shots that may or may not have crept inside the sleeve of a jumper. The game was still everything to them, and they captured its essence perfectly.

We played a 5 v 5 for around half an hour, the game ending all square at 2-2. The lads invited Chris and I for a beer afterwards. Sitting in the shade of the stand, I asked if any of them would be up for a quick interview. "Hey! Dorigo! He wants an interview". Dorigo? No! Couldn't be? I asked the man walking towards me if he was related to ex-Leeds United and England left back Tony Dorigo. "Yes. He's my son". Tony Dorigo's Dad! Here in this park, today of all days. What crazy fortune! Being a Leeds fan, Chris was pretty chuffed to meet him too.

What an absolute gentleman Bobby Dorigo turned out to be. He told us stories of his son's playing days and what he was up to now, and about how much he loves meeting up with the lads in the park every Sunday for a game, a beer and sometimes a barbecue. When I asked Bobby what he thought about the billion-dollar industry that is the English Premier

League, he said, "Money is always helpful, but you have to give it to the right people". He had a keen dislike of referees, but thought the game was generally on the up in Australia. Finally, when asked to sum up his feelings about the game, he took a long, satisfying swig of his beer and said, "It's not a hobby, it's a way of life". With that, the 72-year-old Bobby Dorigo, who looked not a day over 52, rejoined his gang of football-daft mates, whose average age turned out to be 65.

In the car on our way to the airport, conversation turned to the meaning of life. Chris said that we can waste a lifetime thinking about questions like that and it's better just to live. Bobby and his enduring footy warriors were certainly doing that. I was off and running but with no real plan. What would be would be…

GAME 2: NEW ZEALAND

Date: March 10th 2016, 12.30pm
Ground: Central Bus Station, Christchurch

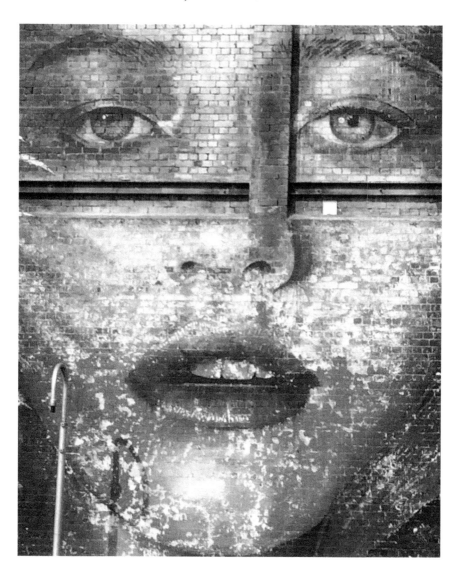

EVERYTHING IS GOING TO BE ALRIGHT

Cranes, drills and artists' spray cans work the streets
to build from the havoc that earthquakes wreak

Distant place but something close
Unity in the face of loss
Here I am in another man's land
But it's mine
It's yours
It's us

It doesn't matter what you throw
We drop, we hold, then throw it back
Says the neon sign to the new tender night
'Everything is going to be alright'

On the 22nd February 2011, 185 people lost their lives in the Christchurch earthquake. Five years on and the city skyline is still dominated by cranes. The streets shake now from the pounding machinery as the people fight to re-build from the rubble.

The city's artists and imagineers were among the first to plant the seeds of renewal. At the forefront of this were Gap Filler, a creative urban regeneration initiative. They began as a response to the September 2010 earthquake, and their work continued after the 2011 disaster. Projects included an outdoor cinema driven by the pedal power of the cinema goers, and the Dance-O-Mat, which is an open-air urban dance space with a coin-operated washing machine powering its four speakers. This proved a real hit with daytime shoppers and night-time revelers alike. Gap Filler quite literally got the city moving again.

Many incredible murals now adorne walls left exposed after the earthquake. Buses turned into bars, wasteland into garden cafes. One of the most striking and affecting ideas was the white chair installation on the corner of Cashel and Madras Street. People were invited to come and paint white any of the 185 donated old chairs, of all shapes and sizes, in remembrance of those who had died. Some of the victims' relatives came and painted a chair that they felt their lost love ones would have liked to have sat on. With the painting now complete, the sight of the empty chairs was both moving and haunting. With the installation now becoming weather beaten, artist Pete Majendie is pushing for it to be relocated, possibly across the road at the site of the old television centre, where 115 people lost their lives in the disaster.

This spontaneous explosion of creative energy breathed hope and colour back into a devastated city and its people. With plans now on the table to create a multi-million dollar revamp, including a convention centre and a 35,000-seater multi-purpose stadium, it would be great to think that those incredible artists and innovators will continue to be allowed to infuse the city with their soul and imagination.

THE GAME...

I met Adam and Mark on their lunchbreak at a cafe right outside Christchurch Central Bus Station. They were scaffolders working on a new-build opposite. Mark was from Northern Ireland and Adam from Macclesfield, England.

As we chatted, Mark took off his work boots, grabbed my footy and started doing some keepy-ups. Adam, despite his knee being tender from a cruciate ligament injury, couldn't resist joining in. Off came the boots and the game was on. A stray pass landed at the feet of one Mandeep Singh, a splendid looking chap who was just about to cross the road. He returned the ball and jumped at the chance to play. Just then, Simon, suitably from Christchurch in Bournemouth, England, sat down for a brew a few feet away. He agreed to play and, before we knew it, the jumpers were down and we had a 2 v 2 going on in a postage stamp space outside the station.

The two strapping scaffolders started well and looked clear favourites. Mandeep had other ideas. The man was on fire, pulling Cruyff turns every two minutes. Some talent for a lad from Chandigarh, India, obsessed with cricket. With Simon in his nets throwing incredibly effective *break dancer meets tantric sex-fiend* shapes, the underdogs quickly raced into a 2-0 lead. The boys in the high-vis jackets were not happy. Sweating like a glass-blowers arse, they worked hard and clawed back the deficit. "Next goal's the winner" shouted Adam, as the lads had to get back to work.

Focus was total. One mistake and it was all over. After a tense period, with players risking their lives to retrieve the ball from the busy main road, the breakthrough finally came. Mark and Mandeep went in for a tackle and the ball spilt invitingly to Adam who tucked it away with some aplomb. Tantric Simon had finally reached orgasm and lay flat out in the nets.

A funny, fast and spontaneous game with some great chaps. I sat and chatted with Mandeep for a good while afterwards in the bus station. He told me how he was not allowed to leave his high school until he could speak 5 languages proficiently and said his parents had saved for over ten years so that he could now study in New Zealand. He was tired of people judging him because he wore a turban and felt that those people should concentrate less on him and more on enjoying life because it was so short. Well said that man.

GAME 3: NEW ZEALAND

Date: March 12th 2016, 7.00pm
Ground: Latimer Square - Christchurch

LOST JOSH AND THE DREAM

Did this day really happen?

Although game two had been brilliant, I was desperate to engage some Kiwi's in a game of 'soccer', the third most popular sport in these rugby and cricket loving islands.

I needed to get out and about, and there is no better way to do that in Christchurch than on the bus. With Canterbury 92.9 FM knocking out the classics, each ride was a real pleasure. I had Neil Young (Harvest Moon), Bob Marley (Could you be loved) and The Stranglers (Golden Brown) all on my first twenty-minute journey. I would travel all over Christchurch for just $3.50 a day. The bus drivers themselves were Gods and Goddesses from Planet Manners Cost Nowt. One driver told me I'd got on the wrong bus at the wrong place, but then drove me the mile to my stop, despite this deviating from his route. All the passengers clapped as I alighted, wishing me a great time in their city. As the bus pulled away, I stood in the street with a silly smile on my face, aglow in the kindness of these lovely folk.

I whizzed around town in these happy carriages all week, until on Saturday March 12th, my friend with whom I was staying, the very wise and wonderful Sine Stewart, dropped me and my ball down at New Brighton Beach. My head almost popped when I saw the stunning white sands and the vast, glorious rolling ocean. Removing my boots and socks, I stepped onto the beach and into another dimension. I came round some hours later with pants rolled up to my knees, wet legs and sandy feet. My pockets were full of shells and the cool wind blowing up from the Southern Ocean felt beautiful on my sun-burnt skin. I was taking a photograph of an ethereal washed-up, bleached white tree when a voice said, "What do you find interesting about that?". I turned to see a woman in her 50s, looking at me with kind eyes. I explained the journey I was on, and she said that she knew it… she knew when she saw me that I had her son's spirit within me. Her son Bruce had been an artist who loved travelling and randomly filming people and places. Sadly, he had taken his own life the year before, aged only 27. She told me that she kept him alive by talking about him and seeing him in others.

This touching moment had the effect of knocking me back into the day. I looked at the time and was astonished to find that six hours had passed.

This place had unlocked an overwhelmingly blissful world within me; the highest natural high I had ever felt. I wandered off the beach and into nearby Rawhiti Park, where a large Māori family were gathered to celebrate a child's birthday. I asked some of the cousins loitering on the periphery if they fancied a game. They said they would if I could find a few more players, so off I went in pursuit. The very next person I spoke to was a huge, huge young man made of granite sat on a wall. He stood up to greet me and blocked out the sun. I felt the size of a flea's willy as he crushed my hand in his huge mitt. "Wrong shaped ball mate" he boomed. "No bother at all big man" I spluttered, with all that was left of me as a man. Wringing my hand to get the blood flowing again, I continued my search for players, but it soon became obvious that the Māori women were not too keen on anyone playing soccer on this celebration day, so off I sloped.

On my way back to the heart of the sleepy seaside town of New Brighton, I noticed a few people on the pier gazing down at the beach. I joined them to see a man raking a perfect giant flower in the sand. Was I back in that other dimension? Leaving the pier and strolling through the remains of the Saturday open-air market, an elderly woman stepped in front of me and asked me to dance. We danced a few steps and she told me that she still had the magic. My dream was complete. It was time to head back to the city.

THE GAME........

Christchurch City Mission feeds and provides shelter for the city's homeless. Returning from the beach, I popped my head in for a nosey and was greeted on entrance by a lovely chap called Keith. There were around twenty people sat at tables in the dining area. Keith insisted that I join them, then recited the Lord's Prayer before food was served. I sat across from Kevin at tea. In another life he would have been a big handsome film-star, with his big black bushy beard, lovely warm brown eyes and a gentleness that belied his size. It turned out he was from Bolton, England originally and had fallen on hard times due to mental health issues.

After eating, the young charismatic Julian Rata Moka, a support worker, entered the building. Julian had only been employed at the mission for a couple of months, but was clearly a popular figure. The first thing he did was offer me shelter for the night and more food if I needed it. I thanked him before explaining my presence. We chatted for a while about his work, the homelessness issues in the city and also the Māori tribal traditions. He explained that his mother was pākehā (a white New Zealander) and his father was Māori. His Iwi (tribe) was Ngāpuhi and his Hapu (sub-tribe) was Ngāti Hine.

Julian suggested I should have a game in Latimer Square, about a hundred yards up the road (Latimer Square had been the site of a rapidly assembled makeshift hospital after the 2011 earthquake). He helped me to recruit for the game, and off I marched to the square with three eager players. Tony was a rough and tough Scouser who had lived in Christchurch for 15 years. He was a bit worse for wear off the beer, repeatedly asking me if I was a Liverpool fan and showing me the "Scouse Forever" tattoo encircling his left nipple. Tall Josh, a young Kiwi, was chatty in a one-to-one situation, but a mouse in a crowd. He could spin a ball on his finger and was spending his first night at the mission. Then there was Lost Josh. He was also a Kiwi. With the muscle tone and grace of a ballet dancer, Lost Josh seemed to exist in a place far out of the reach of us mere mortals. He smiled a lot, hardly spoke and pirouetted around the pitch all night in his vest. He had a kindness, a gentleness, but ultimately a heart-breaking sadness about him.

At the far end of the grassy Latimer Square, some of the city's homeless were gathering for the 7.30pm food van. I wandered over and asked if anyone fancied a game. Three players stepped forward; another Josh, who I'll call Aragorn Josh, as he had the hood and demeanor of that hairy warrior from Lord of the Rings; Shona, who was deaf and all smiles and bouncing with energy, and Johnny, who I think was Shona's partner, all wiry and mountain climber-like. 3 v 3 in Latimer Square. An all-Kiwi affair except for Tony.

Tony, Shona and Johnny teamed up against all the Joshes. It was clear from the start that there was a bit of needle between Johnny and Tall Josh. They could both play a bit. God bless Tony. He ran his little body into the ground until his head turned purple, then went in the nets. Aragorn Josh stayed in goal, quiet in his oversized wellies with his hood up, no doubt plotting the downfall of Sauron. Shona played with guts and determination throughout and never stopped running. Lost Josh went in for tackles like he was auditioning for Swan Lake; a ragged angel now in his dirty vest, laughing at the absurdity of the world.

The odd random person turned up, played a pass or had a shot then moved on, but it wasn't until the stray dogs turned up that we lost count of the score. In all the excitement, these deadly black canines were running wild and literally started biting players' ankles. The game was finally over when some of the troops drifted off to join the food van queue.

Tony, Lost Josh and I sat down on a bench looking up at the evening sky. It was absolutely stunning. The glorious blue peppered with white cotton wool clouds, and the sun, trying to be ignored, sliding out of sight behind us. Tony and I chatted about how amazing our world is. Lost Josh smiled up at the heavens, and the heavens smiled right back at him. Later that night we had a small earthquake.

GAME 4: NEW ZEALAND

Date: March 13th 2016, 2.00pm
Ground: Hagley Park, Christchurch

FETCH IT FELIX

In Christchurch, New Zealand, time just hangs in the air, perfectly balanced. You can push it along or slow it right down if you wish, but somehow it persuades you to leave it just where it is. From my first day in the city, listening to young Scottish busker Paul Shearon belting out my favourite John Martyn tunes from the *Solid Air* album, to Lost Josh and the beauty and wonder of the New Brighton beach dream, I had connected with this stoic south-island city on a deep, spiritual level.

I stayed with Sine and her partner Michael during my time in Christchurch. Sine is an amazingly brainy, caring and astute woman whom I used to work with in England twenty years ago. She works in children's services in Rapanui. Michael is a petrol-head and a hot-crossed bun loving Kiwi with a dry sense of humour. He was a project manager for the Christchurch Earthquake Recovery Authority. They had both been working as I had been wandering, so I was chuffed when Sine said she'd try and rally a few mates for my final game on her day off.

THE GAME.......

On a hot Sunday afternoon, I met with Sine (a Scot) and her friends, Merran (a Kiwi) and James (an Englishman), in the huge Hagley Park, the largest urban open space in the city. We needed more players.

Fabienne 'Fabi' Wagner, John Walcher (both Germans) and Guus Bremmers (a Dutchman) were having a picnic behind a nearby tree. I asked them if they fancied a game. Within five minutes they had packed up their basket and joined us. I then hijacked Felix and Hannah (also from Germany) who had been strolling through the park. Matt (a Kiwi) then joined us and the game was on. A 5 v 5 in very humid conditions.

It was the Germans and Dutch against everyone else. The German keeper, "Fetch it Felix", just whacked the ball for miles whenever it came near him; standing there with a crazed smile on his face, like he had an ice-pop stuck up his bum, whilst some hilariously silent, pissed off player sloped off after the ball. Despite Sine and Merran's work rate, and Matt and James' speculative shots from anywhere, they were no match for Dutch total football and the German midfield machine, who ran out easy 5-1 winners. Although having just met, their collective, telepathic and instinctive passing and movement was a joy to watch. The player of the match was Fabi. Possessed with a real football brain, she operated craftily in pockets of space, silently and skillfully controlling the game.

We all went for a bit of a social afterwards. An international group of strangers brought together through a kick-about. My New Zealand experience had given me the inner peace that I needed to continue on to south east Asia. Travelling so far from home with a health condition can be daunting. My lungs were struggling a bit with the humidity, but I was confident I'd be ok. I boarded the plane bound for Bangkok with a new found energy and optimism.

GAME 5: THAILAND

Date: March 16th 2016, 7.00pm
Ground: F.B.T Sport Park, Lat Krabang

FEELING THE HEAT

Flying up from Christchurch to Bangkok via Auckland and Kuala Lumpur had been grueling.

I landed in Bangkok at 1.25am local time. The heat was incredible. Suvarnabhumi Airport was a giant oven and everyone in it was cooking at gas mark 200. Trying to find my exit for the airport transfer to my hotel was a Crystal Maze special. I needed to be on floor 2, but all the lifts and escalators seemed only to take me to floors 1, 3 & 4. I felt like I was walking about in an Escher drawing. I'm sure all the airport staff were in on the act as they sent my knackered, over-heating pale body in every direction but the one I needed. Eventually, a Spanish dude pointed the way whilst twiddling on his 1920s 'man goes swimming in all-in-one stripy bathing costume' moustache.

I stayed at the Great Residence Hotel in Lat Krabang, an eastern district of Bangkok. The Grand Budapest Hotel it was not. Like every dodgy estate agent's photographs, the hotel bore no resemblance whatsoever to the splendour depicted on the website. The large inviting swimming pool, for example, was just about big enough for two teenage Chihuahuas with armbands. The staff were comically grumpy, though they had their reasons. Super long hours, low pay in extreme heat running after guys like me. I'd be grumpy too. Sod customer service, where's the pay rise and the 5-day week?

After a deep sleep, I woke up in a mentally strange place. All that travelling across different time-zones and those amazing shenanigans in Australia and New Zealand had left me a shell of a chap. I headed to the tiny pool to revitalize myself. When I got there, the two teenage Chihuahuas were drying themselves off and having a beer. It was 6pm in the oppressively humid evening when I gathered up my ball and jumpers and headed out. My head was still battered, and my whole body was showering sweat as I strolled past Lat Krabang's teeming night market. No tourists ventured there. I was the only guy with bright white legs and freckles for a thousand miles, and I drew many a glance and snigger. Headphones in, The Gaslight Anthem's brilliant *"American Slang"* album was keeping me going. I continued walking by the side of the moped-choked main road, until I came across a dream; a park completely over-run with people of all ages playing footy. In my fragile state, I almost wept.

THE GAME........

I had no energy or brain power left. I just went in there, threw down my jumpers and stared at people like a deranged desert survivor, ball tucked under my arm. Two smiley fellows spotted me and wandered over. Fan, a guy wearing a 'Torres' Spain top, said "Me Arsenal. You?" "Liverpool," I said (bit of an upgrade on Tarzan and Jane I thought). We then smiled insanely at each other for a few seconds.

Before starting out on this trip, to entice people to play and to avoid being seen as the pervert in the park, I'd typed up notes in different languages explaining my mission. I showed Fan the Thai version, and his friend then ran off to find players. It was replica shirt-a-go-go. The Premier League tentacles had certainly stretched to this spot, as a group of lads, wearing mainly Liverpool, Man United and Arsenal shirts, darted over to play. The eldest player asked if he could wear what was my last 'Around the World in 80 Games' t-shirt. I knew it was a gonner as soon I gave it him…bleedin' tea-leaf.

A quality 6 v 6 game ensued. Each team played with a good shape and demonstrated neat, incisive play from start to finish. The short passing from the smaller ones especially was joyful to watch, their concentration total. They had learnt the game from football purists, with groans all around if the ball flew in the air. Tackling wasn't the best, but there was a manic desire from all the lads to find space to receive a pass. A small crowd had gathered. Aware of this, the intensity on the pitch increased. The reds took the lead with a neat one-two and finish, then the other reds equalized with seconds to go. In the end, a really enjoyable 1-1 draw.

The game had been a lucky fluke. The lads were already playing and it wasn't as random as I would have liked. However, I comforted myself in the fact that this used to happen all the time when I was kid, with new games breaking out here, there and everywhere on the same pitch. So I'm claiming it and you can all sod off. It had been worth it to see the enthusiasm on those kids faces tonight, and to witness their intelligent passing game for ones so young.

At this early stage in my journey, I was still very much finding my feet. I wanted to document everything, but also join in the games. It was proving tricky to photograph, film and play at the same time. These first world problems were simply awful Rupert. I would just have to be patient and let things evolve naturally.

GAME 6: THAILAND

Date: March 18th 2016, 7.00pm
Ground: Koh Tao (Turtle Island)

PARADISE SURPRISE

Have you ever seen Scooby Doo, Zombie Island? Well if you haven't, and your thing is to party with loads of young, hip, scuba-diving, loose-walking, smooth-talking, toned-bodied world travelers, then Koh Tao is for you. As you can imagine, I fitted right in.

My son Daniel, 20 at the time, had already been travelling for 6 weeks when he wound up on this paradise island. I had a small window of opportunity to surprise him during my five-night stay in Thailand, so I flew down to Koh Samui from Bangkok, then caught the ferry up to Koh Tao. The look on his face when I turned up unexpected in the bar area at his hotel was a classic. It was around lunchtime, and he was nursing a cracking hangover, wrapped in his comforting blue kimono. It was fantastic to see him after so long.

Everyone on Koh Tao had a moped. I tried to hire one myself, but after firing it up and having a try, the rental chap ran out in front of me screaming "Don't do it! You'll kill someone!" much to my son's amusement. So, jumping on the back of Danny's, I headed out to the incredible Freedom Beach where, in the shade of a tree in the warm emerald sea, I finally relaxed for the first time in weeks.

THE GAME.....

So relaxed in fact that I almost forgot about the football.

Danny and some of his fellow travellers were up for a game, but we needed more players. I spoke with Tai, a young Burmese chap who worked in the restaurant at our hotel. He was keen to play and said his friends who worked at hotels nearby would join him, but that they wouldn't want to travel too far for a game after their 12 hour shifts. We managed to find a pitch two hundred yards up the road. Tai, his brilliantly named mates Wai, To and Oo, together with the English boys, met at Koh Tao Wembley for a 6.45pm kick-off. The pitch was a rough patch of land encircled by trees; very sandy and peppered with ankle high stubborn shrubs, a bit like Turf Moor, Burnley, would have looked in 1972.

The game started with mixed teams, but quickly became England v Burma when a couple more of Tai's friends showed up. 6 v 6 and the pace was frenetic, especially considering the intense heat and humidity. The breakthrough took a while in coming, but after a good move, the ball spilled to Danny who squared it for his mate to finish. 1-0 to England. They added a second before Burma replied as night began to fall. These young whippersnappers were navigating the shrubbery brilliantly. Although England made it 3-1, they were sporting enough to play next goal's the winner as the light was fading rapidly. Burma struck soon after, and the lights went out completely. A fantastic game played in a brilliant spirit of sportsmanship and togetherness, and for the total love of this amazing game. The fact that my boy had played too capped off a perfect night.

The following morning I said goodbye to Dan as he boarded an open-backed truck with his mates bound for Koh Pang Yang. Ahh, to be young again. Seeing my son so far away from home had given me a massive lift after such a hectic and exhausting start to this journey. Great game too!

GAME 7: CAMBODIA

Date: March 22nd 2016, 11.30am
Ground: Angkor High School, Siem Reap

THE GREEN SAMURAI

I was asked to lighten my baggage load at Bangkok's Don Muang Airport or risk a hefty penalty. I was feeling hot, bothered and on edge after my Thai Clint Eastwood look-a-like taxi driver's eight near misses on the way to the airport. True to form, Clint hadn't flinched once. Somewhere in the middle of the manic five minutes of swapping stuff from my suitcase to my back pack, and weighing and re-weighing my case, the wallet containing my cash for the next 5 countries disappeared. There were only airport staff around, so it had to be one of them who took it. Bastard! None of the airport's management or security were particularly interested in helping me. After an exasperating hour of getting absolutely nowhere, I trudged off to departures wanting to kill.

Not the best start to the Cambodian leg of my journey. Next, after a comical thirty-minute ride on a crowded transport bus in and out of the aircraft, we were told to return to the terminal as our plane would be delayed for two hours. These things tend to come in threes, right? When we finally got to Siem Reap Airport, Cambodia, the ATM was out of order. Stood outside of the terminal, skint, I got talking to Ayyub Maadani, a Welsh ESL teacher working in Cambodia. Thankfully he offered to pay for our shared taxi to the city. I still owe you £2.50, Ayyub. Good man.

Weaving in and out of the mind boggling traffic, I was eventually dropped off at the Green Park Village Guesthouse. I felt immediately at home. Rachana, the manager, was hilarious. Small, smiley but ferocious, she took the mickey out of me in English and scared the pants off the poor staff. Soon I was lying shirtless in my room, staring up at the large whirring ceiling fan, wondering what the hell had just happened.

Over the next couple of days, in searing temperatures of up to 42 degrees, I wandered around Siem Reap and visited the incredible Angkor Wat Temples, a UNESCO World Heritage Site. I won't go into great detail as the temples are so well documented, except to say that each site was absolutely mind-blowing in both scale and concept. My favourites were the Bayon

Temple, with its towers set with many serene and smiling stone faces, and the tree-tastic Ta Prom Temple of Tomb Raider fame.

THE GAME.....

Day 3 in Cambodia and still no game. I've got to say that the hardest hurdle to clear was the heat. When it's 35 degrees at 10.00am and up to 42 degrees by midday, timing is everything. On Tuesday 22nd March, I decided to set out early and give it a go. Our wheels for the day were driven by Sorn, a tour guide for the Tourist Transport of Siem Reap Airport. He was very proud of his 'professional status' and looked down on the average tuk-tuk driver. To be honest, he was an arrogant, swaggering little schnitzel. My companion for the day was the very courteous and respectful Suzuki, a 21 year old trainee diplomat from Tokyo. Suzuki was staying at the same guesthouse as me and was interested in my story.

Driving along, Sorn spotted a basketball tournament going on at Angkor High School. We stopped and chatted to the pupils watching on. Eight lads, all friends who played in their own team called The Green Samurai, agreed to a kick-about. It was 11am, and they had just finished school (7am start). We headed up to the school's playing field and I placed the jumpers down. We split the lads into Green Samurai A & B teams. Suzuki was chief photographer, and I was chief sweater in the ridiculous heat.

The A team were dominant from the start. Neat passing and great movement off the ball. The B team grafted hard but didn't have the same understanding or link-up play. I loved the intensity of the match. Total focus and desire. They were in the football bubble and, for the next twenty minutes, nothing else mattered. *Spiderman* in the B team's nets was outstanding, like a young Ray Clemence, miraculously tipping away balls destined for the bottom corner. If it wasn't for him it would have been a lot worse than the eventual 4-1 score line.

Talking with the lads afterwards, I discovered that most of them had been working alongside their studies since they were ten years old, to contribute to the family income. They would almost certainly have to migrate to bordering countries at some point to earn a decent living, as staying in Cambodia would mean long, hard, seven-day working weeks on low pay for the rest of their lives. Whichever way you looked at it, there were tough times ahead for these boys. What they did have in abundance, however, as with most Cambodians I had met so far, was a warmth, kindness and generosity of spirit that was absolutely priceless.

GAME 8: CAMBODIA

Date: March 23rd 2016, 7.00pm
Ground: Kjung Yu Field-Siem Reap

DAVY AND THE TUK-TUKS

I visited the striking village of Kompong Phluk with Suzuki. Although referred to as the *floating village*, this cluster of three villages is permanent. It was dry season, and it was an incredible sight to see these dwellings soaring atop their 10-metre wooden stilts, exposed by the lack of water. At this time of year, many of the villagers move out onto the nearby Tonle Sap Lake and build temporary boat houses there. The local economy is based primarily on fishing and shrimp harvesting.

The 'floating village' originated as a result of the genocidal Year Zero regime of the Khmer Rouge, 1975-79, when almost 2 million people lost their lives to execution, disease, starvation and overwork. Hundreds fled to this flooded area near Siem Reap to escape the brutality, gradually establishing their own community. After the Vietnamese army took Phnom Penn in January 1979, the Khmer Rouge moved west. On finding only ruins on their return to their original homes, the people of Kompong Phluk returned to live and settle here. It's such a striking and unique place. I was really settling in to life in Cambodia by now, but time was precious.

There are people you meet in life who make the world a better place for them being in it. Davy Meng, a tuk-tuk driver in Siem Reap, is one of them. Davy is intelligent, quietly spoken, gentle and witty and has patience and humility in droves. He was born in Prey Vent Province, the second youngest of six brothers. Davy knew from an early age that if he wanted to make a decent living, he'd have to learn to speak English and work in the tourist business. After several years of selling street food, then working in gruelling seventy hour a week factory jobs, he finally had enough money saved up to start English classes and own a tuk-tuk.

It was Davy who had carted me about Angkor Wat for the best part of six hours in the incredible heat. During this time we struck up a bond, so much so that when he dropped me back at the guesthouse later, he refused to charge me. He said we were friends now and he could never charge friends for his time. All my superfluous wants and needs were at once rendered ridiculous by this single powerful, spiritual gesture. Rightly or wrongly, knowing what a tough life he had, I forced a few dollars in his hand which he reluctantly took. Friends for life.

THE GAME.....

Through Davy, I met several other tuk-tuk drivers who relentlessly worked the chaotic, baking streets of Siem Reap. One early evening, we left my guesthouse in a convoy of five tuk-tuks to do battle on a nearby field. Piotr and Ola from Poland joined us too, as did the marvellously monikered Men Meng, a young dude who worked at the guesthouse when not studying. The sandy surface at Angkor Kjung Yu Field was perfect for the hot and humid conditions. A 3 v 3 quickly became a 5 v 5 when some youngsters joined in. One of these kids was incredibly fast, talented, skillful and fearless for his age. In another world he'd have been signed up by an academy for sure.

There was a good ebb and flow to the game, with neither side dominating possession or chances. Approach play was generally decent, but both teams struggled in the final third. Shots flew off in all directions, as did the flip-flops. As the players began to adjust to the surface, so the goals started to rain in, but it remained a close affair. When one team got their noses in front, the opposition would peg them back. This pattern continued until the score was 6-6. Playing next goal's the winner, Piotr the Polish predator had the last word, slotting home after a nice team move. A cracking game with much laughter throughout, and big smiles and hugs all around at the end.

Making our way back to the road side, I chucked the tiny young superstar the match ball, and he and his mates skipped off to play some more. We piled into the tuk-tuks and headed back to the guesthouse in the fading evening light. The lads quenched their thirst before hitting the streets again. They had all worked long hours, seven days a week for years. When they weren't driving, they worked in hotels sweeping floors or doing the laundry. Their physical and mental resilience was remarkable, and they handed out lessons in humility, good manners, generosity and respect to everyone they met, free of charge.

GAME 9: VIETNAM

Date: March 26th 2016, 2.00pm
Ground: Indira Gandhi Park, Hanoi

Coming thick from every angle
Stop for no-one swarm of cycles
Risk your own life, true survival
Tip-toe down Old Quarter Street

Masked marauders, beeping bandits
Mum's load babies, goods in transit
Step into the soup and chance it
Cross with Jesus and Tai chi

Human scales all fresh fruit weighted
Coconuts split open, grated
Bun Bo Nam Bo, Pho bò, sated
Perched on plastic infant seats

Same same, shoe-shine, dollars, dong
Lighters, wallets, days are long
For the hawkers in the travelers throng
Trapped inside the city maze

You want massage? Body? Foot?
You want girl to rub you good?
All is known and understood
Eastern eyes and western ways

MOTORCYCLE CITY

I stayed at the splendid Gia Thinh Hotel for a few nights, which is wedged into one of the narrow bustling streets of Hanoi's Old Quarter. Tony, the smart, mild-mannered hotel manager there, discovered I liked footy and invited me to the opening ceremony of the Hanoi 7-a-side super league football season. I clung on to Tony's ribs for dear life as we headed out on his scooter to the ground. There are five million motorbikes tear-arsing around the city; utter maniacs operating at high speed in inches of space, using a highway code of their own making.

Arriving at the ground ten miles away, the four teams due to play were already warming up. The opening ceremony began at 7.30pm, when we were attacked by a super loud speech given by a small, thin, bald man in an oversized blue suit and jam jar glasses. We all recoiled from the piercing microphone feedback, but on he yapped. Why didn't he just switch it off? He could have talked at normal volume to the fifty or so folk gathered just a few feet away from his cavernous nostrils. When he finally finished to no applause, we were all staring around in silence wondering if we could still hear. The impeccably observed national anthem followed, and the super league season 2016-17 was officially underway. There were two great games of footy that evening. Tony himself was a decent player, scoring a cracking 20-yard volley for his side in a 5-4 win. The star of the night though was the short, camp, middle-aged ref who exaggerated all his decisions with matador poses and an accusing pork-sausage index finger.

After the footy, we all headed to a nearby hotel for a celebration meal. Again, there was a loud speech, thankfully with no mic this time. Rounds of delicious food were then served to the hungry hoard of players and coaches. I was feeling a little out of place, seated about half-way up one side of the long table. The fun started when the beer was dished out. Everyone was pissed after one bottle each. Suddenly I had thirty new mates wanting to take selfies with me. The craic was great. I found mild mannered Tony some hours later, arse-holed up a corner. He swore he'd only had two beers as we headed back down the highway to the hotel. If it had been dangerous getting to the ground, it was suicidal getting back. Tony two-beers was off his tits, laughing his head off as we swerved in and out of death. Absolute fucking madness.

THE GAME….

I'd like to dedicate this game to Johan Cruyff, Dutch master, who passed away on March 24th, 2016. The famous orange number 14 shirt epitomized the true spirt of the game. Cruyff led a football revolution with Ajax and Holland and laid the foundations for what Barcelona have become today. We were always either Pele or Cruyff in the school yard. The way our game flowed this day felt like a tiny tribute to the great man.

Hoàn Kiếm Lake is a freshwater lake in the heart of the bustling city of Hanoi, Vietnam's capital. Legend claims that in the mid-15th century, heaven sent Emperor Lý Thái Tổ a magical sword which he used to drive the Chinese from Vietnam. After the war, a giant golden turtle grabbed the sword and disappeared into the depths of the lake to restore the sword to its divine owners, inspiring the name Hoàn Kiếm (Lake of the Restored Sword). Who needs drugs when you can make stuff like that up?

I wandered off around the lake one day but was struggling to find a space to play. As I walked, huddles of super cute kids, joined at the duffle coat, kept stopping me to practice their English. Folk music wafted over from a street band somewhere. To my ears at least, the song sounded like the noises you'd make if you were having your teeth pulled out one by one with pliers whilst having the shits. I'm sure the words were very inspiring though.

I finally came across Indira Gandhi Park on the east bank of the lake. A bronze statue of Emperor Lý Thái Tổ himself watched over proceedings as I placed my jumpers down in the square there.

I managed to cajole three local lads into playing. Soon after, Jason and Jeff joined us. They were US Airforce men on leave from their base in South Korea. The teams were complete when local chap Thoian, plus Rebecca and Andrea from the US, lined up for action. Two mixed teams of Vietnamese and American players. Given the recent history between the two countries you couldn't have scripted it (Well…you could if you tried. It's a daft saying that). A 4 v 4 in near-perfect playing conditions. Rebecca and Andrea ran the show from the off. They had played in teams in the US for years. Rebecca was an outstanding number 10, buzzing around the pitch and pulling all the strings. The local men on her side were energetic and enthusiastic, but just not on her wavelength. Through-ball after deadly through-ball ran idly out of play. It was a fast flowing, end-to-end game. Andrea scored with a fantastic looping effort as the goals began to rain in. Passing on both sides became sharper as the game intensified. The air-force men were trying hard, but the game was alien to them; quarterbacks playing with their feet.

With the score reaching a tense 4-4, Rebecca stepped on the gas and scored a dazzling hat-trick; three brilliant slotted finishes topping off some mazy two footed runs. Despite the languid, almost asleep Chuc somehow pulling a goal back, Rebecca's team eventually ran out 8-5 winners. Great fun and a beautiful, unifying game of footy that came out of nowhere. Best game in the world! As we were leaving the square, I looked back at the statue of the Emperor and he gave us a wink. RIP Johan.

GAME 10: VIETNAM

Date: March 28th 2016, 7.30am
Ground: Ti Top Island, Hạ Long Bay

INTERNATIONAL LOVE WOOD

Some places on our glorious earth leave you spell-bound. Hạ Long Bay, in the gulf of Tonkin, is one such place. This haunting seascape includes some 1,600 islands and islets. We sailed on for a whole day through the mesmeric emerald waters, gazing in awe at the mighty limestone pillars all around. So peaceful and ethereal was it that our pilot, who was steering the ship with his bare feet, fell asleep and narrowly avoided a collision with another vessel. *Dopey Drawers* they call him around here…*Dopey Drawers*. We anchored in the bay for the night, and my young back-packing companions and I regaled each other with far-fetched stories over tea. I learnt two new and great things:

THING ONE……..

Traditionally, on a specific day of the year in some parts of Germany, if a bloke fancied a lass, he and his friends would chop down a tree then secretly transplant it in her garden whilst she slept. On waking, the fair maiden would draw back her curtains before swooning, teary eyed at the sight of the love wood. Three trees over three consecutive years from the same bloke was a virtual marriage proposal (and a forest). Now I don't know about you, but I reckon I'd know about it if someone was trying to plant a 30 foot tree in my garden in the middle of the night? Also, if I was gonna ask a lass out, I wouldn't plant a telegraph pole in her begonias. I'd simply say, "Do you fancy going to the pictures?"

THING TWO……

In Oslo, Norway, *russefeiring* is a traditional celebration for Norwegian high school students (the *russ*) in their final spring semester. This lot make a prom night and limousines look like an outing to Cleethorpes for a brew and a biscuit. Groups of *russ* get together and buy a bus! They spend fortunes pimping it up, pay a driver and then, in splendid colour co-ordination, go on a bender through the city for 17 days! Now that's what I call a leaving do. Unsurprisingly, public disturbances are regularly linked to the celebration.

THE GAME...

We reached tiny Ti Top Island at 7.00am the next day. Some went to explore the caves there, but I stayed on the beach hoping to get a game going. Placing my jumpers down, I sat on the sand for a while and shook my head at the beauty all around. Juan, from Cordoba, Argentina, was first to join me. We just played shots against each other for ten minutes. I asked some of my shipmates and passers-by to play. Eventually, folk from Vietnam, France, Germany, Russia, Norway, Denmark, USA and England joined in.

Played against the incredible back-drop of the bay, this 6 v 6 game on the sand was hard going at first, but the cool air helped the players to keep up a good tempo. Strong tackling was a feature from the start as the ball bobbled and held up on the surface. Victor from Russia and Tom from England were strong in goals for their respective teams. After a few near misses from either side, the super energetic Sam from Vietnam (dressed in all black like the Milk Tray man) darted through and thumped a cracker beyond the helpless Victor.

Allie from Minnesota USA showed skillful, quick feet as she and her team pressed for an equalizer. Flo (France), Melina (Germany) Josephine (Denmark) and Emir (Norway) were working their socks off against each other in midfield, as Tom's impressive young son James pushed for a second for his team. Anastasia (Russia) stuck to the wing, playing with speed and determination. Victor, her partner, sensing defeat with the clock ticking down, left his goal and surged forward like a man possessed. Picking up a loose ball, the man of the match fired the equalizer and the game was done. A 1-1 draw was a fitting result on the balance of play. What a brilliant, fun pop-up international it had been, played first thing in the morning on a tiny island in the most beautiful setting.

GAME 11: CHINA

Date: April 6th 2016, 1.30pm
Ground: Yuexiu Park, Guangzhou

THE LAUGHING GAME

From the narrow, bustling streets of Hanoi to the big wide open city scape of Guangzhou, China. For the first time on this trip I felt a bit lonely and lost. Wheeling my suitcase down from the metro station in the rain to my digs, it hit me square on the jaw that these vast mega cities don't suit me at all. Every place I'd landed in up to now had felt right; this didn't. These feelings of isolation and disconnect were compounded when I got to my hotel.

Using hand gestures, *10 bollocks* the hotel manager came from behind the counter and asked me in raised voiced Chinese (to impress the giggling, obsequious young women behind the desk) to pay for my stay when I'd already pre-paid. After a bit of a toe-to-toe, eyeball-to-eyeball squaring up type thing, my paperwork was finally found and the tension eased. What a total and utter knob chops that fella was. No need... no need at all.

I slunk off to my room, which I was told by his sausage fingers was on the 8th floor, when there were only 4. My room was basic, and my mood was down. With no signal and no wi-fi (so no-one to moan to), I took a walk and found myself at a Walmart. Asda's or Tesco's it was not. There, right next to the crackers and cheese, were live tortoises, fish and water snakes for sale in huge tanks. It was the sight of the tortoises that really got me. These English garden, live-forever cuties were being scooped out and suffocated in plastic bags by happy chatting shoppers, later to be pulled apart to make soup. Not right... not right at all. Lying on my bed that night, I felt like I'd landed on a different planet.

Thank God for music! I woke up to my first proper day in Guangzhou feeling a bit rubbish. I really was out of my comfort zone now. I had only one option - stick my earphones in and have it! I hopped on the city's impressive metro system, and by the time I'd rattled through "Local boy in a photograph" (Stereophonics), "I got by in time" (The Jam), "Waterfall" (Stone Roses), "Wonderful World" (Sam Cooke) and the brilliant "Just a little misunderstanding" (The Contours), I'd happily reached my destination.

Yuexiu Park is a welcome break from the city streets. The best bit about the park for me was seeing the locals practicing their tai chi and ballroom dancing moves on their own. One of the ballroom chaps was superbly grumpy. He'd start the music on his portable cd player, take position and then begin his graceful glide across the paving stones, arms around his invisible partner and totally lost in the moment. I watched him for about ten minutes. Nearly every time he set off someone would walk across his path. His face would turn purple with rage, and the abuse he dished out was tremendous. From a swan to a gargoyle in five perfect steps. So funny. I walked on up through the park until I reached the famous five goats statue at its summit, taking in an impressive view of Yuexiu Mountain football stadium below along the way.

THE GAME

I'd been strolling around for about an hour when I found myself at a small court with spectator stands on two sides. This was where I met the jianzi players. I'd seen the game being played back in Hanoi. The aim of the game is to try to keep a large weighted shuttlecock in the air using only the feet, and to get as many kicks in as possible without dropping it. These dudes were outstanding. The shuttlecock rarely touched the ground as it was passed around in groups of four. I approached one of the groups with the idea of having a kick-about. One or two of the men were unsure, but the women soon sorted them out and the match was on. A 4 v 4 and one of the funniest games yet.

These jianzi masters hadn't played football before, but they weren't going to let a tiny detail like get in the way. *It was football Jim, but not as we know it.* For sheer joy and entertainment, this game would take some beating. The whole gang chased after the ball as one for a good twenty minutes, screaming with laughter. One or two had to keep stopping for breath as they were laughing so hard. The spectators in the stands were laughing too, as were rows of little furry woodland creatures, watching on and eating popcorn on nearby branches. When the troops finally ran out of giggles, the tall chap with the brilliant smile indicated to me that his team had won 2-1, but I swear I never saw a goal being scored!

I was invited to play a game of jianzi afterwards. I started well but faded badly, so bad in fact that my team-mates all sat down and left me to it. Cheeky gits. What a brilliant laugh it had been from start to finish. I thanked these lovely people for their time and went on my merry way. Taking the metro back to my digs, I could feel a thousand eyes upon me, so rare was I with my near blue skin and hairy nose. One woman boarded the train with her head down. The second she looked up at me, she dropped her shopping bags and let out a yelp! I seem to have that effect on women.

The night was again filled with a kind of dread. I couldn't shake off these feelings of disconnection. Was I just being a big baby? Probably. I forced myself out for a bite to eat. There was a string of fast-food shops and street vendors close to my hotel. One shop appeared to be selling the jawbones of different animals to chew on. As I made my way around, being stared at like my face was a ball of fire, I did try one or two things but gagged each time. I'm ashamed to say I ended up on pizza slices and chocolate bars for the whole time I was there.

GAME 12: CHINA

Date: April 8th 2016, 1.30pm
Ground: Shamian Island , Guangzhou

JUMPING BEANS

Have you ever seen the film Logan's Run? For those who haven't, it goes something like this. The year is 2274. On the surface, everything seems ideal in this post-apocalyptic society. Living in a city within an enclosed dome, there is little or no work for humans to perform and inhabitants are free to pursue all of the pleasures of life. There is one catch, however. Life is limited. When the citizens reach thirty, they are terminated in a quasi-religious ceremony known as Carousel. The brainwashed float upwards towards their deaths believing they are heading for re-birth. The city is therefore entirely populated by young ones, apart from the old ones running the city from their hidden lair. Well, I'm pretty sure something similar is happening in Guangzhou. Of the city's 15 million people, it seemed only about twelve of them were over thirty. They were mostly hiding in the parks behind bushes, pretending to prune. Maybe they controlled everything from there? As for the rest, Carouselled, I reckon.

For today's game I ventured down to Shamian Island, a tiny sandbank island that's only 900m from east to west and 300m from north to south. It's bordered to the south by the Pearl River and separated from the mainland by a canal. It was once home to foreign merchants and has a distinctly European feel to it. Setting off from Haunghuagang metro station, I took Line 6 down to Huangsha Station, then clambered over the footbridge to the island, passing begging lepers and exhausted disabled buskers blowing into home-made piped instruments. A young band played beneath the bridge and had drawn a crowd. The brilliant lanky drummer was letting rip on his kit of old tubs and paint-pots.

Once on the island, it was quiet and peaceful with few cars around. I strolled down familiar looking streets, passing beautiful, twisting banyan trees as I went. I eventually reached Shamian Daijie (Green Way), which is a row of tree-lined squares running through the heart of the island. This seemed a popular place to get married, judging by the number of just-wed couples who were having their photos taken in the leafy walkways. Older folk were sat on benches chatting, whilst young friends hurried to the next prime location to take selfies on sticks, like delirious goggle-eyed jousters.

THE GAME.....

Around 1.00pm, a magical explosion of colour and noise flooded the scene. A blur of around fifty red, white and blue, shiny happy jumping beans from Shamian Island Primary School poured into the leafy squares, throwing diablos in the air with ease and skipping around to tunes that only their ears could hear. I spotted one of the learning mentors and introduced myself. His name was Mr Xiu and it just so happened he was football daft. He told me his favourite team was AC Milan and his favourite ever player was Kaka. When I mentioned the famous Liverpool-AC Milan Champions League Final in Istanbul in 2005, he said that he'd been upset, but that God had decided the match in the end. I suggested Jerzy Dudek had.

Mr Xiu was all for getting a game going and took me over to where some of the boys were playing. Jumpers down, we quickly organised a 5 v 5 in a tiny space. Mr Xiu joined in as much for crowd control as anything. The boys went at it hammer and tongs. Typical of their age group, they just followed the ball around at a frantic pace. I joined in the odd time, but the second I touched the ball these little piranhas attacked me from all angles. It's difficult to say what the score was in the end, as every goal was hotly disputed. I reckon it was 1-1, though I'd be outnumbered 10-1 on that one. A brilliant, energetic kick-about with high fives all around at the end. This game took me back to playing in the yard at my own primary school; a swarm of would-be heroes, scrapping for every inch and trying to win at all costs. Marvellous Mr Xiu was a perfect gentleman. He told me his father had taught him the game, and he'd been playing since he was six years old. It was his mission to get as many kids interested in football as possible during his time at the school. Good man.

I had really enjoyed both games in Guangzhou, but I had found it the hardest place so far on my journey to fully relax. Maybe it was exhaustion, the big city, the inedible food, but no. I'd already experienced those things in South East Asia, yet enjoyed every minute. There had been a friendliness here but at arms-length; a reluctance to fully connect, as if the elders controlling things from behind those bushes were always watching.

GAME 13: JAPAN

Date: April 12th 2016, 1.00pm
Ground: The Children's Park, Izumisano City

A FORK IN THE ROAD

My introduction to Japan had not been good. Landing in Osaka at 10pm, I had to make it to the lodge I was staying at in Izumisano City by 11pm or risk being locked out. To be on the safe side, I skipped the train and took a taxi ride across the bridge from the island airport of Kansai. The taxi driver was very charming right up to the point where he stung me for £30 for a 10 minute ride. "No argument. You pay or I call police" he uttered in a very calm and matter-of-fact way. The balls of these highway robbers!

I was greeted at the lodge by the very grumpy elderly owner who couldn't wait to get back to his TV programme. After a half-arsed attempt at showing me around, he tried to slip away into the gloom of the reception area. I asked him for some water as I'd run out and had been on the road from China since 8am. With his back to me and index finger in the air, grumpy arse proclaimed "No water!" then disappeared to watch the Japanese version of "Rogue Landlords".

Just then, the fantastically named Bang, Beach and Oh from Thailand turned up. They told me that grumpy knackers had been like that all week, refusing to help them and generally being an unfriendly shit. We all had a good chuckle at his expense until he re-emerged to tell us all off for being loud. Too tired to complain, we all retired to bed like naughty school children. The whole place was filthy, stinky and musty, and tiny things with pincers moved around all night in the bed. Nightmare. I was so zonked from all the travelling that I spent all of the next day in bed, fully-clothed, sleeping and scratching.

The following day, feeling re-energized, I wheeled my case down to the superb Greenwood Hostel, about half a mile from the flea-pit. Modern and warm with fantastic facilities, the hostel was run by two young men who had escaped the perils of city life. One of these fellas, the super friendly Taiachi, explained: *"Suicide is the biggest killer of young men Japan. It was once known that if you worked in Japan you had a job for life. Not anymore. There is too much pressure. We are expected to follow the rules and say nothing. So many young people now feel pressure from their boss and get depressed, and they feel the only way out is to end it all. That is why we escaped life in Tokyo and came here where we can relax and live our own way".*

After a lovely warm shower, I popped into the local grocery store to buy a fork. I'd been trying to eat with chopsticks, but I was rubbish at it. Eating was proving pretty knackering. This is where I met the incredible Genna Tangog. Genna worked at the store and was a 5ft 2" fireball. After giving me a good telling off for wanting to buy a fork in the first place, she asked me why I was in town. I was then instructed to meet her at 7pm that evening. I daren't refuse.

Genna took me to the restaurant where she worked most evenings. She wanted me to meet the owner, the one and only Kunio "Papa" Kinomoto. What a character! Now in his mid 60s, Kunio had once owned a large restaurant in Osaka City Centre with over thirty staff. He was now semi-retired and ran a tiny eatery/ karaoke bar with his third wife, Mayumi Takeuchi, known affectionately as Mama. When I met Papa, he was wearing bright red pants, a gold neckless with a bullet dangling off it, and showing scars from his triple heart bypass. He was sat at the end of the bar playing his shamisen (Japanese guitar) and guzzling down saki for fun. He cared not a jot. For the next three days, Papa wouldn't let me pay for a thing. He took me to the best restaurants in town and found much amusement in asking me to sing The Beatles' *Norwegian Wood* a hundred times in his Karaoke bar. I used to love that song.

THE GAME .....

Later in the week, Genna introduced me to the staff of Izumisano Cross Cultural Association (ICA) and the city's youth service. The ICA is a brilliant organisation that provides a place "where people from around the world gather and interact without any boundaries in order to learn something new from each other"

After much discussion, we managed to gather enough players together for a game in the nearby Children's Park. Hamano and Daisaku from the youth service and staff from the ICA joined Papa, Genna and I. Two women from a nearby office were also persuaded to play. Jumpers down, I split the players into two teams. "Ready? "Let's go!". I threw the ball in but no-one moved. Tumbleweed as the ball rolled idly under a cherry blossom tree. Eight pairs of eyes were upon me. Then the laughter broke out. This was the very first time that any of them had played footy. After a couple of short demonstrations of how to pass and move, the gang threw themselves into the game.

Hamano, Papa, Genna and Daisaku took on the rest. Hamano was the star, bursting forward at every opportunity and scoring two great goals. She was ably assisted by Papa at the back, his bright red pants scaring away would be attackers. Genna couldn't play for giggling, which got us all giggling. The tall, cool Daisaku was unflappable in the nets and, for their first ever game, both teams did really well. Hamano's team ran out 3-1 winners, but the true winners were these lovely humans and the smiles and laughter that we all shared today. My short stay in Japan had been a very humbling experience. Through Genna, I'd met some wonderful warm-hearted people who had spoilt me rotten with their kindness and generosity. In fact by the end of my visit, Papa had given me his watch and offered me a job in his bar, with a rent-free apartment thrown in. Would I show the same benevolence to a random stranger if they turned up in my home town?

I spent my last couple of days in Japan being a tourist. After finally figuring out how to buy a train ticket at Izumisano Station, I headed out to the colourful and vibrant city of Namba. It was straight out of a comic book and how I'd imagined a Japanese city to be. Buildings were adorned with huge colourful banners and neon signs, displaying lavish Japanese writing and cartoon imagery. Attractive women on massive screens advertised perfume and clothes with perfect hair and smiles. It wouldn't have been a surprise to see Spiderman swinging from block to block. The indoor fish market had to be seen to be believed. It seemed that everything that resided in the ocean was for sale there. The sushi displays were especially eye-catching and kids were tucking into red octopus on sticks like they were toffee apples. Back in the street, vibrant J-pop shops spilled over with thousands of teen records, and I was surprised to see so many adults using vending machines to buy miniature plastic toys. Everything seemed so animated that I felt sure if I caught my reflection in a shop window, I'd now be a cartoon character.

Returning from Namba, I headed down to Rinku Town on the coast and took a walk along the pebbled beach there. I took off my sweaty socks and had a refreshing paddle in the stunning clear waters of the Seto Inland Sea. It felt a long way from the River Irwell in Lancashire, where I used to jump in fully clothed to retrieve the ball when we were kids.

GAME 14: SOUTH KOREA

Date: April 18th 2016, 2.00pm
Ground: Olympic Park, Seoul

PRO-CELEBRITY OLYMPICS

Coming in on the train from the airport, the Seoul skyline looked a bit Star Warsy. Hundreds of white towering apartment blocks, built to house some of the city's 25 million residents, rose up into the vast cornflower blue sky as a Delta-7 Jedi Starfighter glided into view. That last bit isn't true. Arriving at Seoul Station, I had absolutely no clue how to tackle the spaghetti metro map, let alone pay for a ticket. Ray Mears (TV survival specialist) popped into my head, not for the first time in my life, telling me not to panic. Composing myself, I placed my rucksack on top of my suitcase and studied the map once more. Then, just like when you stare cross-eyed at one of those 3D illusions, my route suddenly came into focus and I was off. I would have to sweat for my supper though.

The Inca trail in Peru has got nothing on the Seoul metro system when it comes to steps. With underground escalators as rare as a Korean chip butty, I emerged from a week's subterranean travel with the thighs of a speed skater. In fact, the South Koreans have a thing about steps. Every cafe and bar I visited seemed to involve two flights of stairs and a puff on my inhaler. I didn't so much see the city as have a workout. Alighting at the Jongnu 5 stop, I made my way down the busy street to my hostel, which turned out to be a two-minute walk through the past. With all respect, I felt like I was at a 1970s pro-celebrity golf classic. Loads of the blokes looked like Ronnie Corbett, short with jam jar glasses and serious jumpers, whilst loads of the women were wearing loose pastel coloured pants, open necked blouses and large sun-visors. I half expected Jimmy Tarbuck to greet me at the hostel with a crap joke and an even crapper jumper.

Waking from a long afternoon kip, I decided to take a stroll to clear my head. It was then that I realized my home for the next ten days was slap bang in the middle of a red-light area. Down one side of the street, groups of smiling, frilly knickered women were sprawled out on furry rugs in dimly lit rooms. Many a boob impaired my vision as I struggled to look straight ahead. From the bars opposite, loud, nervous laughter blundered from the mouths of drunken punters revving up for the evening. Needless to say I did not partake in such debauchery.

THE GAME....

After a couple of days resting and eating bananas (didn't fancy the pigs' intestines), I travelled by metro from Jongno-Gu, across the Hangang River which splits the city in two, and arrived at the imposing Mongchontoseong - the World Peace Gate to Seoul's Olympic Park. As I was to discover, the park and all its stadia were still in excellent condition, considering the games had been held there in 1988. It was one of those sunny but chilly and windy days. The square immediately beyond the gate was filled with kite fliers, mini-baseball games, people on bikes and unicycles and parents pulling their children around at high speed in little trucks.

To the side of the square, in a walkway about fifteen metres wide, I spotted a group of young chaps staring and pointing at girls. Within a couple of minutes, the game was on.

Moon Kee Je, Kim Donk Yu, Lee Jae Won, Park Yoon Su, Young Ji Wong and Lee Gyoung Jun were all 17 years old. I thought the lads looked younger to be honest, and by most people's reckoning they were. In Korea you are automatically a year old at birth, and become a year older on New Year's Day, regardless of your birth date. In England, these chaps would have been aged 15-16 years old.

One thing was for sure, the lads could all play a bit. They were all fans of Seoul FC and either Barcelona or Real Madrid. Clearly football daft, they put on an energetic display of flicks, tricks and skills for about half an hour. The game was competitive without ever getting dirty. Park Yoon Su's team raced into an early lead. They had the slightly faster and more technical players, so I decided to go in nets for the underdogs. Big mistake. Within five minutes I'd twisted my knee, fallen over and headed a ball whilst on my bum with my sunglasses on my head, breaking one of the lenses. One of the worst substitute appearances ever made. I quickly returned to my role as official photographer and left them to it.

The game was first to 10, and the score had reached 6-6. Every goal from there on in was hotly disputed, with the troops looking to me to make the final decisions. I felt like a little Caesar, sat there giving thumbs up or down. Park's team deservedly ran away with it in the end 10-6. It had been a really intense, skilled, competitive but fair game; fitting really within an Olympic park. Talking to the lads afterwards, thanks to Moon Kee Je interpreting, I discovered that despite the national obsession with rounders for grown-ups (baseball), they loved their footy more. They enjoyed living in Seoul, but said they spent nearly all of their time studying. It was their dream to travel the world and watch games at all the famous footy grounds. What warm, friendly, chatty young chaps they were.

There is a darker side to the 1988 Seoul Olympic Games. It seems that somewhere high up in the echelons of power, the decision had been made to clear the streets of 'vagrants' prior to the start of the games. This led to the alleged disappearance, enslavement, rape, torture and murder of thousands of Seoul's citizens, mostly children and the disabled. They were thought to have been kidnapped, or arrested and detained on false charges, and kept at the mountainside facility known as 'Brother's Home'. The full extent of the crimes committed there is unknown. It is felt that there has been a huge cover up as the scandal goes right to the very top of government. Many of the victims are still fighting for the truth to come out. This year, some of them gathered to have their hair cut en masse and to demand justice. Their wait looks likely to be a long one.

GAME 15: SOUTH KOREA

Date: April 24th 2016, 2.00pm
Ground: Songjuk Elementary School, Suwon

SUWON SONG

What better way to finish off this leg of the journey than to meet up with a fellow Rossendalian? Mark Trickett - Professor of English at Yongin University no less. He and his wife Mi Young also run their own English Language school in Yongin. Mark has been living in South Korea for over ten years now. We met up to watch a K League Classic derby game between Seoul FC and Suwon, at the impressive Seoul World Cup Stadium. FC Seoul are one of the more successful teams in the league's 35 year history, having won six League titles, two FA Cups, two League Cups and one Super Cup.

Around 10,000 spectators were inside the stadium and the atmosphere was terrific. For a lad from the land of perpetual grey skies, it tickled me watching the colour -coordinated masses raising their red hoods and umbrellas in unison at the slightest hint of rain. I was reminded of the spectacular crowds and colour of the 2002 World Cup when South Korea, co-hosting with Japan, made it through to the semi-final stage, only to be beaten 1-0 by Germany.

Mark told me that he missed good beer, pasties, bacon butties and fish and chips most of all, but that South Korea was a better place to raise children than England: "There is a very low crime rate and no-one really bothers you. No-one's gonna rob your mobile off you in the subway or smash in your kitchen door to rob your stuff. High school kids are too busy with their education to go out spraying graffiti or drinking in the streets. Most of them are studying until midnight at academies."

Although South Korea is one of the four Asian tiger economies, along with Hong Kong, Singapore and Taiwan, the unemployment rate stood at 12% at the time of my visit. Mark explained that most graduates live with their parents, waiting for the day that things improve. In order to get a decent job, adults have to learn English to a good standard and are encouraged to learn Chinese too. This grates with many South Korean's as they are very proud of their own language, and because they have historically been, in Mark's words, *squashed and bullied*" by the Japanese and Chinese. As for the match, Seoul ran out convincing 3-0 winners against a poor Suwon side. Mark invited me to meet him in a few days' time to watch a game at the Suwon Stadium, 40km south of Seoul.

THE GAME….

The Suwon Stadium is pretty impressive, but not as impressive as Mark's son Joshua, a five year old bilingual yoda who translated for us so that we could find our seats. (Told you it was Star Warsy around here. Joshua was even wearing a Star Wars t-shirt). Suwon v Incheon was not a thriller. With the game locked at 0-0, we left just after half-time to pursue our own game.

Walking away from the stadium, Mark spotted some young dudes kicking around in the grounds of the Songjuk Elementary School. We went over for a chat, set the jumpers down and very quickly had a 5 v 5 going. The players included Kim Jong Seo, Lee Min Gyu, Kim Sang Guy, Lee Do Sung, Kim Chan Woo, Lee Hyun Joon, Park Sang Jun and Go Jung Hun. There were first grade middle school students, making them all around 13 years of age.

What a great set of characters. The lads were all football crazy, running up to Mark and I throughout the game shouting out their favourite players names, from Bergkamp to Ribery, Pele to Ji-Sung Park. They all loved watching Spanish football and named their respective teams Barcelona and Real Madrid for the day. Barcelona quickly shot into a 5-1 lead. The game was so one-sided I called the lads in at half-time and asked them if they wanted to mix the teams up for the second half. The Madridistas refused.

In a classic game of two halves, Real Madrid came roaring back into the game and took a 6-5 lead. The Barcelona players were remarkable in their praise, complimenting opposition players for their "Beautiful goal", "So fast speed", "Great skill like Ronaldo". I couldn't believe my ears. There was not a hint of malice or frustration that Barcelona's lead had been wiped out, just pure joy all around at playing the game and an appreciation of the skills on show. It wasn't that both team's didn't want to win, it was just that they wanted to enjoy themselves more. Madrid ran out 10-6 winners in the end but it was smiles all around. A truly friendly El Clasico.

Later, Mark took me to his mates restaurant for fish and chips. He was all excited that we could have a chippy tea together before I set off home. After a long wait, we were both presented with a battered fish head, with the eyes still in it, and one chip each. If we hadn't have laughed we'd have cried. Great thanks to Mark for his friendship and support throughout my visit, and what a pleasure to meet his wonderful son Joshua and all those vibrant young football crazy rascals too.

So there it was. The first leg of my dream to go around the world in 80 games was over. Fifteen brilliant games in eight unforgettable weeks. There is great goodness and much love and kindness being shared in this world.

JUNGLE BEARS

GAMES 16-17

FRANCE AND GERMANY

GAME 16: FRANCE

Date: October 23rd 2016, 3.00pm
Ground: "The Jungle" refugee camp, Calais

I had an idea to keep nipping in and out of Europe, but I only made it to France and Germany the first time around.....

LOST IN THE JUNGLE

Who could forget the shocking image of the washed up body of Syrian toddler Aylan Kurdi, aged 3, lying in the surf near Bodrum? Both Aylan and his brother Galip, and their mother Rehana, perished when their boat capsized as they attempted to reach Greece from Turkey. This was September 2015 and the rapidly escalating European migrant crisis. The United Nations estimated in 2017 that the migrant death toll in the Mediterranean alone had surpassed 2,000. The majority of these people were fleeing violence and human rights abuses in their own countries of Syria, Afghanistan, Iraq, Eritrea and Kosovo.

The crisis threw the spotlight once again on the "The Jungle" migrant camp in Calais. Weekly news bulletins flashed across our screens in England, showing hordes of young men trying to board trucks and trains in their desperate attempts to enter the UK. Some truck drivers I know spoke of being the victims of stone throwing and physical violence and having their livelihoods affected. These were dark days. Britain was under Tory austerity, TV programmes such as "Benefits Street" served to demonize anyone on welfare and take the spotlight off the bankers who had caused the economic crisis in the first place. Murdoch's media were rampant in headlining that the UK was full to the brim, creating a culture of fear and animosity towards the plight of migrants. The conditions were ripe for the rise of the far right and their filthy, divisive, hate fueled propaganda, which led in part, I believe, to the British people voting to leave the EU.

"The Jungle" refugee camp had its origins in the 1990's, when a growing number of migrants gathered in Calais hoping to reach the UK. By 1999, the Sangatte Camp had opened near the Channel Tunnel, housing around 600 migrants. By the time this camp was closed in 2002, over 2000 migrants had gathered in the area. The 2003 Le Touquet Treaty brought UK Border Controls to Calais, making it illegal for migrants to enter the UK and preventing them from seeking asylum in France. Still they came. Men, women and many unaccompanied minors fleeing war and persecution. It is thought by February 2016, when the southern half of the camp was closed down, that over 6000 migrants were living there in dangerous and unsanitary conditions. We arrived a few days before the final eviction of all migrants, on 170 buses to official processing centres all over France.

According to their website, Refugee Community Kitchen (RCK) was created in the autumn of 2015 to help refugees living in the camps of Europe, to *"offer assistance in the form of nourishing meals and access to fresh food"*. So there we were, my friends, John, Helen, Liz and I, just 22 miles from Kent, doing our tiny bit as volunteers at the RCK. Shame on the UK and French governments and the EU. These were desperate people not political footballs you pricks. If it wasn't for charitable support, thousands of our desperate brothers and sisters would have been starving and freezing. RCK was one of a small number of volunteer kitchens set up to support those fleeing the stuff of nightmares.

THE GAME......

Our first day was spent peeling hundreds of garlic cloves, but on the second day I got the *plum* job of whisking the plum tomatoes in huge pans. I was like a kid let loose in a plum tomato whisking shop. We stayed at the house of the incredible Sylvie Vicente, a humanitarian and passionate and committed activist. Sylvie lives in Calais and had been vigorously supporting the cause of the migrants for years, often taking them into her home. On Sunday lunchtime, 23rd October 2016, the day before the final eviction, we broke off from our volunteer duties and followed Sylvie into the camp.

The scene was desperate, but in turns uplifting and inspiring. Using whatever materials they had found lying around, or had donated, some of the more resourceful volunteers had managed to turn the camp into a functioning village. We passed a church, a school, shops and restaurants, thrown together with bits of wood, cardboard and plastic. Within minutes we had met people from across the Middle East and Africa. Yes, there were the groups of marauding young men who were causing chaos with their nightly attempts to make it through the Channel Tunnel, but they were the tiny minority. Despite the lack of sanitation, healthcare and security, the people we came across had held on to their dignity. We were met with smiles and kindness and the offer of tea and conversation wherever we went.

Wondering past the now mostly closed, broken down shops of a thrown together main street, we entered the main living areas. Hundreds of sad, ripped and battered tents sat defeated on the dunes. With the impending eviction, there was a sense of calm before the storm as we continued walking further into the camp. Obtrusive, voyeuristic TV news crews hung around like bad smells, their cameras pointing at the ground; waiting, it seemed, for their chance to film the fires and chaos of the last night of the *animals in the zoo.* Disgraceful. Why weren't they filming the togetherness and community of these people? Not controversial enough?

We walked on until we reached a space no bigger than 8 metres squared by the side of a flooded road. This was the spot. Down went the jumpers and, after a bit of cajoling, a game broke out on this tiny pitch in the heart of the camp. John, Liz and I joined in and Helen took the photos. After ten minutes, a 4 v 4 became a 3 v 3, as one player wondered off and Liz, tackling ferociously in her big wellies, opted out before she could be red carded. Elias (Eritrea) and Ahmadullah (Afghanistan) joined my team and Suleyman (Sudan) and Ibrahim (Iraq) joined John.

The lively Elias played second division football in Eritrea and nutmegged players at will. Ahmadullah was our Zidane, strong and wise with an eye for goal. Together we raced into a 2-0 lead, only to be pegged back when a passing cyclist nudged one of their shots over the line. Still can't believe they claimed it. Game on! Ibrahim was a rock at the back for them, doing the work of two men and allowing Suleyman space to break forward. Me and John were in our respective nets. Aid vans and bikes invaded the pitch at different times, but on we played. I lost count of the amount of times one of our goalposts (a high vis jacket) was picked up by an oblivious pass-er-by. We played first to 10. At 9-7 to us we scored what we thought was the winner, only for Suleyman to claim he'd been fouled in the build-up. What an actor! Anyway, it was all academic as Elias slotted home from our next attack.

Talking to the lads afterwards, it was clear that they all just wanted to go home, but there was no home left for them to go to. Many had lost family members to war and civil conflict, and all faced an uncertain future. Here was the truth beyond the headlines. For a brief moment this day, footy had brought some joy amongst all this sorrow. Tomorrow they would all be gone, but to who knows where. Helen, John, Liz and I will never forget the smiles, warmth and friendship shown towards us by everyone we met. These scared, tired, displaced human beings trying to find peace, safety and direction in their lives. Just like all us all. One love.

Many refugees remained in Calais after the eviction on October 24th 2016, including many children.

Sylvie: *The souvenirs I will bring with me from Calais....people travelling from the Middle East and Africa, in great distress...often traumatised.....the local authorities "welcoming" them with kicks and blows, tear gas ,knife cuts in their tents ,insults and spit....the list is endless ,but above all a local policy pushing them, for many, towards a dreadful life, misery ,or death! Culturally-rich exchanges with refugees and volunteers..... unforgettable.....laughter, smiles, giggles and tears, moments of silence. People who have had the rare chance of creating a future in France or in the U.K. A young refugee, run over on a Calais' motorway very early one morning whilst I was driving another to a job interview in Lille. A young woman and her baby who returned drenched early one morning, they almost drowned...twice! Humiliation, thefts, harassment, police violence towards all these distressed people and towards the volunteers. Undercover police regularly parked in front of my home to intimidate me.....the loss of my job and abusive fines because...I am a humanitarian!*

What can I say about the situation since the eviction? It's worse than ever. The refugees that are left are even more in danger and didn't even have access to drinkable water until a few weeks ago. The showers are allowed for vulnerable people only. We don't have the same meaning for vulnerable as the government. For us they are all vulnerable as long as they live in bushes. For the government, they are the women and sick people only. The CRS (French riot police) sent to manage this are the most brutal and horrible humans in France, they are fierce animals without any brain. It's very very sad".

GAME 17: GERMANY

Date: November 27th 2016, 1.00pm
Ground: The Brandenburg Gate, Berlin

THE BFB

It was to the land of the perfect sausage that we travelled in search of game 17. When I first visited Berlin in 2011, the city's mayor was Klaus Wowereit, Germany's first openly gay high ranking politician. He famously described the city as "poor but sexy". Wowereit showed the same courage to kick start the transformation of this once divided city, as he did in coming out before the German tabloids could do it for him. Under his guidance, Berlin became regarded as one of Europe's coolest places to visit and for businesses to invest.

At the time of writing, Berlin is the second most populous city in the EU behind London (3.6 Million), but you would never guess it. With its broad streets and many low buildings, the city gives you space and reassures you that there's no need to hurry along. Beneath its many beautiful, historical landmarks and shiny modern office blocks, you get a sense of a young, expressive, artistic *and very sexy* city, but one which makes no attempt to hide the horrors of its recent past (Visit the Topography of Terror Museum or the haunting Holocaust Memorial as proof of this).

My brother-in-law Paul, and friends from home Alex and Richard were my companions for this trip. We arrived to find a city dressed for Christmas. Every time we climbed the steps from the U-Bahn, we seemed to emerge near a Christmas market, where currywurst, pretzels, schnitzels and bratwurst were all on display; all washed down, if you so wished, with gluhwein, weissbeer or the delicious local Berliner draft. Happy glowing shoppers, in winter woolly hats and scarves, marveled at the stalls packed with wooden jumping jacks, merry-go-rounds and colourful candy. Storybook stuff.

It would have been easy just to get lost in the magic of it all, but on a mission we were.

THE GAME......

The Brandenburg Gate seemed the most logical but daring place in the city to try and get a game going. This 18th Century neoclassical monument symbolizes for many the reunification of Germany after the fall of the wall in 1989. Many world leaders have given spectacularly pointless speeches here ever since; anything for a free sausage. Passing through its fifteen metre high doric columns, we found ourselves in a spacious pedestrianized place to play. Down went the jumpers and Richard and I passed the ball between us as Paul checked around for cops. Alex began taking photos. We set about trying to tempt players from amongst the many tourists on this chilly lunchtime. First to join us were partners Miriom Dietworst and Ron Mengelers from near Maastricht, Holland.

Josh from England then joined us and we had a 3 v 3 on our hands. Ron was very light on his slippy loafers. So determined was he to score that he lost his footing at high speed and nearly ended up in Warsaw. It was then that the Big Friendly Bear (BFB) of a security guard came over. Pretending to be grumpy, he picked up our jumpers with his big paws and asked us to move on. We did...about 5 feet to the right and carried on playing. Josh left us and a bunch of Spanish chaps from Valencia and Madrid joined in. A marvelous 5 v 5 broke out in the shadow of this great symbol of peace.

I was in the nets for our side, showing all the agility of a gnu with a cracked rib. It wasn't long before we raced into a three goal lead, with Paul scoring a contentious hat-trick past goalkeeper Richard *"First and third were over the bar but you can have the second"*. The game cracked on at a furious pace, sometimes around shoals of tourists who had the cheek to invade our pitch from time to time. By this time, Alex was weaving in and out like a young otter, taking some brilliant action photos. A sizeable crowd of spectators had gathered too. The BFB reappeared and moved us on again. The look on his loveable, hairy chubby chops told us he just wanted to go home, pluck some fish out of the river then go and hibernate. We called it a day after he'd moved us on for the third time. We didn't want to risk provoking him to rear up to his full height and pull us apart like rag dolls. The game finished 3-0 to us, with Paul taking home the match ball for those couple of cheeky chips and a nutmeg.

Once again, I had been bowled over by the speed at which the game came together, but also by how it was played in such a great spirit of friendship and togetherness by a bunch of strangers. Football truly does connect people at random and can even make bears smile too. I can't thank Paul, Richard and Alex enough for coming on the trip and for all their amazing efforts to help get the game going. Vielen dank meine freunde.

On a sad note...

The first Christmas market we visited was at Breitscheidplatz, close to the Kurfuerstendamm, the main shopping street in Berlin's west. On December 19th, a man ploughed a lorry into this same market and, chillingly, through the same area where we had sat and had currywurst only three short weeks earlier. 12 people were killed and 56 injured. The group calling themselves ISIS or ISIL, or more accurately MFB (Murdering Fucking Bastards) claimed responsibility for the attack.

It's hard to know what to say other than the response of people after this attack, and subsequent attacks in other cities, has been incredible. The great majority of folk have pulled together and not divided as these scum would want. Love will always conquer hate. It's what the great majority of people in our beautiful world want. RIP you poor innocent souls.

ACROSS THE FOUR C'S

GAMES 18-27

COLOMBIA-COSTA RICA-CUBA-CAROLINA

Winter 2017

January had been a killer. Despite my best efforts, my asthma had been out of control in this northern winter. I felt light years away from the sprightly chap who'd traveled so far and wide the year before. Getting up the stairs had become hard work again. I had no energy and felt totally fed up. In early February, just to compound the situation, I learnt via a cowards email (after seven years in my job) that I was to be made redundant at the end of March.

I decided to go out for a brew and a chat with my good friend Tony Howarth, a pastor and a Lancashire werewolf (very, very hairy man). He reminded me of my around the world dream and pointed out that, although this situation was pretty dire, it did present an opportunity to travel again. The following morning I awoke with renewed vigor (a cleaning fluid effective on 99% of surfaces). I'm not the kind to wonder sorrowfully through negative land for too long, and I wasn't going to squander all of my hard earned redundancy on rent and bills either. The plan was to hop on a plane to somewhere in May......

GAME 18: COLOMBIA

Date: May 23rd 2017, 11.00am
Ground: Plaza de San Antonio, Medellin

STARING AT MEDELLIN

Mention Medellin, Colombia, and thoughts may turn to the murderous Pablo Escobar drug cartel which, at the height of its operations in the 1980s, was reputed to be bringing in millions daily in drug profits. Everyone I spoke to (especially those who'd seen the NARCOS series on Netflix) thought I was bonkers to want to travel there for a game of footy. After all, it was once dubbed by Time Magazine as 'the most dangerous city on earth'. That was back in 1988, but the prospect of making this trip still weighed pretty heavy.

Landing at José María Córdova International Airport, I took the bus to San Diego Mall at 10.00am. I'd read that it was dangerous to travel this route into the city in the early hours or late at night, due to the real threat of stick-ups and kidnappings. After weaving our way through the mountains for several kilometres, we turned one last corner and there it was. Medellin. Wow! I had never seen anything like it. Situated in the Aburrá Valley, this sprawling Andean city is home to an estimated 2.5 million people. I gazed in awe at the tens of thousands of salmon pink apartment and office blocks crammed into the belly of the valley, and the sprawling barrios stuck to its slopes. I had to pinch myself. I really was staring at Medellin.

At San Diego station I climbed into one of the hundreds of small yellow taxis (known locally as 'yellow spots') which swarm around the city day and night. My taxi driver was brilliant. Somehow, without having a clue what each other was talking about, we laughed our heads off as we made our way through the steaming hot musical streets of the city. I was to stay with a number of other travelers and foreign workers at a homestay in the leafy Laureles barrio, to the west of downtown. The remarkable Rubén Darío Zapata and Anyela Heredia were our hosts. *Guardian*, possibly the cutest dog in the world, was our ferocious protector.

Ruben Zapata is a national prize winning author. His novel, *La resignada paz de las astromelias (The resigned peace of the astromelias)* won wide acclaim for its portrayal of the history of La Sierra, the barrio in Medellin where Ruben grew up. For years he had reported on the forgotten people of the city; the voiceless poor whom successive governments kept in their place by denying them the means to move forward with their lives. He reported on the economic, social and political problems of Medellin, and he and Anyela started their own independent newspaper *ecolectivo* in 2015, covering stories widely ignored by the national newspapers.

Ruben and Anyela are also responsible for the *Chronicles del destierro* (Chronicles of banishment). Using their own words, these five books tell the story of the displaced people from five different regions on the outskirts of Medellin. They'd had their land and homes stolen from them by the government, and many had been subject to torture and systematic violence. Anyela began crying when she told me how transcribing conversations with the displaced had given her nightmares for months, such was her horror and sadness at the persecution of these people. They could not understand why it was happening to them. When they drifted into the city to try to start a new life, they were met with rejection and brutality. Their response, however, was truly remarkable. In the face of such overwhelming odds, they began to develop social projects to help people in their new communities, gradually becoming accepted through their good deeds. These strong and courageous people had fought through it all and were now helping others.

Anyela wept again as she described the fragile peace between the government and the well documented FARC (The Revolutionary Armed Forces of Colombia) as she believed that there would be still more bloodshed to come. One of the main reasons Anyela started to open her home to foreign visitors, was that she needed to switch off. She was emotionally spent and could take no more of hearing about the human suffering in her country.

THE GAME......

This game is dedicated to the victims of the terror attack at a pop concert in Manchester on Monday May 22nd, when 22 innocent lives, many of them children, were tragically taken. Rest in Peace.

Walking out into the blazing sun of Medellin on Tuesday morning, my heart was heavy with what had gone on in Manchester the previous evening. Manchester is close to my home and to my heart, having worked all over the city down the years. I was more than a bit paranoid and anxious too. I'd read that there were over two hundred gangs still operational in Medellin. I'd been warned to be careful as it was difficult to know who was or wasn't a gang member. My new house mates had all been mugged for their phones, money or back-packs since their arrival. Great!

I took a deep breath and climbed into a 'yellow spot' to the city centre, Plaza de San Antonio. A bomb had been detonated in this plaza in 1995, during a pop concert, killing 23 people; a sickening parallel with what had just happened in Manchester. I sat on a wall in the shade of a tree, looking out across the plaza as a tall, slender man in virtual rags first ran, then fell to his knees. Tilting his head back and lifting his arms, he offered his despairing soul up to the vast blue skies. A few homeless men lay next to the famous voluptuous sculptures of Fernando Botero which are dotted around the plaza's perimeter, some of which have been left in their twisted, mangled state as reminders of the 1995 atrocity. I was listening to Morcheeba's cool classic "Part of the Process" but I was feeling anything but cool myself.

Nervously, I plonked my jumpers down and looked around. The ball tucked under my arm felt like my only friend in the world. What was I doing here? Why didn't I go to Accrington instead? It was then I spotted Albert Aguilara Cancino and Alexis Marin Duuan sitting chatting close by. I went over and showed them my mission note written in Spanish. Thankfully they agreed to play. What a relief! My paranoia completely evaporated. I was in the centre of Medellin, I'd met some locals and I was still alive! Before long we were joined by some other young chaps who were mulling around, including the very cool Ricardo Esteban Canola (20), Yimy Romano Perez (27) and Dubenas Bemal Espinosa (28). With one or two more additions, it was game on. 4 v 4.

I was in the goals for Yimi's side. He was a fantastic player; rangy with great skill and energy. Ricardo was very composed on the ball too, but we were no match for Albert's team. They quickly ran into a five goal lead, largely due to a sweaty mound of Lancashire lard in the nets. None of them had broken sweat and I looked like I'd just been chucked in the sea. (Ahh, so this is why European teams rarely win this side of the equator?)

The opposition were rock solid in defence. Albert in particular was Bobby Moore-esque, coolly breaking up play and intelligently laying the ball off. The swift and skillful Señor Espinosa in attack was proving deadly too. Spotting my deficiencies, Yimy went in goals and I turned official camera man when another player showed up. This badly needed tactical switch seemed to do the trick. Ricardo pulled a couple of goals back in quick succession. We even got to 5-3 before Albert's team ran in comfortable and deserved winners at 7-3. A brilliant, technical and committed game with plenty of flare on show. The South American way I guess?

The best part about today's game was the absolutely natural and cool way that this random group of lads joined in, played the game, then sat chilling together afterwards like they were brothers. Like every Colombian I had met so far, they exuded warmth, kindness and friendship. They could all play a bit too. Not for the first time on my trip, I felt truly humbled and uplifted. Even in one of the toughest cities on earth, love, respect and kindness had found a way to survive and prevail amongst these marvelous folk.

GAME 19: COLOMBIA

Date: May 27rd 2017, 7.00pm
Ground: Inder Park, Laureles, Medellin

GILMA

Medellin had pulled me in completely. I didn't stand a chance. To my rural northern eye it was a fierce and feverish, frantic and intense place. The combination of the pressing heat, those tough, warm, smiling sentinels of hope that were its people, the sheer volume and madness of the city traffic and all those stunning women had left me delirious. And then there was Gilma.

On Sunday 21st of May, I met a beautiful and special woman. Gilma Munoz Sabogal stoked a fire in my heart that had been dying for so long. Over the next week, we spent several days and evenings together. We rode the metro by the rampant chocolate coloured river to the end of the line, then took a cable car up the mountain side, looking out as the vast sprawling city before us melted into darkness at sun set. We laughed together in the afternoon sun, sharing fruit and ice-cream, and held each other tightly as we gazed down at the city lights from the lovers look out point of Las Palmas. We were kindred spirits. There was no other way to describe it. She couldn't speak English nor me Spanish, but the hours we spent together were so easy and natural. I was falling in love and my heart ached for her.

One evening, as I was making my way back from Gilma's home city of Itagüi in the south, I missed the last metro connection to my homestay. It was after 10.00pm as I walked out on to the pavement outside of the city central San Antonio Station. The streets were deserted. As I stood pondering my next move, I heard quickening footsteps behind me. I turned to see a policeman drawing his gun. Before visiting Medellin, I'd read stories of how corrupt some of the city police were. My heart was pounding, but then for some strange reason I totally relaxed, resigned to my fate I suppose. The policeman was now stood almost toe-to-toe with me, gun held across his chest James Bond style. He waved the index finger of his other hand in my face as if to say "What are you doing stood here alone at this time of night you daft bugger?"

He waited by my side, gun still drawn, until a taxi came by. He flagged it down and asked the young, heavily tattooed driver to step out of the car. He then patted him down, asked to see his documents, then took a photo of his number plate before ringing through to the station to do further checks. Satisfied that it was safe for me to travel with this dude, he motioned for me to get in the taxi and issued what sounded like a threat to the driver to get me home safely. That was the longest 20-minute taxi ride home of my life, such was the reputation of some of these drivers to take tourists up into the barrios to be robbed and worse by fellow gang members. I arrived home safely and spent the next hour in silence, staring at the ceiling in my room.

THE GAME…..

Mario Gomez from Madrid (No, not footy player) was also staying at Ruben and Anyela's. Mario is a journalist and translator and had been a massive support to me all week, especially when I was trying to buy stuff to make a shepherd's pie for everyone, and I couldn't even say *onions* in Spanish. The very lovely Shefali from India and Giulia from Italy were also living at the house. I persuaded them all to come for a game of footy at the nearby Inder Park. Ruben and Anyela invited their friends Raul, Johnny and Alejandro to play too. This would be the first game under floodlights. Some young chaps were already playing when we got there, so we invited them to join us.

Game on. 7 v 7. What a game! It took a full 15 minutes for the deadlock to be broken. Diving to my right, I managed to paw away a fierce shot, but only into the path of the Delhi Dazzler Shefali, who tucked it away inside the far jumper. Good finish for someone who had never played before in her life. Things rapidly went from bad to worse for our side. 2-0 down at half-time, with Shefali notching another (goal-hanger), we paid for missed chances and went 4-0 down not long after the break.

The match was fiercely competitive, with Johnnie, Raul, Ruben and the local lads in particular biting into the tackles. Giulia was turning on the Italian class for us at times; neat turns, penetrating runs and precise passing. Mario was everywhere, forcing the play, making big tackles and trying with everything he had to get us back in the game; some engine that fella. Anyela was brilliant. She just hung about in front of me, putting blocks in and laughing. We eventually pulled one back.

It was pretty clear that we were going to struggle to close the gap, so we exchanged one of our players for their best player, whose name I didn't get. Let's just call him the orange flash (he had on a bright orange t-shirt). This guy was brilliant. Early 20's, fit as a fiddle with unbelievable tekkers, he started to run things for us and I hardly had another shot to save. It wasn't long before we got the score back to 4-4. Everyone looked knackered by this time so it was next goal the winner. Fortunately we got it. What a brilliant and joyful game with brilliant people. We all went back to house after, ate my shepherd's pie and listened to Raul and Johnnie knocking out South American folk songs on guitar and percussion until four in the morning. My Gilma came too. Perfect.

GAME 20: COSTA RICA

Date: June 1st 2017, 6.00pm
Ground: Cerro Plano, Monteverde, Costa Rica

MADAME BUTTERFLY

Leaving Colombia had been upsetting. I'd had ten of the most overwhelming days of my life there and made some great friends along the way, not least with my beautiful Gilma.

Arriving in Costa Rica, I honestly didn't know what day it was. Needing some peace, I headed out to Monteverde, a breathtaking mountain nature reserve west of my homestay in Sabanilla, San Jose. After a day's trekking through the lush tropical jungle, I got talking with one of the five brothers who owned and ran the beautiful Manakin Lodge, my home for the next three nights. Here, the jungle touched my veranda (Oo er missus!) and a charm of mesmerising colourful humming birds played around the balcony in the mornings.

Edgar Vargas Sulcedo, 31, is quite a character. He grew up in Alajuela, the country's second largest city after San Jose. Edgar's mum moved to Cancun, Mexico when he was just ten years old, leaving him devastated. He didn't get along with his father and was kicked out of the family home when he was just fifteen. He moved in with his girlfriend, but it wasn't long before they had both developed a cocaine habit. Things came to a head when Edgar, by now in his early twenties, went into town with a knife, looking to mug someone so that he could score. He cornered his victim but couldn't go through with it. He knew he had to change and, luckily for him, he was thrown a life-line.

Edgar's father was a wealthy man. He decided to give Edgar and his brothers their inheritance before he died. They pooled their resources and bought Manakin Lodge. This proved a great stroke of luck for the lost, chaotic Edgar, who went on to thrive in his new responsibilities. Now, in addition to his stake in the lodge, Edgar owns a beautiful house, set in 1600 sqm of land in the San Luis area of the Monteverde Cloud Forest. He rents this out for part of the year as he spends so much time working at the lodge. Edgar taught himself to speak English and has an English girlfriend. He hasn't touched drugs for over five years and this big, bouncy, lovable chap wouldn't now dream of living any other way.

THE GAME…..

Edgar was really enthusiastic about my journey. One afternoon, he asked some kids from the local neighbourhood to spread the word, and at 6pm that evening, ten footy mad kids came bombing around the corner on their bikes ready to play. Brilliant! Edgar joined one side and I the other. We would end up playing on well into the night. 5 v 5, first to 10 in the back-street to the lodge.

These little warriors competed for every single inch; the concentration on their beaming faces total. The most ferocious player joined in later; a tiny, wiry girl with a butterfly t-shirt on. She proceeded to boot the lads all over the place, score a few and at one point make a gravity defying, acrobatic goal-line clearance. Her mum called her in a few times but she refused to go. This was life and death. Even when her mum came out to send her on an errand, she got on her bike, rode a few yards, checked her mum had gone back in then dumped her bike and carried on playing. Fantastic!

The game had the lot. Elbows, name calling, boots in the ankle, the ball getting stuck under bikes, disputed goals, volleys, headers, a dog on the pitch and a 100 miles an hour determination to score which didn't let up for the whole hour and a half that we played. It was almost pitch black by the time Edgar's team sealed the win 10-7, the game encapsulated by the fearsome courage of madame butterfly. These wee troopers, and being in these stunningly beautiful and peaceful surroundings, had cheered me up no end.

GAME 21: COSTA RICA

Date: June 4th 2017, 11.00am
Ground: The Blue River, Tirasses, San Jose

PABLO AND NELSON

I awaken, wash, get dressed and head out feeling uneasy. The streets are unfamiliar. People stare. I don't belong here and they know it. I get on the bus to San José. It's one of those days. People whispering, staring, laughing. I take a seat. The bus gets crowded but still no-one sits next to me. I'm the odd one out, the foreigner. Then I put my headphones in, press play and The Who's "The Real Me" floods my brain and restores my confidence. I look around and no-one is staring anymore. No-one's interested. When I get off the bus I couldn't care less about who might be looking at me. This is my world too, freckles and all.

San José is Costa Rica's capital city. Its centre is packed with familiar shops and American fast-food chains. Walking through the Plaza de Juan Rafael Mora, the first thing I notice is a bare bum. A poor woman, high on something or other, has unbuttoned her jeans and is having a pee right there in the middle of the street. Everyone just carries on with their day around her. Amputees, elderly women and people with learning disabilities congregate in front of the stores looking for handouts.

I wander into the Central Park area, a big wide-open space where the tall, beautiful palm trees are shaking off the morning rain in the breeze. Some women hold umbrellas up against the mid-afternoon sun and music blasts out at a daft volume from a nearby sports shop. Why? It's a worldwide insane phenomenon! It's the people who work in these places who should be sent to war. You can use all the sound torture you want, you'll never break 'em.

There seems to be a barbers every 100 metres. I pop into one for a neat and tidy. My barber is a dapper young bloke with a pencil moustache, resplendent in what could only be described as a black satin smoking jacket. So razor sharp is he that his parting could cut through a tree. I sit down and place my overgrown hedge in his hands. He is gentle and meticulous; the consummate professional. I leave a slightly younger man, replete with the essential over 40's ear trim. After a couple of hours walking, I am struggling to see a place where I can put my jumpers down. Police on bicycles are buzzing around everywhere. I had been told back at my digs that a missionary lived next door who might be interested in meeting me.

THE GAME…..

I met with the brilliantly named Pablo Rosendo de León Custodio on Sunday and we headed down to Tirasses for a game. Pablo is a missionary from Guatemala and an absolute gentleman. He has been working in some of the poorest neighbourhoods in and around San José for over four years. Tirasses is such an area. Most people there earn a living by picking through the huge rubbish dump nearby for recyclable materials. They are known as Buzos (divers). The pitch we played on this day, Rio Azure (Blue River) is built on part of the dump.

Arriving at Tirasses, we met with the tall dreadlocked Nelson Paez, a huge Bob Marley fan, community volunteer and top bloke. Nelson and Pablo had been working with the young people of the town, helping them with their school work, teaching practical life skills and running a football team. Almost all of them would have to leave Tirasses if they wanted to secure employment and build a better life for themselves.

At around 11am, we gathered a group of lads together and had a 5 v 5 in very hot and humid conditions. There were some brilliant players on show. On my side, Antonio stuck to the wing and reminded me of Neymar without the antics; brilliant close control, skill, vision and speed. Like all good players, he always seemed to operate in plenty of space. Ariel was a serious box to box midfielder, playing as if in front of 50,000 people. Keilor, known as The Bullet, was the maverick- the Gazza, the Worthington or the Best. He was a fantastic player who had an inert hunger for the game, always trying the extraordinary. Alberto was the cool guy, quietly affective like a Carrick or a Whelan. Then there was some joker in the nets making up the numbers.

Despite having such a good team, we were quickly 4-2 down. Nelson, on their side, was brilliant with the lads, tripping them up and rugby tackling them if they got past him. It was clear they all loved and respected him. Pablo was performing heroics in their nets for such a diminutive chap. Finally we got our act together. Antonio and The Bullet went into overdrive and brought the game back level. The suffocating humidity was starting to take its toll, especially on the opposition. We scored a couple more to make it 6-4 and the game came to a natural end through sheer exhaustion. As we drifted back into the town, I couldn't help but think about the tough struggle those boys now faced. Thankfully, there are millions of incredibly hardworking, kind and caring volunteers all over the world like Pablo and Nelson, bringing the light of hope to people. This global love being shown for others should be headline news every day.

GAME 22: HAVANA, CUBA

Date: June 8th 2017, 2.00pm
Ground: Parque Cervantes, Old Town Havana

THE TWO RASCALS

…. and so it was that I reached the land of revolution, fantastic cars and big cigars. I'd always been drawn to Cuba. Maybe it was because Che Guevara had been an asthmatic too, or maybe it was the astonishing music of the Buena Vista Social Club…or maybe it was the island's steadfast refusal to cower to the big bully across the water. Whatever it was, I was chuffed to bits to be there.

Landing around 4pm, I took a taxi into the city. The roads were virtually deserted. Only around 5% of Cubans own their own car, and petrol rationing was still in force on the island. It was only when we were approaching my digs in La Habana Viejo (old town Havana) that I finally saw them; Cuba's famous and colourful 1950s vintage Chevrolets, Buicks, Chrysler Plymouths and Ford Lincoln's, gliding by or posing at the side of the road, like stunning metallic birds of paradise designed by poets.

My room for the night was on the first floor of a gorgeous colonial casa in old town. A narrow stairway led up from the street entrance to a long, beautifully tiled corridor, off which must have been 4 or 5 bedrooms. I was shown to the room closest to the front of the casa. Flopping on my bed I looked around at the cream walls and up to the high ceiling painted salamander orange. Did you like that? Salamander orange? No doubt named by the same berk who brought us *sensitive crimson, ballet slipper pink, air superiority blue* (I kid you not) and *moonlight over Rochdale cream* (I kid you). A deep window was cut into the street facing wall, housing a stunning multi-coloured stained glass pane. I particularly liked the shade of *custard at the point of boiling yellow* in this.

I drifted off to sleep and woke around 8pm. Feeling relaxed, I wondered barefoot through the lovely large communal room at the front of the casa, on through the huge shuttered window and onto the balcony. Gazing down the narrow dusty street, I could make out a few locals sat chatting on their doorsteps and others just mulling around in the warm air. I decided to take a stroll. What a fateful decision this turned out to be.

After a minute or so of walking, I found myself in Parque Servantes, a square named after the Spanish author of Don Quixote, Miguel de Cervantes.

Although nowhere near as paranoid as I had been in Medellin, I was still quite wary. I appeared to be the only tourist around in this hazy place with pale street lights. Groups of men stood chatting in doorways and seemed to be looking in my direction. I heard footsteps behind me. Someone was getting closer and closer. "Hey mister? ". I turned around thinking "Here we go ...robbed, kidnapped or murdered". My eyes met those of a slim young man in his early twenties in a grey vest. He'd stopped about three feet away from me. "You want a girl tonight mister?" "No thanks" I replied. "Do you fancy a game of footy?" That was a conversation stopper I can tell you.

It was then that a stocky fella of around 40, wearing a yellow vest and baseball cap, came over to where me and slim Jim were stood gawping at each other. This guy was full of questions "Where are you from? Where are you staying? How long are you here for?". It was his last question that I struggled with "Come Steve. Me and my friend here will take you on a tour of our city. Come. Why not?" Were these two fellas in league with each other? Was this a classic pincer movement? The offer of a girl ... a city tour… really just smokescreens for the inevitable dark-alley-knife-mugging to come? No. Something in my gut told me that these chaps were genuine. Yes, I knew they were chancers who might want a few bob at the end of the 'tour' as gratitude, but neither of them struck me as dangerous. I turned to the statue of that dreamer and adventurer Don Quixote for permission. He gave me the thumbs up. "Ok lads. Why not?" and off we trotted.

These two rascals, the young handsome Alejandro Aguirre and chatty Antonio Olive would show me around the city for the next two hours. We wandered past the Catedral San Cristobal del la Habana, the Museo de la Revolución, then down a stretch of the famous Malecón sea front. I also got to call in on "Granma'. This is the yacht that transported Castro, Guevara and 82 fighters from Mexico to Cuba in November 1956 to kick start the overthrow of the Batista regime. It is now on permanent display in a glass enclosure adjacent to the Museo de la Revolución.

Although this was all really fascinating, the best bits came later. Explaining my mission to the lads, they led me down some back streets and through a low entrance into a dramatic looking courtyard. Here, around twenty young men were playing 5-a-side (winner stays on) in a space about half the size of a footy pitch. A magnificent mural of a reclining woman stretched the length of the wall behind the far goal, and the steep walls flanking the pitch were crowned by tall, whitewashed dwellings. The players were very serious and committed and the standard of play was excellent. Antonio explained that although the Cuban league had only ten teams, football had overtaken baseball as the country's most popular sport.

We watched on for about half an hour. I was getting hungry and asked Alejandro and Antonio if I could buy them food as a thankyou for their time. We wandered off down several dark narrow streets until we came to a doorway. Had the whole night led to this point? Was I finally about to be done in? Antonio pushed the door open and in we stepped to be greeted by a big happy chef, a very smiley waitress, two tables and a battered tv wedged in the far corner showing a baseball game. There we sat for the next few hours, stuffing our faces with ropa veija and drinking beer like old friends 'til the chef chucked us out. What a tour and what a night! Who said you shouldn't talk to strangers?

THE GAME......

Antonio and Alejandro agreed to meet me the following day to play footy. We met at 1pm outside my casa just as a storm broke. I can't tell you how refreshing that warm rain felt on my baking body. I'd been cooking since Colombia. To the shock and horror of my new mates, I placed my jumpers down in the middle of the road at Parque Cervantes and asked folk to join in. Alejandro shook his head, smiled then wandered over. Next, two kids of around 13 years of age joined us. The shoeless Christian joined my side and Larry joined Alejandro. 2 v 2 in a spectacular rainstorm. It was hammering it down. We quickly drew a crowd. The locals found any shelter they could to watch and the kids at the adjacent Agustin Gomez School stood packed at the classroom windows.

Barefooted Christian was a fearless athlete, covering every inch of the pitch and slamming into tackles. We quickly ran into a 4-0 lead, this despite the silky skills of Alejandro and the very serious Larry, who plainly didn't like getting beat. Me and Christian were getting all the breaks. Fifteen minutes in and we were soaked to the skin. A kid called Raisal came on for Larry and Marlon for Christian. Raisal changed the game. He had a few tricks but knew when to pass, and he certainly knew where the goal was, bringing it back to 4-4 within ten minutes of coming on. I had a quick word with the very cool Marlon. We shut up shop for a bit then scored 2 lucky goals on the break. 6-4 the final score.

I loved every second of today's game. The little guys were so hungry for the ball that I doubt they even noticed it was raining. Antonio, Alejandro and I wandered off for a drink afterwards. By great chance, I got to see them again a week later to say farewell on my last day in Cuba. Lovely humans.

GAME 23: VINALES, CUBA

Date: June 10th 2017, 5.00pm
Ground: Sergio Dupro Baseball Stadium

RUM LOT

Before setting off, I'd been advised to book on a group tour of the island if I wanted to see more than just Havana, as getting around by public transport would be impossible in the time I had. I joined my group in the early evening after the rainy game. For the next eight days, our merry band of twelve amigos and amigas bombed around the empty motorways of this time capsule of a country. We visited rural Viñales, the stunning coastal town of Cienfuegos, via the Bay of Pigs, and the colourful and vibrant town of Trinidad before returning to Havana via Santa Clara, where we visited the Che Guevara mausoleum. We all got along brilliantly.

As well as Mexican-Americans, Chinese and Australians, there was a brilliant chap from Poland in our party by the name of Kamil Stibinski. I got on with Kamil right away, which was a good job as we were designated room-mates for the whole tour. Kamil is a tall Polish chap in his early 30's with a wicked sense of humour and a thick Irish accent, after having lived in Galway for ten years. Oh what fun we had.

THE GAME......

To the west of Havana lies the quiet village of Viñales. Tobacco is their main crop and grows well there due to its special micro-climate. I took a walk down main street. Many of the locals were been busy converting their casas into colourful tourist homestay's. A local fella named Ariel spotted the ball tucked under my arm and came over for a chat. He told me he was an excellent footballer who had once been on Barcelona's books (like he'd also been a butter bean and a griffin in previous lives).

We agreed to meet at the nearby Sergio Dupro Baseball Stadium at 5pm for a kick about. When I got there, Ariel had yet to arrive. I walked on to the pitch and called over some local teenagers who were busy getting drunk in the stands. The 5 v 5 that followed was intense, probably due to the ale. This was the first game where I had witnessed aggression and dangerous slide tackles. Thankfully things didn't spill over too much.

Wherever I had landed so far, I'd seen talented players who would stand a chance of making it in the game, if only they had the opportunity. There were three such players involved in this game. Philippe was the best player on the park; low centre of gravity, technical, super quick feet and imaginative. His only fault was that he was a bit greedy. Marco on my side was a composed, Alan Hansen type player. At over 6 feet tall, his touch for a big man was almost faultless, as was his reading of the game. Manuel was the brains; a very cool sweeper for the opposition. He was comfortable in possession and displayed precision passing with both feet. The younger, smaller dudes were tough and didn't give an inch. Little David the Lionheart in our nets was a beast.

Ariel had arrived by now, but after a quick five minute burst he sat out the rest of the game. (Must've been saving himself for his trail with Paris Saint Germain. Nice bloke, tall stories). This relentless game was locked tight at 3-3 after 45 minutes. Some players had a breather and were replaced by others who had stopped to watch. I subbed on and off with Kamil. Philippe played throughout, making surge after surge forward. Unfortunately for him, apart from Manuel, the rest of his side couldn't sustain his appetite for the game. Marco's side ran out 5-3 winners in the end. We took a few photos and chatted and laughed for a while after the game. The boys offered me the last of their rum before wandering off back to the stands.

And so it was that with visions of Che, rum in my belly and the spirit of these lovely welcoming people in my heart, I headed across the water to a very different land.

GAME 24: GEORGIA, USA

Date: 19th June 2017, 6.30pm
Ground: River Street, Savannah

THE GEORGIA QUEEN

After incredible scenes in Colombia, Costa Rica and Cuba it was time to head off to the USA for the last leg of this part of the journey. It would take some mental adjustment. My brain was struggling to make the cultural leap from 1950s Havana to the slice of American pie that is Irmo, South Carolina. The fact that I was absolutely cream crackered played its part too.

Neil Murphy is from Millom, Cumbria, and a great friend of mine from our student days at Lancashire Polytechnic. After four marvelously debauched years there, it truly was a miracle that we passed our degrees. Landing at Neil and his wife Michelle's beautiful home, and meeting their children George (18) and Elle (20) and Summer the beagle, I finally got some much needed kip. After a couple of days, me and my old mate set off to tour the steaming hot south, propelled by Neil's super cool, jet black Wrangler Sahara Jeep and Fireball Whiskey. I felt a wee bit lost as we headed out. There wasn't a single hill in sight. Being from the Lancashire Pennines this completely threw me. I had no concept of where I was and felt like we were in a pac-man game. Cruising down the freeways, the air-waves were dominated by country music, and it was all really shite. The same song sung by a hundred different folk, with crap lyrics like "Got it goin' on Like Donkey Kong' and "Whoo-wee shut my mouth, slap your grandma". I love a bit of John Denver, Willie Nelson, Johnny Cash and Kris Kristopherson, but this modern stuff was just red chubby cheeked bollocks in a Stetson.

Our first stop was Savannah, Georgia. What a place! Steeped in history, Savannah is the oldest city in Georgia and was a strategic port during both the American Civil War and War of American Independence. Millions of visitors flock there every year to stroll through its southern storybook scenes such as Lafayette Square. We headed down to River Street in the late afternoon for a beer. This is a stretch of century old former cotton warehouses running alongside the Savannah River. The buildings have been tastefully converted into shops, galleries, bars, restaurants and hotels. After drooling through the gluttonous cake and sweety fest that is Savanna's Candy Kitchen, we popped into a bar a couple of doors down.

THE GAME……

From where we were sat, we could see the red and white splendor of the huge Georgia Queen steamboat, a vessel capable of taking up to 1000 passengers at a time. We *had* to have a game by this magnificent beast. Supping up, we strolled over and down went the jumpers on the quayside next to it. We asked three lads sat on a nearby bench if they wanted to join us. Jonathan Andersson, Martin Sand and Anton Ryberg were all on holiday from Örebro, Sweden. Louis Jassmeier from Germany then joined in to make it a 3 v 3.

Martin and Louis were on my team, but it was the energetic and forceful Jonathan who looked most likely to score first for them. Against the run of play though, Louis slammed us in to the lead from close range. It was so hot. Even these strapping mountain trekking Swedes were finding it tough going. Big Jessies. A dodgy goal at the far post brought them back into it. 1-1 at half-time and we changed ends. Shortly after the re-start, the ball sailed into the Savannah River. The response was heroic. A Georgia Queen crew member, who had been spectating, hurtled down the decks with a long pole in hand to try to save our ball. Tourists and boat staff alike stopped to watch the rescue effort. I'm surprised ABC News didn't show up. Between us we scrambled it back into play and cracked on.

Gaps started to appear in our defence as Louis and Martin began running out of steam. For them, Neil was having more of an influence coming forward, with Anton hanging back to plug the gaps. Jonathan continued to press. By this time I had melted into a sweaty immovable mess. The humidity had done for me. Unable to stop a fart let alone a ball, I was entirely responsible for us losing the game 3-1. The game ended for good when the ball rolled into the river again. Superb game with lovely friendly folk. We sloped off for a well-deserved beer together afterwards.

Neil : " *Now I get it and commit to be at Game 80 in Stacksteads, because this project means something. I'm a conforming type of chap who holds compliance in high regard and abides by social norms and generally accepted behaviours. So having a pop up game of football in a public place where other folk are entitled to their right of access bothered me a bit. I did it though because I trusted Steve and he knew it was going to be Ok. It was definitely Ok.*

Steve threw his four jumpers down on the tiled quayside adjacent to where the Georgia Queen had berthed. Folk were milling by and boarding. I wondered what they were thinking as we started booting the ball about as they queued to get on board. We could have lobbed it into someone's chops at any time. My next series of concerns were centred around the dimensions of our pitch in relation to my questionable first touch. As was said of Rangers and Leeds United beanpole marksman Mark Hately, I can trap a ball further than most folks can pass it. I was watching out for octogenarians sauntering by and keeping an eye on the Georgia Queen's crew, respecting their authority, thinking that folk would frown on the whole thing. It was the opposite. They were watching on from all decks smiling, approving, really enjoying what we were doing.

I was to learn that I was reading it all wrong and being far too serious about stuff that nobody else was bothered about. I've probably been doing that for years in many situations. The first time the ball went in the river, the Georgia Queen staff were right on it, almost desperate for the game to continue. We weren't the non-conforming thugs causing an obstruction at all. We were a spectacle in their eyes.

There were very few words needed when we were playing. From the moment Steve threw the ball in play, game faces were assumed and pass and move was what it was all about. When the ball went out of play and careered towards the face of a woman in her sixties, I was all ready to blurt out my sincere guilt ridden apology. However, she caught the ball, fixed me with a very deliberate stare then started bouncing the ball, giving it the full Le Bron, and tossed the ball back to us with a massive smile.

What we did that night meant we connected in friendship with some strangers who had all been sat within 20 feet of each other but who would never have ended up talking otherwise. It was a powerful social experiment that seems to work like a treat every time. Why is that? It's all about the earth shaped ball."

GAME 25: SOUTH CAROLINA, USA

Date: 24th June 2017, 11.45am
Ground: Folly Beach, Charleston County

PELICANS AND SINNERS

"Well sir. I'm sorry to tell you, but you're a sinner". What!? This little freckle faced boy in a baseball cap was staring up at me shaking his head. He'd just recited the juicy bits from the Book of Genesis at me in a squeaky voice, then asked me if I was still a non-believer. I said I was and he branded me a sinner! I just about resisted the urge to pick him up by his little gerbil cheeks and dunk him in the ocean.

Folly Beach is a city in Charleston County, South Carolina and has a stunning coastline of soft, grey sand and warm water. Neil's son George and his partner Darcie had joined us for the day. It was around 11.00am when we arrived and the beach was starting to fill up with holiday makers. Squadrons of pelicans patrolled the skies and would later dive bomb for fish just out to sea. An amazing sight.

THE GAME......

I plonked my jumpers down on the beach and had a kick-a-bout with Neil and George for a while. Neil and I then strolled around asking if anyone wanted a game. It was slow going and who could blame folk? It was a beautiful day to do nothing at all. I spotted a few people walking under the pier towards us wearing lanyards. They were part of Fuge, a Christian based summer camp. We had a chat and five minutes later it was game on with around fifteen young people and their leaders from all over the US.

Neil and I joined in for a bit then left the troops to it. There were some impressive talents out there, especially Annabel and Hayley who were clearly the best players. Hayley was captain material; super serious, hard-working, skilled and leading by example throughout. Annabel was quick, intelligent and a good finisher. Austin the cool cat in shades was impish and could play a bit too, scoring a cheeky back heel from a tight angle at one point. We were joined later by a young chap called Jonah, not with the group. He was twelve years old and a naturally gifted footballer, doing the difficult skills for fun. We lost track of the score early on and, for the first time on this whole trip, no-one seemed too bothered about it either. They were all just loving playing footy, stopping only when lunch was called an hour later.

Talking with group leaders Gabrielle, Rebecca, Lucas and Holly, we discovered that Fuge had around twenty summer camps throughout Charleston. On top of having fun, these young dudes would be asked to form small groups at certain times (like this afternoon) then go and talk to strangers about Jesus and the bible. Neil and I couldn't help but get the vibe that these kids just wanted to have a laugh for the rest of the day, and not do the religious bit. At the end of the game, after Little Zach had branded me a sinner, Lucas gathered everyone in and said a prayer for my safe travels. Thankfully I didn't catch fire or dissolve. A really enjoyable day on the sands with these vibrant young souls.

GAME 26: SOUTH CAROLINA, USA

Date: 25th June 2017, 6.30pm
Ground: Fall's Park, Greenville

NUKA DA KID

During my stay, Neil took me to see the Williams-Brice Stadium, which is home to the South Carolina Gamecocks. Remarkably, this 85,000 seater stadium is only the 20th largest college football stadium in the National Collegiate Athletic Association. So it is true? Things *are* bigger in the US…even the people, as I later discovered watching a procession of super inflated bottoms take their seats at a Denny's Diner. *"A Lumberjack Slam, a side order of clutch my chest I'm gonna die cheese pancakes and a peddle-bin full of cola please. Hold the salad."*

Part way through our road trip, Neil did me the courtesy of dropping me off for a couple of days at my cousin Katy's in Greenville SC. She is my Dad's sister's lass and I hadn't seen her since we were kids. Katy and I visited her father, my Uncle Graham, in a nursing home during my stay. He was very poorly after a series of strokes. Graham sadly passed away a few short months later.

THE GAME

Katy's explosive, drumming playing husband Ian was very supportive of my cause. Together with their two children, Hunter (18) and Keegan (10), we took a trip to Falls Park, a short walk from town centre Greenville. Peering down over the splendid Reedy River Falls from Liberty Bridge, we spotted a patch of green where we could play.

Even though the park was busy, it took a while to persuade people to join in. Church goers were still dressed in their finery, white trainers didn't want to get dirty, mysterious blisters appeared on big toes and muscle bound young poseurs in vests and shades were too cool for school. Although people were very polite with their refusals, I couldn't help but feel that our recruitment efforts were intruding on ancient southern traditions. Eventually Darryl (15) and his sister Kayleigh (8), out strolling with their grandparents, joined us. We needed one more player.

Julius Huntley (17), AKA Nuka Da Kid, is a rapper from Niagara Falls. (Check him out on sound cloud) Living in a poor part of Greenville, he was working for next to bugger all as a cashier at the local 2 Chefs fast-food joint. He looked super-cool on his bike, wearing a red 70's Stevie Wonder-like shirt, and smiling more than anyone in the world has ever smiled before. We got chatting and he told me he was doing his best to impress the ladies in the park by pulling wheelies. It seemed a long shot to me, but he seemed to be enjoying himself. He was well up for a kick-about.

A 3 v 3 in the mid-afternoon southern heat. I was on the same side as Kayleigh and Ian. At one point, a blocked shot sent the ball speeding down the slope towards the river. Ian bolted after it, slipped on his back and continued to hurtle towards the water, hollering and flapping like a drowning man. Hilarious. The spectators watching from the bridge yelled and whooped as only American's can. Ian came to a stop just a foot from the water, and got a standing ovation from the onlookers as he peeled his muddy body off the grass. Hunter waded in for the elusive ball and on we played.

On the pitch, little Kayleigh on our team was defying the odds against the big boys, scoring two and saving a few on the line. The quicksilver Darryl nutmegged me one too many times for my liking and, depressingly, I couldn't do a thing about it. Cheeky git. Hunter was brilliant in the nets for them and little Keegan retired when he got hungry. Julius just laughed and smiled all the way through. Not a footballer by any stretch, but priceless in the transfer market for sheer enthusiasm and fun.

Ian was working hard in our nets but he couldn't do anything about the eventual 8-5 score-line. Two old blokes and an 8 year old couldn't quite cut it again those young whippersnappers. Toughest day yet trying to get a game going, in what my cousin Katy calls the buckle of the southern Baptist bible belt. We got there though, and on a Sunday too.

GAME 27: SOUTH CAROLINA, USA

Date: 3rd July 2017, 6.00pm
Ground: The Stonewall Stadium (outside my mates house), Irma SC

WHY DON'T WE DO IT IN THE ROAD?

This unbelievable chapter in my journey was almost over. I was totally knackered, and so it was with great relief that the final game before flying home was on our doorstep. Neil and his son George put the word out in their neighbourhood, and it wasn't long before a fine bunch of young warriors drifted over to Neil's house to play.

THE GAME

On a lovely warm American evening, three teams of four, calling themselves Unicorn FC, Khaki and the Trousers FC and Doubters FC, would go on to play winner stays on for just short of three hours. We played in the middle of the road and the action was unrelenting and super competitive. At first, I was concerned that the youngest team, Unicorn FC, would struggle against their elders, but my fears proved unfounded. Miles, Noah, Landon and Karic were fearless little rascals, taking great pleasure in snapping at the ankles of the big boys. Karic's tackling in particular was as wild as his moon cat eyes. Khaki and the Trousers FC proved to be an immovable object though, too strong and technical for the other teams. So for the final game of the evening, we decided to combine the Unicorns and the Doubters to take them on.

The impressive Rachel opened the scoring with a long range belter for the combined eight. Big Andy, Hunter, Jay and Neil's son George scrapped hard against the odds for the Khakis, but there was little space for them to work in. Neil stayed at the back, determined not to let his lad score. The eight took a 3-0 lead through sheer weight of numbers, so I joined the Khakis for the final ten minutes. After some frenzied play, we miraculously clawed it back to 3-3. Next goal's the winner! Focus was total. All joviality stopped. Silence reigned. You could have heard a moose fart in Wyoming. Little Karic again carried the flag into the decisive battle against the Khakis; a lion heart not short of a trick or two (Robbie Savage with skill). A tense stalemate ensued with no-one wanting to make the fatal mistake. The breakthrough came when a deflected shot looped over to George at the back jumper. He coolly slotted home to seal victory for the Khakis. What a fantastic night of footy!

From the two rascals of Havana, to the cloud forests of Monteverde; the frantic musical streets of Medellin to the majestic Georgia Queen. Unforgettable memories so rich and life affirming, all conjured up by that earth shaped ball.

It was time for home.

RED EARTH

GAMES 28-40

UGANDA-TANZANIA-KENYA

Flying back from the America's, my mind was flooded with incredible visions. Had all that really happened? Reality hit me like a brick when I landed back at Manchester Airport. I had nowhere to live and no job. I turned on my mobile phone and couldn't believe the first two messages I read. One was from a landlady I'd met the year before, telling me her house was now free and would I like to rent; the other was from my brother offering me some labouring work. Lucky boy. I called the landlady and explained my situation. She was brilliant and allowed me to move in straight away without a bond, and pay my first month's rent at a later date. Within a week, I'd sold all my precious guitars and amplifiers to pay my dues, and started work on the building sites.

I had to find a way to get to Africa in January, when I knew my health would be at its worst in the freezing English winter. With encouragement from friends, I decided to go down the crowdfunding route. Initially I was very uncomfortable with this, but my friends convinced me that there was growing interest in what I was trying to do, and that people genuinely wanted me to complete the journey. After thinking it over for a while, this felt like a better option to me than seeking corporate sponsorship. I didn't want to have to appear in company newsletters and wear branded T-shirts to suit them. Everything was branded these days and this whole project was about getting away from all that stuff. By crowdfunding, I could maintain the freedom and integrity of the idea, and it felt good to know that my friends were now part of the journey. Thanks to them, a thousand pounds was raised which paid for my flights to Africa. I will be forever indebted to their generosity.

Some other mates connected me with the Granada TV News Team, and the brilliant, funny and down to earth reporter Paul Crone came over to my house. He did a very skilled job of filming, interviewing and putting together a cracking three minute clip, which was shown on the tea-time news the same day. He found it hilarious that I had a 'no ball games sign' outside my house:

GAME 28: ENTEBBE, UGANDA

Date: 26th January 2018, 10.00am
Ground: City Park Motel, Entebbe

STAR OF IZRAEL

I was sat with two Ugandan women on the plane as we climbed away from Addis Ababa, Ethiopia. We viewed the breathtaking moonscape from our window, stretching out to the blue horizon of mid-morning, and wondered how people survived out there.

Rita and Farida were on their way back home to Kampala from China. They'd been out to Guangzhou sourcing materials to make jewelry back home. You wouldn't mess with these two. They both gave me a good bollocking for having only one child and for never having been married. I was a small boy again and I wanted some vimto and some crisps.

They told me to beware in Africa, that many people would see the colour of my skin and try to rip me off. Rita warned me that African's were always 'doing business'. As we chatted, they both softened a bit and we were having a good laugh by the end of the flight. Farida kept asking me if I fancied the air stewardesses, and which one I thought was the cutest. She told me she knew a woman in London I could have for the right price and did I want to WhatsApp her? Rita asked me if I wanted to buy some rings and necklaces...cheap price. I'd been warned about these people...by these people.

Landing in lush, green Uganda, Farida helped me to sort transport to my digs as the owner hadn't shown up as planned to pick me up. I would be staying at the City Park Motel for the next week, only seven miles from Entebbe airport. My host was the young, savvy Bruno K Kato. Only 20, Bruno was the clear leader of his posse who were gathered in reception on my arrival, watching footy on telly. Bruno had left his village for Kampala when he was a teenager and had found himself on the streets. Kampala had proven too dangerous a place for him, so he made his way to Entebbe and took any job going. Through a cleaning job he had, he met the owner of the City Park. She took a shine to Bruno and asked him to help her run the place. The owner had then moved on and left the motel and all its staff for him to manage.

THE GAME......

Barely had my hairy big toes touched African soil that we had a game on. Explaining my mission to Bruno on arrival, I arranged to meet him for a kick-a-bout in the motel compound the following morning. We managed to gather enough players for a game. On my side were Jamalad Bbuye, a fellow guest and Ugandan now living in Dubai, and Moses Kibeke. We took on Bruno and his mate, 20 year old star player Izrael Abaho (Izrael is spelt with an S but its cooler for him with a Z).

I'd asked the women working at the motel if they wanted to join in. Both Eva and Stella were well up for it, but Bruno decided they were too busy. They didn't look too busy to me, watching on smiling from the hotel entrance. I asked Eva if she would film the game, which she kindly did, shooting a half hour of footage of just our feet. Very arty.

Moses, the security guard, went in our nets. He spent most of his days tending to the plants in the compound and hiding out in the tiny guard hut near the entrance. A 6 ft 2" bloke, boxed into a 5ft X 3ft space, comically peeping out of the tiny square cut in one side. He had the whole deserted compound to sit in, but there he crouched with his two remaining teeth, voluntarily trapped for hours.

The strong, hardworking Jamalad bludgeoned us into a 3-0 lead. The brilliant Izrael for them was a joy to watch. A quick, intelligent, natural athlete with fantastic close ball control, he hungered for the ball and clearly loved the game. He would be scouted by professional clubs at home but, sadly, because of geography and economics, he may never get the opportunity to fully realize his talent.

Bruno was a neat and tidy player with instant ball control. He and Izrael combined well to pull a goal back. There was no stopping Jamalad the tank though, striking for goal whenever he got chance. The game finished 8-4 to us. I got my first hat-trick of the whole trip so far. A good laugh all the way through and the game was played in a fantastic spirit. Once again, I had been absolutely humbled by the welcome, support and kindness I had received. A perfect start to the African leg of the journey

GAME 29: ENTEBBE, UGANDA

Date: 26th January 2018, 2.00pm
Ground: Police Field, Entebbe

SUNDAY

Two games in a day? Unheard of! Bruno and Izrael wanted to help me get another game going in the afternoon. My motel was just off the main road linking Entebbe and Uganda's capital city Kampala. A mad blur of matatus' (mini-bus taxi's) tear-arsed up and down this 40km stretch of road day and night; the drivers with heads out of windows, constantly honking their horns and looking out for fares.

At around 1.30pm, I set off on foot down this crazy road with Bruno, Izrael and another guest at the hotel, Mathew Atuhiarwe. Mathew was a Ugandan computer engineer on holiday from his home in Dubai. He would prove to be both a real support and a bit of an actor over the coming days. We wondered around for a while by the schools, markets and shops nearby. Many lovely local folk came up to me for a chat and welcomed me to their country.

THE GAME......

We wondered around for about twenty minutes until we came to Police Field, a red sandy footy pitch. Like pine needles after Christmas, I think I'll still be finding traces of Uganda's red earth on my things in months to come. There were loads of kids and teenagers hanging around and within minutes we had a 7 v 7 going. The opposition decided to play in skins. Izrael joined them. Me and Bruno played for the shirts (you wouldn't want to see me in skins).

These young rascals were just fantastic! Wearing deadly serious faces, they scrapped for every ball, and sighed heavy, puffed cheeked sighs at every wasted chance. They never stopped running. There were some cultured players too. Colline, on the wing for the skins, seemed to glide along and had a wand of a left foot. Izrael carried on his scintillating form from the morning's game, exhibiting a dazzling array of passing and dribbling. He covered so much ground too. Like Agent Smith from The Matrix, there seemed to be Izrael's everywhere. It was little Sunday who was the absolute star though. The smallest player on the park with the biggest heart, slide tackling the big boys and totally fearless. This little warrior in rags left the field at the end still wearing his game face, covered from head to toe in the famous red dust. My hero.

The skins took an early 3-0 lead before our elegant centre half Travis ventured forward and poked home. 3-1. Game on. The giant Wadri Christopher deserved his goal for us when it came for his all action display. Wadri was

18 but played for hours with these kids every day because he loved the game so much. 3-2 and all the momentum was with us. Unfortunately, everyone (the adults mostly) started to run out of steam and we finished the game with a narrow defeat. A brilliant, all action competitive game played with total dedication.

Wyclif, Eddy, Faizol, Wadri, Sunday, Steven, Daniel and the gang, could have powered Blackburn for a month with their sheer energy. It was a real privilege to be part of it. As the lads all drifted away, I caught sight of little tenacious Sunday sat leaning some railings, and I just knew he was playing the game over and over again in his head.

GAME 30: LAKE VICTORIA, UGANDA

Date: 27th January 2018, 1.00pm
Ground: Lake Victoria at Entebbe Botanical Gardens

BASHIR THE CAVEMAN

What a day this turned out to be. At the end of yesterday afternoon's game, Mathew and I spoke to Wadir and agreed to meet him for a kick-a-bout at 10am the following morning. I was to learn that it's pointless setting specific meeting times in Africa. 10am could mean any time from dusk 'til dawn.

Mathew was rough off the beer on the morning of the match. He'd been partying till 4am the night before and had drank himself half to death on Guinness. Unfortunately he was my guide for the day and a terrible sight he was too. We ambled our way through the stunning Entebbe Botanical Gardens and onto the small beach at Lake Victoria. Thankfully for the recovering Mathew, this was only a ten minute stumble from our digs. We found a couple of plastic chairs and chilled out on the near deserted sands. Mathew fell asleep. A bar was opening at one end of the beach. Some young lads then showed up, combing for litter around the faded glory of the three raised beach huts.

I gazed out at the water in wonder. Lake Victoria is the world's second largest fresh water lake behind Lake Superior on the Canada/US border. Mainly laying in Uganda and Tanzania, it also borders Kenya. I love the natural world, but outside of the obvious stuff I can't name bugger all. All I can tell you is that there were many different varieties of colourful birds gliding, diving and noseying around the lakes edge. I did spot a couple of Marabou storks though and later I was told that the thing I thought was a crocodile was actually a Nile monitor lizard, slowly and menacingly making its way through the water to its submerged lair amongst a patch of reeds.

THE GAME......

Wadir showed up around 11.30am. It was great to see him. This tall, quiet, football mad man of 18 was a pleasure to be around. We had a bit of a kick-a-bout whilst we waited for more folk to come onto the beach. The ruined Mathew finally gave up and skulked off home, rough as a wrestlers armpit. More young lads joined in the litter picking near the beach bar, enough for a game I thought. I walked over to speak to the bar manager, who also managed this stretch of beach. He told me that all the lads were regular volunteers who hoped to get a few bob off any visitors for their efforts, and so it was ok to ask them to play. They all jumped at the chance. By this time, the brilliantly named Birol Bulbul and his mate Mehmet Demir, two Turkish Embassy workers, had appeared and were quickly roped in to a 4 v 4. This turned out to be a short warm up game for the main event, as the two Turks had to leave soon after kick off.

Around 12.30pm, two more blokes had wandered onto the beach. I asked the big guy with the muscles, wearing the "Jesus Christ Love" t-shirt, if he and his mate wanted to play. He told me they couldn't right now as they were looking for a quiet place to bring some young people later that day. He had the air of a pastor looking for a spot for a prayer meeting. They then wandered off, but returned twenty minutes later with seven smartly dressed young men ready for a game. David, the muscle man, was carrying a guitar …definitely a kum ba yah Christian I thought. Turned out he was a highly trained killer and sometime security guard at the US Embassy in Iraq. Good lad to know. He was spending his home leave doing some youth work.

Some street kids joined us. Amongst them was Bashir Amanya (16). His story was incredible. Bashir was abandoned by his parents aged 9 and lived on the streets of Entebbe until he was 14. He had swam in Lake Victoria every morning since he could remember and had an encyclopedic knowledge of the adjacent botanical gardens, where he'd occasionally make a few bob giving unofficial tours to gullable tourists. A true nature boy, he now lives in a cave (yes a cave) near the lake with five fishermen. He told me that the fishermen drink heavily every night and fights often break out. Bashir doesn't trust them, so he leaves the cave in the early morning and hides his belongings up a tree in a bin-bag, returning late at night when the men are asleep.

Game on! A 7-7 and it was getting hot. "Machine gun preacher" David's well-dressed teenagers against the rough, tough, ragged battalion of older street kids and beach combers, plus Wadir. It looked for all the world like a mis-match, but how wrong I was.

David's shiny young team were just far too quick and energetic for the beleaguered, shell shocked opposition, who kept looking over at me with pained expressions for help. Stretched, pulled and swamped, they just couldn't get hold of the ball and ended up conceding five without reply, before collapsing in a sweaty heap and giving up. David's victorious team ran around the beach together singing songs. Brilliant fun on the shores of one of the world's great lakes with so many wonderful characters.

After the game, I walked back through the botanical gardens with Bashir and Walid. Bashir did his party piece for us, shinning up a tall tree in ten seconds flat. Considering what he'd been through in his young life, he was so well mannered and polite. As we reached the busy main Entebbe-Kampala highway, I asked if the boys were hungry. They nodded so we headed over to Victoria Mall for a bite to eat. To enter the mall, we had to go through a security checkpoint. Bashir had never been allowed inside and Wadir had never had the money to spend there, so hadn't visited either. Security saw that the boys were with the white guy and let them through.

What a team! Bashir the 'caveman', six foot Wadir with legs up to his ears, lolloping along to his own tune, and a pale blue chubby guy from another planet. I suggested KFC and Bashir just couldn't believe it. He told me he'd

143

always wondered what a KFC would taste like. As our order was being taken, I couldn't help but notice that a lot of people in the restaurant were staring over at Bashir. "And?" I said loudly, staring around the room at all the gawpers, who then sheepishly looked away. I couldn't help myself. Bashir and Walid had a right laugh at my outburst.

I saw Bashir a couple of times again before I left. He'd call by my motel and we'd go for a stroll and pick up some blankets, shoes and warm clothing to help keep the cold away in the cave at night. I gave him my number in case he found some work, that he was constantly looking for, and was able to contact me. It was a brilliant surprise when he finally did call. He was selling art prints in Entebbe and was now living in his own rented room in shared accommodation. That young engaging, knowledgeable and polite young man, who owned virtually nothing, had enriched my life so much with his spirit; defiant against all the odds.

GAME 31: KAMPALA, UGANDA

Date: 29th January 2018, 1.00pm
Ground: City Square, Kampala city centre

FIZZY POP RIOTS!

To me, Uganda's capital city of Kampala had always meant Idi Amin and death. I remember being frightened by his big round aggressive face on the news when I was a kid, dressed in a military uniform adorned with self-bestowed medals. Amin was President of Uganda from 1971-79, having gained power through a military coup. His regime was characterized by mass murder, corruption and disastrous economic incompetence. Reportedly fathering over forty children from numerous wives and mistresses, Amin fled to Saudi Arabia after his failed Uganda-Tanzania conflict. He lived there until his death in 2003.

My companion again for the day, Mathew Atuhiarwe, told me to be extra vigilant when we reached the city. My skin colour would make me a target for beggers, a mugging or worse. He didn't exactly fill me with joy and optimism. As we drew closer to the city, stuck in heavy traffic, desperate young women in rags carrying babies begged at our matatu window. Arriving in downtown, heavy spots of rain started to fall on the madhouse of motorbikes and human traffic. The air was thick with dust and fumes and the need to graft for every little inch to survive. Tiny shoeless tots held out their innocent hands on the teeming streets for something… anything. One wee girl tried to hold my hand as I walked. It was devastating beyond words.

THE GAME……

Mathew guided me up to City Square where some of the city's homeless congregate. Some young blokes were laying down in the early afternoon sun on the grassed area there. We went over for a chat. Moments later we had a 4 v 4 going. These tough young men came to life. The game turned out to the roughest yet by far. None of the lads could be seen to be backing out of the tackle. Literally wrestling for the ball at times, they started to draw a crowd. Most of the lads were shoeless and slipped on the grass, drawing loud derisory laughter from the raucous spectators.

There was plenty of talent on show. Malumga Mukisa is a hell of a player, a left midfielder full of darting runs and quick turns. Godfrey Wegulu in the nets for one of the teams was as strong as a bull and wore a very serious face throughout. In contrast, Hassan Samari, tall and rangy with a good touch, played with a big beaming smile on his face. Other smilers were Benjamin Boringo, Brian Esgwagwe, Sadat Zimula and Michael Mucks. I joined in for the side who had quickly fallen 5-1 behind. We ended up

147

winning 6-5! (Nothing to do with me, I was knackered after ten minutes in the heat, although I did curl a pearler in the corner with my left).

Some women nearby were calling people to buy drinks and snacks from the tubs balanced on their heads. I called them over so that I could sort the lads out for refreshments at the end of the game. Nice idea in theory. Clocking this muzungu (white man) buying drinks, about thirty rough sleepers in the square shot over to where we were, raided all the fizzy pop and biscuits they could from the hapless venders, then danced around the gardens in celebration. It was chaos. One of the women was screaming at me to pay 5000 schilling per bottle, about three times what they were worth. Another wanted the same for her biscuits. The atmosphere had turned sour. Someone was gripping the back of my shirt through the railings asking me for money and my guide Mathew just gawped and did nothing. The footy lads were trying to help me any way they could but were helpless in the malaise. Fizzy pop riots! Two reporters from the local TV network turned up and the police were glancing over from across the street. It was not a good scene.

That's when the dreadlocked Antonio intervened. Appearing as if by magic, he calmly diffused the whole situation; waving at all the lads who hadn't played footy to return their booty and assuring the distressed venders that they would be paid the correct amount. Who was this fellow and why did he hold such power over these men? It didn't feel appropriate to ask. My guide Mathew said later that he was just about to help me when Antonio stepped in…and I'm a Russian bag-pipe playing squirrel with athletes paw.

With peace restored, I chatted to the footy lads for a while. A tougher life than theirs is hard to imagine. Most of them had come into the city from surrounding villages seeking work, but instead had found hunger and homelessness. They told me that to survive in Kampala they would have to hawk black market goods all day for little pay or turn to crime. These polite, well-mannered young men, without two pennies to rub together, had welcomed me without prejudice. Respect was mutual and I'd felt totally safe with them. I've certainly had more bother dealing with power mad pillocks in offices back home and Saturday night drunks. For the half hour or so that they'd played football, they had become alive and invigorated.

How long this inner vitality could survive in such a harsh and brutal reality was anyone's guess.

Later that day, Mathew took me to meet his lovely mum at the plush 5 star Sheraton Hotel up on the hill. The contrast between the expensively adorned lobby, with its fountain and leather settees, and the tough streets of downtown could not have been greater. Mathew's mother turned out to be none other than the Honourable Proscovia Bamutura, the Deputy Prime Minister of the Kingdom of Bunyora Kitara, one of the four kingdoms of Uganda. For a person holding such a prestigious position, Proscovia was refreshingly warm, open and friendly. Keenly intelligent, she told me that she spends a great deal of her time travelling the world to encourage investment in her kingdom and in the country in general. She said that although the task to improve things in Uganda was mammoth, there was great cause for optimism. As Mathew's Uncle Fred, a Ugandan National and philanthropist now living in Canada, would tell me later, *"the people of Uganda are not stupid or lazy, they have just been continually neglected by corrupt institutions at every level'*.

Arriving back at my digs around midnight, I lay on my bed exhausted by all the powerful emotions I'd felt that day. The poverty of downtown, the mad footy riot and the Deputy Prime Minister. What a day! I couldn't get the image of those poor toddlers out of my mind though, and shed a few tears as I fell asleep.

GAME 32: ENTEBBE, UGANDA

Date: 31st January 2018, 6.00pm
Ground: Katabi Field, Entebbe

RESTY

I was more than aware that not one of the four games I'd had so far in Uganda had featured women. This was not through lack of trying. Back at the motel, I spoke to Izrael about this and he arranged for me to meet Emmanuel Amati, the coach of the women's team at his university. Izrael and I jumped in a taxi and headed to nearby Katabi Field at around 4.30pm. Emmanuel had assembled a mixed women's team from Tagy High School and Nkumbu University to take on the reigning national league champions, Kawempe from Kampala, in a pre-season friendly. Emmanuel was a very impressive, passionate chap. Six years ago he had been tasked with stimulating interest in women's football in Entebbe. He told me how it had seemed like an impossible task to begin with, due to lack of interest and having no kit, footballs or boots. Geography was a barrier too as many of the young women attending schools and the university in Entebbe lived in villages some distance away. Slowly but surely, through his sheer persistence and belief, Emmanuel began to build Entebbe's very first women's football team. His philosophy was that the team may not always have the equipment, but this should not stop the development of their skills. He was qualified up to Level 3 of the 5 coaching levels available in Uganda, and encouraged his teams to play different formations, with the emphasis on hard work, possession football and defending as a team without the ball. The proof of his dedication and determination was on the field tonight. These women were brilliant. Although narrowly losing the match to the champions 1-0, the team-work and hunger on display was phenomenal. The tackling was brutal at times, but unlike some of the big diving babies at the top level in the men's game, these young women just dusted themselves off and carried on without a peep.

The Headmaster of Tagy School, Ayubu Asiimwe, was also there to watch the game. He told me that participation in football had fostered a sense of attachment and belonging to the school, which had resulted in a sharp increase in attendance levels and educational attainment. Ayubu believed that football was helping to broaden the players' horizons and their sense of freedom and independence. Emmanuel agreed *"By promoting women's football in this way, we are keeping young women busy and free... helping young women to see that there is more to life that getting married as soon as possible. There are a lot of child marriages here."* Ayuba also explained that sports scholarships were offered to the best of the older players, which meant, crucially, that their tuition fees would be met by the university.

THE GAME......

*Uganda is home to 5 million child brides. Of these, 1.3 million married before age 15. Source: UNICEF global databases, 2020.

I nabbed eight of Emmanuel's team for a game after their friendly match. This was undoubtedly the best technical display of footy I'd seen on the whole trip so far. By 'eck these lasses could play; so good that when I asked them to play two-touch they bossed it. Resty Nanzii was the best player on the park. Quick, technical and strong, she had the lot. Sarah Nakuyu was a box to box number 8 and Lillian Matuuzo was a brilliant finisher in tight congested spaces. Judith Sanyu's work-rate was mind blowing. Cucu Fatumata could play everywhere and her passing was fantastic. Raphaelina Nakabuubi was a neat and tidy committed midfielder, Joweria Babiiye a tough, no nonsense defender whilst Halima Kanyago made brilliant runs constantly. 4 v 4, first to 5, and it was gripping stuff. The pace was relentless; pass and move at its best. The game finished 5-4 to Resty's side but on they played. Emmanuel's coaching had definitely paid off. After the game, Cucu summed up the feelings of her team-mates: *"The love I have for this game is just too much"*

What a mesmerizing week it had been in Uganda. Huge respect to Bruno, Izrael and Mathew for their support throughout and to the nature boy himself, Bashir the Caveman. Unforgettable.

GAME 33: MOSHI, TANZANIA

Date: 3rd February 2018, 2.00pm
Ground: Mai Moria Market, Moshi

ANARCHY

Kilimanjaro Airport, Tanzania, is a short hop from Entebbe. On arrival I jumped in a taxi for a forty minute drive to the beautiful Secret Garden Hotel, Moshi, where I would stay for four nights before moving on to Zanzibar.

Each morning at breakfast, sat in the roof-top dining area, I was met with a magnificent view of Africa's largest mountain, Mount Kilimanjaro. It looked like a ginormous Christmas pudding with a big dollop of icing on top. Most of the residents of the Secret Garden had come to climb this pudding, or were waiting for friends and relatives who were attempting it. What if it really was a pudding? Would there be any left by now? On my second day there I met a young Danish chap by the name of Mads Sørensen. He was up for a game so off we popped.

THE GAME

Mads and I walked out into the blazing early afternoon sun. Mai Moria Market was only ten minutes' walk from our hotel, but it felt like an hour in that heat. The market was rammed with stalls selling donated clothes and shoes. We weaved our way through its narrow passage ways, the air filled with the beautiful sweet music of the female traders calling us with song to buy from them.

Reaching the edge of the market, we were surprised to find a footy pitch. I invited four friends chatting nearby to play. They alerted a few mates and news spread like wildfire throughout the market. Within ten minutes we had a nuts 15 v 15 game going on.

A shoal of whooping, hollering young chaps were darting up and down and left and right in pursuit of the ball, as if pulled by strings. Most of them had two left feet and spent much of the game doing air shots, falling over and kicking up dust. Mads was right when he said it was *"Anarchy! There are no rules!"*. Corners were goal-kicks, blatant penalties were ignored and there was hand balling going on everywhere. Some just picked the ball up and ran with it 'til they were rugby tackled. Crackers. Taking a breather, I went to speak to some of the watching crowd. The impeccably polite and well-mannered Gilbert Justin was the conductor on the bus which brought many of these lads to work. He knocked on for them all in the mornings to make sure they made their 6.30am - 9.00pm shifts, on the six different market days in the area.

Mads by now was rolling around in the dust. He'd decided to go in the nets for one of the teams and was performing heroics in the chaos. His team eventually ran out dubious 2-0 winners. Posing for a team photo at the end, the very wise Donald Machange, who had earlier helped me to get a good price for water for the boys at half time, gave a great speech about one love and unity, which just about summed up the atmosphere around today's game. Superb and a great laugh.

GAMES 34 & 35: NJORO, TANZANIA

Date: 4rd February 2018, 2.30pm
Grounds: Njora streets and basketball court

THE GOOD, THE BAD AND THE BALL

I know I keep saying this, but what a day!

I wanted to get out into the heart of one of the Moshi villages for a game. I grabbed a taxi into town with some lovely folk I'd met at the hotel, Sam, Jaheda, Toni and Mulenga. It was ridiculously hot. As luck would have it, we bumped into the gentleman that is Donald Machange again from yesterday's game. He was working at the market in town. Donald was a tough, resilient, street wise-man who had seen a lot, but still managed to maintain a striking kindness and humility.

Donald suggested we try near Moshi's long disused railway station for the game. Reaching the platform, Jaheda, Toni and Mulenga decided not to go any further because of the heat. Donald, Sam and I carried on over the tracks and down into the village of Njoro.

THE GAME

The good

The village consisted mainly of small mud, breeze block and wooden dwellings. We walked around for a while until we came to a street near to the market. This was the spot. I chucked the jumpers down in the middle of the uneven, slippy road near a couple of shops and began cajolling people into playing. Sam, a big guy from Northern Ireland, who didn't even like football, a local bloke called Hans Rubin and two small boys from the village made up one team. Donald, myself, a young kid called Ezekel and Hilary Machang took them on. A 4 v 4 on one of the worst pitches ever.

Slowly but surely all the villagers came out to watch. There was a lovely neighbourhood and family feel to the afternoon, and much hilarity when the tall slim Sam in his floppy hat kept losing his footing on the treacherous surface, like a daddy long-legs trying to get out of a window. Hans for them was greedy for goals, and despite having both me and Ezekel in the pegs, we quickly went 4-0 down. Donald was scrapping hard trying to claw back the deficit. Hilary pulled one back for us, but he was clearly high as a kite on something or other and couldn't sustain his energy levels. They got another and at 5-1 down we stopped for half time and sat in the shade.

The bad

This is when things turned a bit bad. I tried to buy water for everyone from the nearby shop, but was quoted well over the odds by a bad tempered shop keeper on the make. Then, two lads in their twenties turned up and the taller clever dick one picked up our ball and tried to sell it back to me. It was a threat not a request. There was silence and the mood had turned sour.

I couldn't believe what happened next. Donald, Hans and another lad who'd joined us, Jamal (a Kilimanjaro expedition leader), rallied around me and Sam, telling us they would keep us safe because we were their brothers. Donald very coolly stood up and asked big-gob to play the ball to him. Thinking Donald was on his side against the *mzungus*, the aggressive one obliged. You should have seen the look on his face when Donald picked up the ball and gave it to me. Donald then whispered in my ear that we needed to get out of town quick. This fella was dangerous and would most likely go and get some mates and attack us. What a shame. I was gutted. Game 34 had come to an abrupt end. It had been a real laugh and a great spectacle for the village too.

...and the ball

Game 35 followed straight on. Loads of chatty curious kids followed us as we made our way out of the village and back up towards the railway tracks. They were desperate to play. We spotted a sandy basketball court and out came the jumpers. Donald divided the lads up into two teams of 11 (which eventually swelled to 14 -a -side) and off they went. I learnt later that this was the first real football these children had ever played with. They'd usually fashion something like the one little Gifi John showed me today, made from litter, banana leaves and string. The sheer delight on these children's faces to be playing with a real football will stay with me forever.

I started the game but had to quickly find shade. The heat was punishing. Watching on with Sam, Donald, Hans and the boys, was pure magic. Unusually for ones so young, 10yrs-14 yrs, they didn't chase the ball in packs, but held their positions given to them by the older kids. So organised were they that it took a full twenty minutes for the first goal to be scored. After an hour, with the score at only 1-1, we called the lads together for a photo.

I was in awe at how well-mannered and respectful these kids were. They had nothing but they had everything. Sam and I bought them all sweets which Donald and Hans helped to give out. They formed two orderly queues to gleefully receive their lollies and gum drops, with many coming up to us to say thank you. We then gathered everyone around and told them, to an ear-splitting cheer, that the football was now theirs to keep, but someone had to look after it. They all immediately pointed at young Muhamed Kimuaga who looked well chuffed to be nominated. I chucked him the ball and off they all charged to play some more.

Crossing the tracks, Sam and I took Donald, Hans, Jamaal and Hilary for a beer on the old train station platform. United through football, we chewed the fat, got drunk and laughed in the cool of the early evening breeze. One of the best days of my life.

GAME 36: ZANZIBAR, TANZANIA

Date: February 9th *2018, 11.30am*
Ground: Maandalizi Sogeani School, Zanzibar

CORRUPTION

Corruption is ruthless and heartless and bleak
It's cold by design and it targets the weak
It worm's its way on, breaking hearts, breaking will
Corruption sends lesions of fear in to kill

Corruption robs nature, robs futures, robs hope
Smiles wide with a wink and a brown envelope
Self-serving, unswerving in its righteous domain
Corruption spits pity like acid rain

Corruption lives there in the kids on the street
In their ripped, dirty t-shirts and bloodied tough feet
In their swollen empty bellies and at the law makers banquet
Corruption wraps a baby, dead, up in a blanket

Corruption leaves you pleading and helpless and lost
It ages you, murders you, counts at your cost
It lies to itself, rusts a mother's smile
Corruption bewilders, blinds truth with its guile

Corruption swells waistlines and coffers and heads
Buys votes, rubs in oil on a yacht on the Med
But for all of its silver and all of its clout
The best folk I've met are the ones who have nowt

After fantastic scenes in Uganda and Moshi, the romantic in me was really looking forward to getting to Zanzibar. It sounded so exotic. Tanzania was formed in 1964 when mainland Tanganyika and the island of Zanzibar were united.

Well, the bubble had to burst at some point. I just didn't expect it to be here. Apart from those few strange days in China, I'd loved every place I'd visited so far on this journey. I found Zanzibar sad. Sad because, as many locals would tell me, ingrained widespread corruption had meant that the housing, education and employment needs of the people here were not being met. The extensively sourced GAN Business Anti-Corruption Portal Report (Updated 2016), found that corruption is "pervasive throughout Tanzanian Society" and is a serious problem across all sectors of the economy. The report goes on to highlight ten areas in which corruption is rife, including the judicial system, police, public services, land administration, tax and customs administration and public procurement. (www. business-anti-corruption.com).

My stay got off to a bad start. The first night was spent in a really dirty, stinky, ant and rubbish infested "guesthouse" in Stone Town, with dangerous electrics everywhere. I arrived late so had to stay the night. I don't usually mind where I stay, but this really was the pits. In the morning, after a sleepless, boiling hot night with a broken fan for company, I had a walk around Stone Town. With its old, picturesque narrow streets, souvenir shops and the beach being only a stones throw away, Stone Town is a real tourist trap. I must have arrived at a bad time. Maybe it was just my lack of sleep, but I found no joy in the air there. Gone were the smiles and vitality of Entebbe and Moshi.

On the second day, I moved to a decent place near the airport, and on the third day I jumped on a vespa with tour guide Ali and headed north. Big mistake. Ali was totally uninterested in me as a person. It was plain that he was just going through the motions for the money. He promised me the earth and came up with virtually bugger all by way of a tour. Leaving my hotel near Stone Town, we scootered on through a busy township and out to the west of the island, with its stunning vista of palm trees, white sands and blue sea. After an hour or so on the road, my arse was completely numb and my helmet blew off and was crushed by a lorry behind us. Ali was not amused. That made two of us.

We traveled up through the rural north of the island. Apart from the few people working in the bicycle repair shops and small garages, or selling mangoes and bananas from small roadside stalls, loads of people seemed to be hanging around with nothing much to do. I was looking for positives everywhere, and as always found them in the beaming smiles and friendly waves of the people we passed by on the road; beaming lights amongst the procession of broken down buildings.

THE GAME.....

It was the children and young people who saved the day. My first game of the 80 was in Australia with the oldest players so far, aged 65-75 years. This would be a game with the youngest, all 4-5 year olds.

We stopped at the Maandalizi Sogeani Kindergarten, where I met the lovely Mwanaisha Hassan Hasi. Mwanaisha is a teacher who kindly allowed me to into the classrooms to meet the young ones and invite them to play footy. As I walked into the first classroom, I was greeted by a very loud "Jambo" (Hello) from around thirty tiny, shiny tots in uniform. They were sat at big round tables and were all incredibly well behaved.

Mwanaisha picked a few children out to play and soon we were having a 4 v 4 game in the garden outside. As tiny people do, they totally forgot where the goals were and ran with the ball all over the place. Ali *'my guide'* joined in at one point. He dribbled the ball near to some fencing and four tiny-terrors waded in for the tackle, leaving him on his arse with his sunglasses flying off in the air. I laughed a very satisfied and sinister laugh. Well done boys!

The lads were having a great time, chasing everything and laughing their heads off. I joined the team playing against Ali's four and we ended up 4-0 winners. Our keeper, with his hilariously vigilant face, was rarely troubled. As we finished the game, a hundred kids poured into the garden and made a b-line for the mzungu. 'JAMBO !' They all crowded around me and started to pull at the hairs on my bleached legs, nip my cheeks, grab my hair, stand on my toes, press my nose and make horn sounds. Savaged I was, savaged! They had great fun watching some of the video I had taken of the game, poking fun at each other.

Great great joy in the sunshine.

GAME 37: ZANZIBAR, TANZANIA

Date: February 9th 2018, 1.00pm
Ground: Makunduchi Secondary School, Zanzibar

GIRLS V BOYS

As previously mentioned, my tour guide Ali was not the best. Everything seemed to be geared around his needs. Instead of taking me to all the places we discussed...the universities, townships, and the nature reserve, we dropped in at a few of his friends' houses without explanation. It quickly became clear that this was a ploy for me to give his friends a few bob. He'd introduce me, they'd tell me how skint they were and Ali would watch on intently waiting for me to dig deep. I'll share anything I have with anyone, but not a bean if I feel I'm being used. Ali looked pretty miffed that I didn't part with any cash and had to slip folk a few bob himself.

He was a helpful tour guide in some ways though, pointing at a melon and saying 'look, a melon" and at a cow saying "that is a cow" (I kid you not). David Attenborough must be shitting himself. I wouldn't have minded as much if he was a cheeky loveable rouge, but he was a conniving, obvious little smart arse. Full up with the lid on, as my grandma used to say.

Eventually we ended up at his old high school, again so he could talk to some of his old mates who worked there. I saw my opportunity and wandered away from this self-consumed nut to chat to some teachers. They allowed me into a classroom to talk to the pupils. This could have been any high school classroom in England. All the bright, interested young women were at the front, working hard on a science problem, whilst most of the boys were at the back being rowdy and chucking stuff. I asked if I could have a kick-a-bout and was told I could, for ten minutes, but not within the school grounds. No sooner had I asked one or two pupils to play, than a large crowd followed me out through the school gates.

THE GAME.....

Minutes later we were having a brilliant game by the side of the school. Girls v boys, 15 v 15 at a rough estimate. I had been told by one of the teachers that over 90% of people living on Zanzibar were Muslim. It was quite a sight to see that team of young women in full flight, their white hijabs flowing in the breeze, taking the fight to the boys. They scrapped hard, laughing hysterically, but the lads had a bit more football nouse, quickly taking a 3-0 lead with some well-placed shots. I encouraged the girls to pass more instead of just wellying it, but they totally ignored me and ran about everywhere having a great time. I joined in for them and the old magic fleetingly returned. I beat four before my back-heel was cleared off the line. My thirty-second cameo in that humidity had left me gasping for breath. I had to sit on a rock for a bit, sucking on my inhaler like a new born on a nipple.

Three of the boys joined the girls team and they helped close the score to 3-2, but the boys ran out eventful 4-2 winners. A colourful, frantic, loud battle of the sexes played in a fantastic happy spirit. By the time we'd taken photos and chatted, at least half an hour had passed. I was in the bad books with the teachers and narrowly avoided detention.

As it stands, there is no universally free education for secondary school age children in Zanzibar. If your parents cannot pay then that's you snookered. It's sad that many of those happy, tiny tots I'd met earlier at the kindergarten may grow up never having the chance to explore their potential. For those who do complete secondary school, the future is not much brighter. University fees exclude the majority of school leavers, with most going back to their families; some to work but most, according to one of their particularly pessimistic teacher's, to 'remain idle for the rest of their lives'.

GAME 38: ZANZIBAR, TANZANIA

Date: February 9th 2018, 3.00pm
Ground: Makunduchi Village, Zanzibar

VESPA

After two marvelous games earlier in the day, we decided to head to the east of the island for a bite to eat. If you've read games 36 and 37 you will know that my guide for the day, Ali, was a self-serving numpty of a chap. We'd motored up to the north of the island on his vespa, which conked out as soon as we started to head back. Vespa is Italian for wasp and the more the day wore on the more waspish I was becoming with this twerp.

Thankfully, we were in sight of a great mechanic who was fixing scooters on a patch of land behind yet another delapidated building. Ali said the repair would take minutes....it took two hours. In true Ali style, he even tried to get me to pay for the new parts! I just stared at him then walked away quickly before something daft happened. Whilst we waited, a crowd of young lads appeared pushing a broken down truck. I took the chance to get a game of footy going with them. I was told that they all went to a school nearby, Miwaleni.

THE GAME.....

The game turned out to be a cracker. A 5 v 5 on the dirt track leading to the main east coast road. Rajabu, Abdallah, Panama, Hakim and Mwaeb were on one side, Riduli, Fani, Hakim, Idrissa and Ma were on the other. Idrissa was an elegant player; captain material, holding the fort at the back. Ma was a ragged and rugged all action box to box player. With these two in attack and defence they quickly jumped into a 2-0 lead. Abdullah in his torn Liverpool top was having none of it. It was clear that he was a bad loser. He almost single handedly got his team back in it, ploughing into tackles and levelling the score with two powerful drives. At one point he smashed his ankle on a rock, wiped the blood clean with his top and cracked on with the game. Have that Neymar you toddler.

Fani made it 3-2. He was the eldest of the gang and seemed to be well respected by all the lads. On the side-lines, Panama was too cool for school. You could tell he wanted to join in, but he had to save face in front of his mates watching on. Hakim was the youngest player but sharp as a tack. He was intelligent and had the ability to slow the game down and find space, despite the relentless pace. It was Hakim who scored the equaliser. 3-3 the final score. Fitting for a game as evenly matched and competitive as this.

A great game with these bright, polite, well mannered and energetic lads. They were rich in spirit and brotherhood, but living in abject poverty. Football had worked its magic again, bringing joy where it was so hard to find. These communities have been totally and criminally abandoned by government for decades. At least these chaps had each other.

Vespa repaired, we said our goodbye's and drove the one and a half hours down the east coast to Ali's favourite eating place. I was pretty hungry by now, having not eaten since 11am. We pulled up around 6pm, just as this road side cafe was closing. Ali was full of beans, laughing and joking with his mates who worked there. Then, unbelievably, instead of proposing we go somewhere else, he grabbed the last plate of food, sat down to scoff it and, with his back to me, started playing on his phone!

Zanzibar was definitely not the kind of place to cause a fuss and get arrested, so I crossed over the road and lent against a tree, seething like a teased cobra. Then I reminded myself that I'd just been playing footy with a bunch of semi-starving kids. What had I to moan about? I'd be in my hotel room soon, having a nice hot shower and eating good food. Yes, this pillock was rude but I had to rise above it. It took some time for Ali to notice I was gone. Sensing his payment might be in jeopardy, he quickly brought his little, full, tubby belly across the road and asked me with a fake smile where I wanted to go next. "You'd better take me home now mate". Comedy gold this bloke.

The Zanzibar traffic police are well known for being corrupt, frequently waving drivers over to pay them a few bob for any 'offence' they can invent, threatening them with jail for non-payment. Heading home, we passed one such policeman who tried to flag us down. Ali ignored him and sped off with the policeman waving his arms about then writing something in his note book. Ali took a sharp turn off the main road and we spent the next 45 minutes ducking and diving down the backstreets to avoid the cops. I was turning into the deranged Chief Inspector Dreyfus from the Pink Panther films and Ali was my Inspector Clouseau. I started laughing like a maniac. This nut job…the non-tour, the 'money tour' of his mates houses, the knackered vespa, him scoffing the last plate of food, the cops…it had to be a set up.

Arriving back at my hotel at 8pm, after nine hours without food, covered from head to toe in thick road dust and with a nasty case of scooter arse, this priceless little git asked "Where can I take you tomorrow sir?" My reply was short and succinct, "Absolutely fucking nowhere Ali".

GAME 39: ZANZIBAR, TANZANIA

Date: February 11th 2018, 6.45pm
Ground: Mkunazi Wapilii, Zanzibar

GRUMPY CAT

We were always disturbing the neighbours when we were kids. Booting the ball against garage doors or constantly kicking it over the same garden fence. There was always one grumpy neighbor too. "Clear off you lot! Get round yer own end!" This game could have taken place in Lancashire in 1977.

When I moved hotels on my second day in Zanzibar, a group of kids spotted my football as I got out of the taxi. *"Mister! Football! Play! ".* I told them I'd play the following afternoon, but I'd been late back from my tour of the island and missed them. I paid for it the next day. These tiny tots hijacked me on my way out for tea. *"Hey mister! Where were you? We waited - no football! Bad man!".* Bloody 'ell kids, give me a break! *"5 tomorrow, ok!?", You'd better be there mister!".* Threats I tell you, threats! So there I was the next day, sat on a wall with my ball at 5pm and not a cherub in sight. I went back to my room, got changed, but when I left the hotel later to go for a stroll they had appeared. *"We had homework!"* Poor excuse.

THE GAME.....

I introduced myself to their mums who gave them permission to play and watched on. We had a 2 v 2 (occasionally 3 v 3) in an ally at the back of my hotel. Jeremiah was on my side. He was a brilliant, brave and tough goalkeeper. His bare feet must have been made of iron. David and Nizack took us on. David was super enthusiastic, trying to nutmeg me every two minutes. Nizack was a nutter in his nets, diving wildly across his goal line. His timing was comically out of sync though, a second too slow or too quick to stop the shots. Little Peter watched on under the watchful gaze of Humaina. They both joined in occasionally, then returned to perch on the neighbour's wall. A fantastic, end-to-end game ensued until the score became locked at 11-11 (first to 12 in the fading light). This is when the grumpy neighbour came out. He shooed the tiny kids off his wall and barked his displeasure at the racket we were making. "This is not a play-ground! You are harassing me!" "Look mate "I said "Sorry and all that ..but it's next goal's the winner " "It better be !" rapped Grumpy Cat. With that. He went back inside and slammed his door shut. We all looked at each other and fell about laughing. The light had almost gone when David struck the winner with a long range effort. A funny, magical and nostalgic game with some proper wee characters and Mr. Grumpy Cat.

Apart from the games and the amazing young dudes I had met along the way, Zanzibar had left me feeling low. Widespread corruption is robbing the islanders of a decent standard of living and its children of a bright future.

GAME 40: KENYA

Date: February 14th 2018, 4.00pm
Ground: Tonanoka Park, Mombassa

VALENTINE'S SURPRISE

It was on Valentine's Day that I decided to take a walk along Mombasa Beach. What a beautiful sight it was. Miles and miles of white sand and crystal blue water, with just a few shacks dotted about selling touristy stuff. It was mid-morning and I was alone…but not for long.

After ten minutes of strolling along in paradise, I turned to look behind me and saw a vision in a purple swim suit and shades. This beautiful young woman was shouting something to me, but her words were lost on the breeze. I stopped and waited for her. 'Hi. My name is Valerie. You like to swim?". I gulped. "Aye. Sometimes". "Would you like to swim with me today?" Shish kebabs! This stunning lass must have only been 20 years old. Old enough to be her Dad, I said I'd pass on the swim. Valerie continued to walk with me until we reached one of the shacks where she got talking to a couple of lads working there. I carried on walking and got chatting to a jovial old fella with three teeth who offered to take me out on his boat. I looked out at the choppy waves then back at his ancient boat and decided to choose life. It was heading towards scorching hot midday and I decided to go for a dip. How beautiful that water felt around my sweaty blue carcass. I floated along looking up at the bluest sky and felt like the luckiest boy in the world.

Some-time later I raised my head to see how far I'd drifted, and there stood the beautiful Valerie, not two feet away from me. Bloody 'ell. She proceeded to give me her best chat up lines and the story of how her Slovakian ex-boyfriend had ditched her for another local girl. She was now looking for someone exactly like me. Really? A middle-aged Lancashire chap with athletes foot, pasty skin and hairy ears? She asked if she could show me around Mombasa the following day and visit some beautiful islands and beaches. I politely refused. My suspicions of a honey trap were confirmed when she followed me out of the water, off the beach and onto the road side, where she glanced to her left and shook her head at three dodgy blokes sat on a wall nearby. I gave her my flat cap and wished her all the best. As I walked away, I looked back to see that she'd drifted over to these three rascals, probably for comfort; so distraught was she that the man of her dreams had rejected her.

•

Skin tone can tell you a lot about people in Kenya. That was according to my mate Richey Ndongo, the 21 year old chef at my home for the week, Tulia House Backpackers. Richey had kindly offered to be my guide as we headed out into the steaming hot madness of Mombasa one afternoon. Pimped up matatus swarmed everywhere at crazy speeds. The first one we climbed into was fitted with TV's blasting out African pop vibes at a ridiculous volume. I got out half an hour later feeling like I'd been aurally molested.

With my head still ringing from club-taxi, we made our way to Tonanoka Park. This sandy pitch was deserted when we got there. We spotted some lads walking by and asked them to play. Within minutes we had more than enough for a game. 7 v 7 in the blazing sun. Richey, who has dark black skin, pointed out that the lighter skinned lads who'd gathered to play today were Swahili. They had no tribe, came from Arab decent and only spoke English and Swahili. One look at their clothes and footwear told Richey that they came from rich families. He told me that it was frowned upon in Kenya for Swahili's and African's to marry or even mix, even the children. What a silly bloody divisive idea, no doubt driven by outdated traditions and religious lunatics who don't know the true meaning of peace and love. I respect culture and tradition but not division.

As always, footy was the great equalizer. A white bloke from Lancashire, a black bloke from the Luos tribe of Kisumu (northern Kenya), and a bunch of fairer skinned Swahili's, just kicking a ball about and having the craic for an hour.

THE GAME…..

GAME 40! HALF WAY THERE!

A great game ensued with some belting little players. Little Ali Sombwana was everyone's man of the match. He was a fearless keeper during the game, and the coolest cat from 12 yards in the penalty shoot-out. I was on Ali's team and we were blessed with talent. Brothers Ali and Muhammad Faiz were electric up front. Both technical and quick, but a little greedy.

For the opposition, the tall Shariff Jaffar was a constant threat, though the much smaller but very tough Ali Amed dumped him in the sand more than once. All the lads could play and it was end to end stuff. We'd begun to draw a crowd. My mate Richey the chef was a big strong chap, but he was knackered after ten minutes. He hadn't played for years. He still managed to notch the winner for us though. 5-4 the final score. We then had a penalty shoot-out which went to sudden death, with Super Ali Sombwana emerging victorious. Great fun in the burning sun.

At the end of the game, Richey asked the boys if they'd like to meet him the following week to train. He would be their coach and they'd work towards being good enough to join a league. I'm happy to report that this happened and has continued ever since. Magic.

Later, Richey and I visited Frere Town, where I gave away my last football to a bunch of kids. You'd have thought it was Christmas Day. There were huge smiles and singing all around now that they had a proper ball, and not just the one they'd fashioned from paper and string. What a Valentine's

Day it had been, full of love, joy and togetherness. I wonder if Valerie's still wearing my flat cap?

Speaking of flat caps, it was time for home. My African adventures were over. It would take me weeks to digest what I had seen and experienced. Once again it had been the human spirit that had shone through despite the harsh realities of life, leaving me feeling very humbled, grateful and inspired.

And we're off...

Game 1: Australia - *With Chris (left) and 72 years young Bobby Dorigo. A perfect gent.*

Game 2: New Zealand – *Mandeep - Cruyff turns from the cricketer from Chandigarh*

Game 3: New Zealand – *Lost Josh – a ragged, balletic angel in a dirty vest - Latimer Square*

Game 4: New Zealand – *"Fetch it Felix", grins his dastardly grin*

Game 5: Thailand – *Football intelligence in Lat Krabang*

Game 6: Thailand – *Burma warm up on Turf Moor, 1972 – Koh Tao*

Game 7: Cambodia – *The Green Samurai do battle at Angkor High School*

Game 8: Cambodia – *Lessons in humanity from Davy Meng, Siem Reap*

Game 9: Vietnam – *Brilliant Rebecca bosses the Airforce blokes. The keeper's had enough -Hanoi*

Game 10: Vietnam – *Halong Bay- an incredible setting for our morning international*

Game 11: China – *Don't pass it to me! Trying and failing to play jianzi in Yuexiu Park*

Game 12: China – *These mega cities don't suit me at all - Guangzhou*

Game 13: Japan – *Erm…now what?*   **Game 14: South Korea** – *Old before*
Footy for the first time - Izumisano   *their time? Fast and furious at*
Seoul's Olympic Park

Game 15: South Korea – *Mark and Yoda, I mean his son Joshua -*
the brains of the operation in Suwon

Game 16: France – *"It's anyone's!" A bit of light relief in "The Jungle" refugee camp, Calais*

Game 17: Germany – *The Troops! From left: Richard, myself, Paul and Alex in Berlin*

Game 18: Colombia – *friendly faces in tough places. San Antonio Plaza, Medellin*

Game 19: Colombia – *Shefali the Delhi Dazzler (left) and Anyela*

Game 20: Costa Rica – *Madame Butterfly (centre) terrorized the boys all night- Monte Verde*

Game 21: Costa Rica – *Nelson was brilliant with the lads, Blue River, Tirasses*

Game 22: Cuba – *Road warriors in the Old Havana rainstorm*

Game 23: Cuba – *Philippe was the best young pirate on the pitch - Vinales*

Game 24: USA – *"It's all about the earth shaped ball" Savannah River, Georgia*

Game 25: USA – *Pelicans and sinners - with the dudes from Fuge on Folly Beach, Charleston County*

Game 26: USA – *Cheeky git!*
Daryll put the ball through my legs
far too many times, Greenville SC

Game 27: USA – *Cheers Neil!*
Thanks for everything me old mate

Game 28: Uganda – *Star called*
'Izreal' warms up at the City Park
Motel - Entebbe

Game 29: Uganda – *Sunday the*
Lion Heart commands the ball at
Police Field, Entebbe

Game 30: Uganda – *David's boys danced around the opposition at Lake Victoria*

Game 31: Uganda – *In Kampala with the Hon Proscovia Bamutura, Deputy PM*

Game 32: Uganda – *Resty! What a player! ...and very cheeky! "Can I have your t-shirt?"*

Game 34: Tanzania – *Slip sliding away. Donald and Sam try to stay upright - Njora village*

Game 33: Tanzania – *Anarchy! With the Mai Moria Market boys, Moshi*

Game 35: Tanzania – *The Njoro village kids do battle*

Game 36: Zanzibar – *Oh dear! What a shame! Ali gets flattened by the cherubs at the kindergarten*

Game 37: Zanzibar – *all smiles at Makunduchi Secondary School*

Game 38: Zanzibar – *Tough kids with tough feet in Makanduchi Village*

Game 39: Zanzibar – *Winding up the Grumpy Cat. A magical little game.*

Game 40: Kenya – *This is serious! Ali bosses the penalty shoot-out in Mombassa*

In the summer of 2017 we lost our beautiful little beagle Honey to cancer. Honey had been my little hairy companion on hundreds of long walks as I attempted to stay fit to complete my journey. She was my little pal. Anyone who's ever owned and loved a dog will know how heart-breaking it is to lose them. Here's a little tribute to my Honey-Pie.

HONEY

Following the wind through the willows and on to the lane
Over the bridge we go, brazen and braver than brave
Up by the factory and on to the fields on show
Then the sun comes up and everything feels like before

And I know you're alive again

Past the shimmering trees talking to me, tellin' me everything's ok
These hills are my protection, they are knowledge, they are ancient, they are safe
How many times have I been lost in life, just to find myself out here again?
Where it all makes sense, in the wild and it's so far away from them

And I know you're alive again

All night shows, the moonlight glows in your eyes
You're down by the water's edge, making friends
While the new washed stones say hello, then home we go

Look out of the window, see us working for peace in the fight
Sometimes I don't know if we're gonna make it, but I know it's alright
Because I'll always find you waiting for me, playing in the light
Of a big December moon, a blazing June
A lightning sky, a silver noon

UP ON THE ROOF

GAMES 41–48

INDIA-NEPAL

Nothing prepares you for India. When I arrived home, I felt compelled to ring my old mate from my student days, Dipak Patel. I was worried that the things you are about to read would sound like the utterances of a flippant white colonialist. Dip reassured me that my worries were unfounded. He too had witnessed the same madness I had in the land of his parents and ancestors. Another great friend, Tracey Kim, told me that you cannot un-see what you have seen. This is true. So here is what I saw.

GAME 41: INDIA

Date: January 10th 2019, 12.30pm
Ground: Vinayak Guesthouse roof, Jaipur

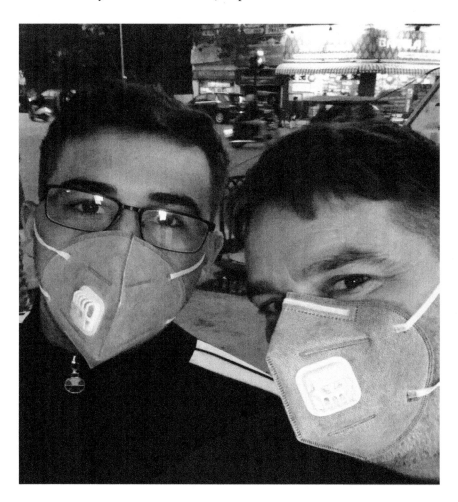

UP ON THE ROOF

To celebrate my 50th birthday, my son Danny flew up from Sydney Australia to travel with me throughout this part of the journey. We'd had a go at some site-seeing in India's capital New Delhi, and I'd been hopeful of some games there, but we were both suffering from breathing problems within a couple of days.

Delhi kills people. It's one of the most polluted cities in the world. When we arrived, we literally couldn't see it for the smog. The Times of India reported in 2016 that poor air quality in the capital irreversibly damages the lungs of 50% of its children. Diesel exhaust fumes, natural dust and crop burning all contribute to the engulfing haze, leading not only to respiratory problems but heart attacks, strokes and cancer.

What little we did see of Delhi during our two night stay looked post-apocalyptic. Homeless people were everywhere, setting up 'home' with a few sheets laid on the pavements. Clothes were hung on the city's walls and railings to dry and men were urinating and defecating wherever they liked. Random street cows stood staring into the gloom, pigs gorged on piles of roadside rubbish and a steady stream of fawn coloured dogs trotted about looking for food, or slept exhausted under the poisonous skies.

The anarchic roads were jammed with scratched, battered and bruised taxis, tuk-tuks and motorbikes, driven by suicidal maniacs who had never seen a theory test. Four lanes became seven, and how the number of ridiculous, heart-in-mouth maneuverers didn't end in a crash every five-seconds is beyond me. Mad Max would have declared himself no longer mad, parked up and started walking. Add to this the cloying smog and the picture was very depressing. And so it was, with my asthmatic tubes closing up rapidly, and without properly exploring the city or meeting its people, we decided to depart for the pink city of Jaipur, Rajasthan.

•

Rahul Kumar was his name….possibly. He was also possibly from Goa and when he wasn't driving a tuk-tuk in Jaipur ("the best tuk-tuk in India") he was possibly a kick-boxing instructor back home ("the best kick-boxing instructor in India"). So shady and Trumpesque was he, that in reality he could have been a door to door conservatory salesman from Halifax. Rahul looked like an Indian Argonaut. Over 6 feet tall, handsome with a thick beard and intense brown eyes, he had charmingly bullshitted our tired brains at Jaipur train station, and off we sped in his ornate tuk-tuk to our guesthouse.

Later that day, Rahul would take us around the city for what turned out to be an extortionate price. He drove in a state of theatrical paranoia, constantly looking around at other drivers in the packed roads, occasionally whipping his hood up if he suspected someone had recognized him "People around here don't like people like me" he would say as he nipped in and out of the tiniest spaces.

With echoes of Ali in Zanzibar, it quickly became clear to Danny and I that Rahul was devising our city tour around his needs…stopping off for a cup of chai here, a bite to eat there and a chin-wag with some mates somewhere else, then asking us to hurry up when we stopped off to see something. He said he had to go and pick a shirt up at one point, but we both told him to bugger off and carry on driving. He sulked like a big baby Argonaut for the rest of the journey.

THE GAME……

We stayed at the brilliant Vinayak Guesthouse, a few short miles from the city centre. It was run by the very funny and smiley Raman and his lovely welcoming family. We had the world's greatest veggie curry there too, cooked by young Sanjay. Raman told us that there were no decent spaces nearby to play footy, but we could have a game on the roof of his guesthouse if we liked? Brilliant!

At 12.30pm on January 10th, Rohan, Sanjay, Rajan and Mukesh, who staffed the guesthouse, joined Raman, Danny and me for a game. Rohan and Mukesh were on my side and the others on our Danny's. We had to redirect the laundry filled washing lines on the roof to create space. I looked like the quiz master from Slumdog Millionaire, playing with a Bollywood bouffant hairdo given to me by a barber earlier in the day, much to Danny's amusement.

It was a 4 v 3 and first to ten. For them, Sanjay (18) was a good, fast technical player. Rajan (30) in his sandals looked scared to kick the ball; never smiling, always staring as if he'd just arrived back on earth twenty years after abduction. Danny was playing great and scoring far too many goals for my liking. Raman in their nets was comically competitive. Every time the ball came near him, he'd kick off his slip-ons and dance manically along the goal-line as if he was on hot-coals. Mukesh (13) for us had a cannonball for a right foot, and Rohan (18) was a brave and energetic keeper.

Spectators started to appear on nearby rooftops as the game intensified. It was nip and tuck all the way. It became a 3 v 3 when Rajan literally vanished! Had he been beamed back up? We eventually ran out 10-8 winners, with Mukesh the Cannonball scoring a double hat-trick. The vibe throughout the hour we played had been superb. These chaps had been a pleasure to meet and play footy with today; very gentle and friendly folk. We finished with a penalty shoot-out then grabbed one of Sanjay's ridiculously good curries.

GAME 42: INDIA

Date: January 11th 2019, 1.30pm
Ground: Nehru Park, Jaipur

MISSIONS TO MARS AS PEOPLE STARVE

The city of Jaipur was painted almost entirely pink to welcome the Prince of Wales and her Royal Glumness Queen Victoria in 1876. Pink denoted the colour of hospitality at that time and it's still really cheery seeing big blocks and strips of it as you travel through the manic city streets.

There are some ace buildings in Jaipur. Tourist spots like the fairytale Amber Fort, and the huge strawberry ice-cream gateaux Hawa Mahal Palace are brilliant creations. The view over the city from up at the Monkey Temple is impressive too. On the way down from this we came across a bloke making tourist photo money out of a cow with half a cow growing out of its arse-end (a holy cow if ever there was one).

On our last day in Jaipur, Danny and I made our way down to the Albert Hall Central Museum, another superb building dreamed up by the architect responsible for the Royal Albert Hall in London. There are many verdant lawn spaces in front and to the sides of it. In England, this sunny scene would have been awash with people picnicking, lovers loving and office workers stretching out on the grass in their lunch break. Here it was a very different story.

India's caste system is thought to be more than 3000 years old. This hierarchical system divides Hindus based on their karma (work) and dharma (cosmic law/duty). There are four main categories – Brahmins (Priests and teachers), Kshatriyas (warriors and rulers), Vaishyas (farmers, traders and merchants) and the Shudras (labourers). Dalits are those who fall below the four main castes and are regarded as untouchables; less than human.

No doubt many of the scores of homeless people we saw in the museum gardens this day were Dalits. I was shocked at how normalized this heart-breaking scene appeared to be. A group of happy young people chatted excitedly just a few feet away from an emaciated begging woman holding her hand out for alms; a serious looking businessman barked instructions down his gold i-phone as he strode through a corridor marked out by beaten desperate people asleep on the ground.

The Scheduled Castes and Scheduled Tribes (Prevention of Atrocities) Act 1989 was passed to deter offences against scheduled castes, providing relief and rehabilitation to the survivors of such offences. Despite this, there is still widespread discrimination and violence perpetrated against the so-called untouchables. Many continue to experience restrictions in terms of education, housing, work and access to justice. Women and girls are vulnerable to trafficking and early and forced marriage. Rape of Dalit women is commonplace and perpetrators are rarely brought to justice, as access to justice is limited for women from less privileged castes, especially in rural areas.

It seems the politicians have more pressing issues. India has a near $2 trillion dollar economy and spends $1 billion each year on its space programme, whilst 78 million of its people are homeless (India Today magazine, 2016) and only 1.2% of GDP is spent on public health (The Times of India, 2017). What the fuck is that all about?

THE GAME......

It seemed daft to play footy today. Daft to do normal everyday things with such depravation all around, but this is the way in India.

We wondered on across the road, away from the museum and into nearby Nehru Park. Here we got chatting to a group of five friends. They were first year bachelor degree students from the nearby Maharishi College. A couple of minutes later we had a game on our hands. My Dan, Sandeep C and Amit were on one side; Baskhar, Ajay and Sandeep Y were on the other. Sandeep C was crackers! How much energy could one boy have? He was everywhere! Slide tackles, wild air shots and, just occasionally, composing himself for long enough to actually pass the ball to a team-mate. Early on there was very little football being played by these mad cricket fans. The ball flew in all directions. Danny ended up getting one right in the eye ball, a real stinger.

The impressive Baskhar provided the composure the game so desperately needed. He was a left pegger whose mazy runs brought his side a two goal lead. Amit was trying to play whilst chatting on his phone, so I replaced him between calls in the nets for Dan's team. We clawed it back to 2-2. Ajay tried hard in the opposition nets but couldn't keep the irrepressible Sandeep C down for too long. By sheer law of averages, this Milan Baros impersonator managed to score 3 goals from about 300 shots.

At one point a long shot sailed well over my head, so off I trotted to fetch it. The ball had come to a stop by a stand-pipe. Here, an elderly lady was squatting, cleaning her tiny hands and finger nails with a small rock. I'll never forget this image as long as I live. Here was a woman preserving her dignity and femininity despite the horror of her starving existence. She will always appear to me now if I ever catch myself moaning about what I don't have.

Baskhar continued his brilliant form, weaving in and out of tackles and scoring from acute angles. Half an hour in and the game became locked at 8-8. The lads were loving it, playing with big smiles and winding each other up. With the next goal the winner, man of the match Baskhar fittingly slotted it away. A great game.

We chatted for a while after with the lads and what well mannered, funny, vibrant chaps they were. Great mates just starting out in life. In fact, the only frustration for these rabid love tigers seemed to be that theirs was an all-boys college and the girls college, which was tantalizingly close by, was strictly out of bounds. After a wee while we thanked them for their time and Danny gave the match ball to two overjoyed tiny tots who'd been watching on.

Jaipur...for all of your pink and all your splendid buildings and all the smiles of these five great lads and Raman, my lasting memory will be of the human catastrophe that has unfolded in your streets and parks. India is the world's fasting growing economy but, from what I'd read and what I'd seen in Delhi and now Jaipur, there's no urgent push to help the millions of most needy, or to address the horrific levels of trauma being experienced because of the caste system. Nothing's trickling down anytime soon from your economic boom is it fat-cats? Still, I'm glad the mission to Mars is going well you bastards.

GAME 43: INDIA

Date: January 14th 2019, 11.00am
Ground: By the Ganges, Varanasi

GHOSTS

The journey to Varanasi from Agra had taken 17 hours on the Marudhar *Express* train. The train is known as the Murder Express because of how slow it is. In Agra, we had again witnessed the incongruence of India. Here stood one of the most visited and breathtaking wonders of the world, the Taj Mahal, yet many homeless women and children were living on the Agra train station platform. Where are all those tourist millions going? Looking around, certainly not on public health, housing, education or infra-structure. Corruption really is a rapacious, murderous beast.

THE TEN MINUTES IT TOOK TO WALK THROUGH THE HORN BLARING, BRAIN SMASHING, CHOKED STREETS OF VARANASI TO THE RIVER GANGES ......

BEEP BEEP ! BEEEEEP! a flood of humanity **BEEP** you need driver? best price... **BEEP** ! where you staying ? **BEEEEEEEP** ! man with no legs on floor in rags pulling himself along by his elbows **BEEP BEEP** ! hungry line of beggers sat holding out trays looking up **BEEEEEP** ! two non plussed cows strolling through the crowd towards us **BEEEEEEEP** ! vibrant red, gold, yellow, green, purple everywhere **BEEP BEEP** ! a street cobbler kneeling working **BEEEP** ! screaming monkeys up high on the temple roof **BEEEEEEEP!** stray puppy struggles to get at an orange garland placed around its neck. Danny stoops to remove it **BEEP** picture postcard old man - orange turban, orange robed silver bearded guru **BEEP** green army shirt - serious face, serious moustache grips big brown serious stick **BEEP BEEP** ! Namaste ! **BEEEEP** ! bike wheel runs through cow shit **BEEP BEEP** ! man pushes cart loaded high with rosy red pomegranates **BEEEEEEEEP** ! **BEEEEP** ! moped runs into Daniel's heel **BEEEP** ! you need money exchange? **BEEP** ! line of pilgrims walking behind a banner **BEEP BEEEP** ! a smile BEEEP two mysterious, attractive women in stunning blue silver saris cut through the chaos like a pure clear stream **BEEP BEEP** ! traffic stops - herd of cows lying in the road **BEEP** ! **BEEEP!** men stood drinking chai from small clay cups around the merchants cart **BEEEEEP** ! **BEEEEEEEEP** ! **BEEEEEEP** ! **BEEEEEEEEP** ! trying to cross at the car/bike/rickshaw/people/animal anarchy round-a-bout **BEEEEEEEEEP** ! confident young woman driving moped, wearing shades using phone in traffic soup **BEEEEEEEEEEEEEP** ! curled up fawn dogs sleeping in the road nonchalantly risking death **BEEEEP** ! your first time here? **BEEP BEEP** ! old frail street seller demonstrates small children's yellow toy with propeller **BEEP** ! **BEEP** ! man urinating against a wall **BEEEP** elderly shirtless shoeless man with bent broken body following us, begging with arthritic hands **BEEEEEEP BEEP BEEEEEEEEP** ! you need a boat ?

Our hotel was right on the Ganges. The view each morning from the roof-top restaurant was breathtaking. Row boats stroked slowly through its sun-kissed waters as the river bank curled away from us into the distance. The river was flanked on our side by some of the 88 ghats, or riverside steps, and on the other side by an expanse of sand. In Hinduism, the river Ganges is considered sacred and is personified as the goddess Gaṅgā. Hindus believe that bathing in the river brings absolution from sins and facilitates Moksha (liberation from the cycle of life and death). We'd watch as pilgrims bathed in the holy waters each morning, and families brought their disabled and frail relatives down for a spiritual and hopefully healing paddle. Hindus believe the water to be pure. I hope they mean this in a spiritual sense because it is in fact one of the most polluted rivers in the world.

We'd arrived at the beginning of the festival season, and the festival of kites was in full flow. What a sight it was. Hundreds of children flying their colourful gliders and dive bombers from flat roofs all over the city. Stunning, especially in early evening as they soared and dipped against the orange tinged deep blue.

THE GAME......

It was mid-morning when I headed to the Ganges waterfront. The steep ghats are scored through the middle by a walkway. Strolling along I spotted the ghost children; ragged street urchins, repeatedly scrambling to the top of a steep tiled embankment to slide down in their bare wee feet. Ghost children because no-one was acknowledging them. Was it only me that could see them? Why were all these hundreds of *spiritual* pilgrims walking past them and not offering support?

I stopped at the bottom of the embankment with my ball tucked under my arm as they slid towards me. Just then a chap named Yasir Khan walked by. Yasir turned out to be a weaver in Varanasi who works 10 hours a day, 7 days a week, 362 days of the year. I asked him to ask the children if we could have a game of footy. Yasir explained to me that these children were all orphans and lived on this promenade by the Ganges. Little Gita, Jamun, Karina, Rinu, Rinda, Golu, Resab and Ramesh stared up at me with sad, unsmiling and aged faces. They looked lost and bewildered.

I quickly organised a game of penalties and it wasn't long before their little smiles broke out. Everyone had a couple of shots before we attempted a game, which, after a promising start, just turned into a free for all. Just kids being kids; vital, excited, hollering and screaming and poking fun. The game ended when the ball looped into the holiest of rivers and took an age to retrieve.

I popped into town for hot food, sweets and toys for these young rascals, which they quietly and graciously accepted on my return. They then went off to huddle in a circle nearby, filling their hungry bellies and playing with their toys with big smiley faces. For a moment, they looked like children anywhere in the world should look. Sadly, their reality is very different.

The only other person who seemed to notice these children was a big chubby restaurant manager, who came out of his fine establishment a couple of days later, barking at Danny and I to stop feeding them. He said it only encouraged them to hang around and was bad for tourism. Staring at his big belly with shirt buttons ready to burst, I asked him what these kids were supposed to live off, and how was it that supposedly spiritual people like himself could ignore hunger. He spluttered some nonsense and I just walked away before it got personal.

India leaves you feeling completely helpless at times. The contradictions between religious fervor and the caste system, stupendous economic growth and mass hunger are so stark but so embedded and accepted. Religion in particular is such a double edged sword; it so clearly controls and dopes the masses, but if the millions of India's poor didn't have it to cling onto, what would they have?

GAME 44: INDIA

Date: January 16th 2019, 1.00pm
Ground: By the Ganges, Varanasi

BLACKPOOL

We were served beer in a teapot in our hotel. The owner couldn't be seen to be serving alcohol in this holy land. He told us to tell folk it was iced tea if they asked. Just thought I'd tell you that.

During our stay in Varanasi, Danny and I paid a chap to row us down river towards Manikarnika; the largest, and most famous of the two burning ghats on the Ganges waterfront. It was a beautiful, warm early evening as we took our seats on a wooden slat at the back of young Rami's boat. The river, by day so dark and gloomy, seemed to have taken on a creamy consistency and had taken on a magical sheen from the lights on shore. Rami paddled us slowly towards the fires.

Hindu's who prefer to be cremated here, do so to break the cycle of death and rebirth, allowing their souls to proceed directly to heaven without pesky karma and reincarnation getting in the way. As we neared, Rami instructed us not to take any photos of the cremations as this could interrupt the souls journey to nirvana. We saw at least a dozen burning funeral pyres on different steps above the water. As we sat watching, bearers carried bodies wrapped in white cloth down to the river, there to be immersed in, or doused with, handfuls of the sacred water. Bodies were then placed in a neatly laid firewood sandwiches and set alight. Rami told us that these cremations took place all day every day. It was by turns a morbid and spectacular scene.

We headed back up river and joined the twist of tourist boats and row boats gathered in front of Varanasis liveliest and most colourful ghat, Dashashwamedh Ghat, to watch the colourful ganga aarti (river worship) ceremony with puja (prayers). Hundreds of pilgrims had gathered to watch. The ceremony itself consisted of very loud music and blokes in ceremonial burgundy and cream robes whirling flames around their heads for twenty minutes. They were stood in a row of seven separate, brightly lit platforms facing out to the water. What a scene! Like something from Mummy Returns or Raiders of the Lost Ark.

Danny and I would later walk along this ghat in the daytime. We were super hassled there by boatmen, flower sellers and worst of all, supposed holy men. These mostly bald, chubby chaps with their big welcoming smiles, marked our foreheads with red tikas, without permission, then asked for money for doing so. Very holy that mate. I'll also have a 1975 Ford Capri if you've got one?

The ruse that made me chuckle the most was the handshake that turned into a full body and head massage. I fell for it straight away. Dan and I were sat watching the world go by, when a lovely gentle chap walked up and shook hands with me. He then proceeded to massage my forearm as if the deal had already been done. So slick and sure was he that before I knew it, he was rubbing my ears and wobbling my head about. You just have to go with the flow sometimes...cheeky git.

For all the technicolor and utter madness on our side of the Ganges, we wanted to find out what was going on across the water.....

THE GAME......

Well I never. At lunchtime on the 16th January, the boy and I took a row boat with our ball across the river and discovered Blackpool. A sandy beach, kite fliers, games of quick cricket, families picnicking and frolicking in the water. The only difference was that donkey rides were camels rides. We wondered further on the sands. Clocking our ball, two young chaps started to follow us and asked for a pass. A minute later and we were playing a 4 v 4 with some young fellas who had been sat on their bums nearby.

Like the second game in Jaipur, the play was full of wild shots and mad hoofs from these mad energy balls. The tall Amar tore about like a wasp on speed before collapsing after two minutes. He was on Dan's team, as was Shaijesh, and Abuj. Dan and Amar scored two quick goals past me. That's when Suman stepped up for us. He was a clever Zola like player, showing great technique to lob our Dan for 2-1. Smelling blood, Aviaitpul pushed on and, between him and Suman, took us into a 5-3 lead at the break.

Amar rejoined the game in the second half, playing another incredibly energetic cameo and scoring two goals before retiring in a heap. Ankit for us was a proper actor and more interested in being photographed than playing footy. Eventually, we ran out 8-5 winners then had a penalty shoot-out. Great game with the children of pilgrims from all over India.

Danny helped push our row boat back on the water and we headed home. Sitting with a tea-pot beer on the roof of our hotel, with the kites flying all around us on the cool evening breeze, we reflected on the madness of our time so far in India. We agreed that it was time to move on to the mountains of Darjeeling for some peace.

GAME 45: INDIA

Date: January 18th 2019, 11.30am
Ground: Chowrasta Square, Darjeeling

GORKALAND

The journey to Darjeeling had not been good.

Time becomes suspended on India's dank railway platforms at night. Our 9pm train east from Varanasi to New Jalpaiguri would turn up 6 hours late. As we sat there into the gloomy small hours, we'd been entertained by a procession of white pigs, monkeys and dogs all chasing after rats on the railway lines. Had these creatures really been there, or was this just magical realism borne out of our exhaustion?

We awoke after eighteen grueling hours on the sleeper train to find that Danny's wallet, containing his phone and bank cards, had been stolen. He'd fallen asleep listening to music and some thief had spotted an opportunity. Indian sleeper trains are infamous for this. As they move slug like across country, stopping for long periods in remote places, bandits sneak on board and steal stuff from dozing passengers.

Danny paced up and down the carriages to see if he could spot someone using his phone. It was long gone. What a sickener. He'd taken some brilliant photos since arriving in India. The major worry was that his Australian working visa was about to expire. The official documents he needed to arrange his follow on visa had been in his wallet, leaving the very real possibility that he would have to return to England prematurely. He loved Australia and had set his sights on settling there. As you can imagine, the mood was marvelous.

Step in the very lovely Tulshi Modi. Tulshi had slept in the bunk above Daniel and was on her way home to Siliguri. She was very sympathetic and expressed her sorrow that this had happened in her country. She alerted the train staff and said she could arrange for us to report the theft to police if we wished. With a few hours still to travel, Tulshi attempted to lighten the mood by playing us her favourite tunes. Her main man was the multi-talented Salman Khan. In addition to knocking out cheesy 'man stalks girl 'til she gives in' pop videos, Mr. Khan is a very famous actor, producer and tv personality in India. "He can do everything!" gushed Tulshi. "Bet he can't do a rubik's cube in twelve seconds using only his bum-cheeks?" I thought.

With Tulshi's kindness and guidance, we eventually reached the jeep stop at Siliguri; the quickest mode of transport to Darjeeling. It was late. We'd had a punishing journey and our heads were battered. Add to that the fact that we were both pissed off about Daniels stuff being robbed, the last thing we needed was another Billy small balls trying to rip us off. I can still see him now; that greedy, shameless little piggy face, with a wad of cash in hand, asking us for double money to squeeze into the one remaining seat on the jeep that was about to leave. I was in no mood and just stared at him until he moved away.

We waited an hour for the next jeep and finally, finally, finally we were on our way to some peace and tranquility.

THE GAME......

Situated in north east India, in the state of West Bengal, Darjeeling became a hill station for the British in the mid 1800's, acting as both a sanatorium for soldiers and a retreat for British officials during the hot Indian summers. It would continue to be the summer capital of India during British rule (1858-1947).

At an altitude of 6,710ft, Darjeeling's stunning mountains and valleys are blanketed in sprawling tea estates and indented with many small colourful villages. Unfortunately, Danny had to spend our first day there trying to block bank cards and retrieve the information he'd had stolen the night before. I gathered up my ball and jumpers and went exploring.

It was a cool, crisp sunny morning when I wondered down to the fairy tale Chowrasta Square, the pedestrianized town centre. This flat open square is surrounded by colourful shops and stores and has that striking mountainous vista as its backdrop. The best shop in town was the Oxford Book and Stationery Company book shop, packed with brilliant novels and many mystic Himalayan and India titles.

I wondered on past the golden statue of Nepali poet Shri Bhanubhakta Acharya, and found a space to play at the foot of some steps leading to a big screen and bandstand. I was to learn that the whole community had been out to watch the World Cup on the big screen the year before.

Plonking the jumpers down I beckoned some of the many students hanging around to come and have a game. After about 5 minutes, Akshal Rai, Gourav Poudhan, Milan Baxaiky and the marvelously musically named Nawang Tamang joined me. They were all 17 year old art students at the nearby Ramakrishna School. A couple of little guys joined us and went in the goals for each team. They were Enock Subba and Masuring Risa. I helped Masuring in nets because he was so tiny.

Nawang and Gourav were on our side. They had an immediate chemistry; quick one-twos and plenty of flicks and tricks on show. We quickly took a 2-0 lead. Akshal was a cracking player for our opponents, using his bamboozling body movements to open up space and draw his team level. Enoch in their goals had found his confidence and was diving about like a little De Gea, saving the impossible and getting rounds of applause from the gathering spectators. My tiny side-kick in our nets, Masuring, was loving it; drop kicking the ball out of his hands and tackling the big boys.

There was some real posing going on too. About ten minutes into the game, a group of female students had gathered on the steps to spectate. The body language of the lads completely changed. The game suddenly became much more serious. Some of the chaps started to toy with their hair between passes. Shots and skills were followed by a glance over to see if the young women had been suitably impressed; hormonally hilarious. It could have been a scene from Grease or the dance of mating birds. As for the game, it really was end to end stuff. Trading flurries, strikes and body blows, our two teams slugged it out to a 5-5 draw like evenly matched boxers. A brilliant fast paced game played in a great spirit.

Talking to the chaps afterwards, they told me how proud they were of their heritage. They described themselves as Nepali speaking Indian Gorkhas, not to be confused with the Gurkhas of Nepal. Their people had been demanding independence from West Bengal for over 100 years as they were so culturally and ethnically different. This demand for their own recognized state, Gorkhaland, had led to violent uprisings and bloodshed over the years. After school, the lads would all join the army, not only for financial reasons but also because it was seen as a great honour. What a great set of polite, well-mannered lads and the first people I'd met in India who preferred football to cricket.

After the madness of the past ten days, it had felt so good to breathe pure clean air and be left alone to wander unmolested. I hadn't heard a horn beep all day.

GAME 46: INDIA

Date: January 20th 2019, 6.00pm
Ground: Lower Bhutia Busty, Darjeeling

LADS V DADS

What a wonderful experience this was.

Me and Dan headed out for a walk around lunchtime. It was another bright, beautiful day in Darjeeling as we strolled through the town centre and on to Padmaja Naidu Himalayan Zoological Park. The zoo is internationally recognized for its conservation breeding programmes. Here we saw many highly endangered species including red pandas, black bears, a snow leopard, a bengal tiger, a tibetan wolf and a bloke from Barnsley wearing shorts, white socks and sandals.

After this, we wondered down a mountain to the Happy Valley Tea Estate. It was out of season so there were no tea-pickers to be seen in the gardens. This was very much to the ire of a big, purple faced German tourist who complained loudly " Ver are ze pickers ?! I paid gut money to see ze tea-pickers picking in ze fieldz ! I vill never visit here again! " Thank Lord Krishna for that ye big daft tit. Me and the boy had a chuckle with the reception staff as he stormed off back to his jeep. We then drank a wee cup of Darjeeling's finest before continuing on our way.

THE GAME......

Throughout our walk I'd been constantly on the look-out for a flat space to play footy, but they are scarce in this very steep terrain. Landing back at our digs, Dan went to rest up and I grabbed my ball and jumpers and headed out; there was no way around it. I would have to wander off down a steep mountain side to one of the villages if I wanted to play. It wasn't the wandering down there that bothered me, it was the wondering back up with my gasping lungs that filled me with dread.

After descending for about twenty minutes, I bumped into a chap coming out of his house. This turned out to be 65 year old Santosh Chettri, and what an absolute gentleman he was. He gave me a big hug, listened to my drivel then showed me down to a space by the community centre of his village, the brilliantly named Lower Bhutia Busty.

Santosh alerted his mate Ashok Rai (also 65) and his grandson Avinav Chettri (16), who asked his mates of the same age Nadeem Siddique and Nikhil Tanang to join in. It was an incredible feeling to play a game in such a spectacular setting, half way down a mountainside. The lads brought the jumpers in to make the goals smaller. They then put barriers behind each, as any wayward shot could literally mean a sprint down the mountain to get the ball back.

A 3 v 3; lads v dads. Santosh, Ashok and I held those young whippersnappers at bay for a good 26 seconds before conceding. At 65, Santosh and Ashok put me to shame with their energy levels. However, we were no match for the rapid, technical Nikhil, the intelligent passing of Nadeem and the calm, assured play of Avinav. I was in nets for most of the game, trying to stop the constant barrage of shots. Resistance proved futile in the end. It was like Dads Army playing against skillful cheeky cheetahs. Needless to say we lost the game and 3-0 greatly flattered us.

I spoke with Santos and Avinav for a little while afterwards. It turns out that Avinav, Nadeem and Nikhil, a Muslim a Buddhist and a Hindu, had been close friends since they were small. Avinav wanted an independent Gorkhaland and was unhappy that the profits from Darjeeling's tea gardens were going into West Bengal's coffers, but that the Gorkhas saw little investment in return. Santosh pointed to the nearby disheveled primary school as an example of how West Bengal fails to adequately fund important public and social institutions in Darjeeling. He was also unhappy that all the high ranking officers in the army in the region were West Bengali. Avinav was concerned about the effects of global warming, telling me that orange yields were massively down year on year in the region and that 2019 was the first time they had seen snow for 15 years.

I was concerned about my own internal weather system, and worried that my whistling lungs may not make it back to the top of that mountain. I'd resigned myself to snailing my way up there over the next hour or so. The astute Avinav picked up on this, ran off and reappeared a couple of minutes later on his motorbike. Clinging on to him as we wound our way up the steep mountain road, I whispered to myself repeatedly "thank fuck for that, thank fuck for that, thank fuck for that".

GAME 47: NEPAL

Date: January 22nd 2019, 1.30pm
Ground: Tri-Chandra College, Kathmandu

COMEDY GOLD

Leaving Darjeeling at mid-day, Dan and I headed to our hotel in the nearby city of Siliguri. We would catch our plane to Kathmandu from there, via Kolkata, the next day. The hotel was very dirty and stinky, with piles of rubbish and broken masonry strewn across the floor on each level. The windows were cracked and broken and loads of soldiers were mulling around. It looked like it had been under heavy siege for months.

We decided not to stay. The hotel manager came running after us as we bundled back through reception with our suitcases. "Why you leave sir? ", "Because your hotel's a shocker". "No problem for me sir. I just work here" came his giggling repost. Comedy gold this bloke; no hint of an apology, just a big daft smile and a dopey eyed stare. Now I'm not a violent chap, but for some reason I wanted to poke him in the eye with a pickled onion.

It was baking outside. We were struggling to flag down a taxi when an elderly fellow in a blue Hawaiian shirt pulled up beside us in a peddle powered tuk-tuk. This had to be a set-up. He seemed like a very lovely chap, smiling at us with his one tooth and waving us on board. We climbed in and asked him to take us to another hotel we'd just booked across town. After thirty minutes of slow, sinewy peddling it was clear he had no clue where we were going. We knew this when he turned to us and asked "do you know where I'm going?"

We asked him to pull over, paid him then climbed into a motorized tuk-tuk nearby. The old fellow seemed taken aback at this turn of events and started running after us shouting all kinds of expletives. Whatever next? We finally arrived at our hotel, checked in and went for a beer in the restaurant. We were gasping by now. It turned out to be a dry hotel. We took to the streets in our quest to be quenched and ended up in a brand spanking new shopping mall, which was completely at odds with the poverty stricken urban sprawl all around it. We searched up and down this palace of decadence, until finally finding a bar on the top floor. All the signs were good. Photos of beers and spirits adorned the walls as we wondered through to the long inviting bar. "Two beers please ". "Sorry sir, we do not serve alcohol". What the …. !?

In the end we plumped for a pizza. This is where we had the bottled water which gave me and Dan the Eartha Kitts for the next three days in Kathmandu; what a marvelous day we'd had in Siliguri.

THE GAME......

Danny got the lurgy worse than me and spent most of the first day in Kathmandu exploding at both ends. We finally made it out and tracked down a phone shop. To get a sim card for his new phone, Danny had to show his passport and have his finger prints taken. Imagine that in Tesco's? Dan went back to the hotel where we'd later meet up with his mum. Natasha had flown out to do some Himalayan trekking with a group starting the next day. It was great that Dan could have a good catch up with his mum half way across the world.

I nipped into the city to see what I could see. Arriving at Durbar Square, famous for its temples, I was told that it was closed until Wednesday. Trundling on down the busy main road into Ghantaghat, I came to a little open fronted cafe and stopped for water. Taking a swig, I spotted Tri-Chandra College directly across the road, one of the oldest institutes of higher learning in Nepal.

I walked by its high perimeter wall for a good ten minutes trying to find my way in. Once inside I saw quite a few students hanging around in groups. I headed past them and onto the basketball court at the far end of the campus. I was greeted with smiles and handshakes from the moment I set foot on the grounds. Walking on court, I plonked the jumpers down and didn't really need to ask anyone to play; a group of young chaps were already making their way over.

We had a 5 v 5. Jay R Dhamala was our star man; bleached blonde hair and fond of the nutmeg, he drove us forward every chance he got. Suman Kharel was a cool player, very clever at finding space. Prashant Banjara was a languid player with a wicked shot who never seemed to lose the ball - Nepal's very own Matt Le Tissier. Completing our team was Biraj Khadra who was ..erm....enthusiastic. I went in nets. The lads were playing so well that I only had two shots to save. One was blasted past me from close range and the other I turned acrobatically around the post (it smacked me on the left cheek and went out). The game was played in a great but serious spirit. A healthy crowd gathered and kindly cheered every time I picked the ball up. I think this had more to do with me flashing my builders bum than anything else. We finished up 3-1 winners.

The lads were all budding scientists, aged 18-24 years. The college has over 10,000 students and this was their winter break, but many still came down to socialize. They have to pay to attend college and competition for jobs post-graduation is fierce. None of the lads were too keen on their Indian neighbours to the south, and all were eager to tell me that the Nepalese were much more welcoming. A couple of the lads gathered my jumpers up for me at the end. Many others came over to say hello and all welcomed me to their country. The vibe throughout the afternoon had been brilliant. Being a college, I had walked in expecting a bit of mickey taking, but instead found genuinely kind, interested and considerate young people. Another uplifting and inspiring experience, and a reminder how daft making assumptions and having expectations can be.

GAME 48: NEPAL

Date: January 23rd 2019, 2.30pm
Ground: Nayabasti Kuwatole, Kathmandu

SKY MONK BUDDHA AND THE THREE POISONS

I spent the early part of my 50th birthday in a taxi with a Buddhist Monk. With Danny still feeling rough, I went for a late morning stroll around the bustling narrow streets of Thamel. I bumped into a Tibetan Monk named Aley Lama (43) and his young friend from Rajasthan, Akash, meaning sky (17). Aley, who lives at the Monastery at the Monkey Temple in town, teaches Akash to paint incredible mandalas at a local arts centre. I visited there later and was astounded by their work.

After chatting for a short time, we jumped in a taxi to the outskirts of the city where Akash lives, close to the Boudhanath Stupa. This is a world heritage site, dated from 600 AD and sacred to Buddhists. On the way there, Monk Lama told me about the three poisons that we all must release from our minds if we are to live a happy life. They are represented by animals: the snake is anger/hatred; the pig is ignorance/ delusion; the cock is desire/ attachment. Well, I've certainly been a bit of a pig, snake and cock at times in my life. Hopefully those three poisons have left me now for good.

THE GAME......

Arriving at the sandy pitch in the Nayabasti Kuwatole neighbourhood, I saw the brilliant sight of little Saroj sat on a football with his goalie gloves on, waiting alone on the empty ground for someone to turn up and play. With the jumpers down, Akash shot off to spread the word. We didn't have to wait long. Within ten minutes we had a cracking 5 v 5 going.

Saroj turned out to be a fearless little lion in the nets for us. The smallest chap on the park by far, he'd go crashing into 50-50's with the bigger boys, dive at their feet and abuse them if they left a foot in. He put his absolute heart and soul into keeping the ball out. Despite his heroics, we had fallen 5-0 behind by half-time. The main reason for this was a young chap named Buddha. He wore a 'Hazard' Chelsea top and was playing just like him...in sliders! Incredible twists and turns, close control, vision and light years ahead of anyone else on the pitch. I think he scored 4 out of the first 5 for his team.

At 5-0 we swapped ends and our fight back began. Slide tackling maniac Sabin was not happy at the drubbing we were taking. He burst forward at every opportunity, scoring two quick goals to get us back in it. I passed in a third before Buddha struck again. Try as they might, the creative and skillful Hirajan and the strong Ngawang couldn't claw back the deficit for us and we went down fighting 10-6. Fantastic game.

The two man of the match awards had to go to Saroj the keeper and the mesmeric Buddha. The outstanding achievement award had to go to the Nepalese people for their deep sense of humanity and inherent kindness. The incredulously named Bibasgelekngawang Bibasanima brought me over a cup of tea at the end and I chatted with her and some of the locals for a while. The Monk said it was Karma that we met today. It certainly felt that way.

Danny and I spent the rest of our time in Kathmandu bombing around on a scooter. I didn't trust myself to drive one, so jumped on the back of Dan's. He was brilliant on it. In the tight city streets on Thamel and on the wild dusty highways around the city, Danny boy weaved in and out like a local, cheekily pushing in and stealing space just like everyone else. We only came off it once. Thankfully we were going very slowly at the time and landed in a load of mud. We drove for miles, visiting temples and finding vantage points to look down over the city. Up and up we went until we could finally see the majestic Himalayas in the distance, reaching to the stars.

What an adventure we'd had.

RAPID VIENNA: POSTCARDS FROM EUROPE

GAMES 49-64

POLAND-CZECH REPUBLIC-AUSTRIA-SLOVAKIA-HUNGARY-SLOVENIA-SWITZERLAND

I know what! I'll visit 7 European countries in 19 days! Silly sod. It's a great idea when you're 18. My knees are still creaking. Here's what happened…

GAME 49: POLAND

Date: August 4th 2019, 1.00pm
Ground: Rynek Glowny, Krakow

JUST THE TICKET

First world problems indeed. My plane to Krakow had been delayed by four hours. On arrival, with no taxi's in sight, I managed to catch the last bus into town from the airport. I was dropped in a place with no streetlights, cars or people. It was midnight and the battery on my phone had just died. Luckily, I'd made a note of my hostel's address. I dragged my squeaky suitcase towards the city lights flickering in the distance. After an age a taxi appeared like a glowing angel in the now cold deserted night. Arriving at my digs in the wee small hours, I buzzed to get in, only to find the reception was on the 8th floor. There was no lift. I dragged my suitcase up the big wooden staircase, only to be told by the young whipper snapper on the desk that my bed was on the first floor. When I climbed back down again, with the help of two sherpas and a St. Bernard, I bundled into my dorm, turned on the lights and got bollocked by nine of my fellow sleeping hosteliers. Welcome to Krakow.

The next day I awoke early and went for a wander. Krakow is clean. The cleanest place I've ever been. That's why it was such a surprise when a chap in the street asked me if I wanted to see some pole dancing at 1 o'clock in the afternoon. Now, would that be a Pole dancing, a pole dancer or a pole dancing Pole? I felt poleaxed and just said no. I wandered around the huge ten-acre main square, Rynek Glowny, where I got chatting to Robert Paluch. He works for the city's refuge department and was sweeping the square all day this Sunday for double pay. He supports Wiarusy Igolomia, a team low down in the Polish pyramid. He told me they were rubbish but "What can you do? Your team is your team".

Robert was a funny chap. He told me it wouldn't be a good idea to play in the square because the police might give me a ticket. I guessed this wouldn't be for the Lion King. I took a chance and went about trying to cajole the locals into playing. They were having none of it. After all it was Sunday. Lovers were loving, shoppers were shopping and parents with screaming toddlers were trying to keep a lid on things in the hot afternoon sun. A policeman came over at one point and asked me to move on or risk a ticket. What if it was for the Lion King and I was missing out? I decided not to ask him that question. I stepped into Cloth Hall (Sukiennice), an historical building in the centre of the square which dates back to the Renaissance. An important trading point in the past, it now houses a shopping centre and a museum. Emerging from Cloth Hall on the other side of the square, I continued my quest to get a game going. It had been over an hour now.

THE GAME....

Just when frustration had started to set in, salvation came walking towards me in the shape of a Geordie stag do. (Krakow is becoming a popular destination for the doomed). Callum was the stag and had eight staggerers in tow. Alan, Rob, Mark, Paul, Gary, Ben, Sean and Connor were absolute top blokes, but none too pleased that Steve Bruce had replaced Rafa Benitez at their beloved Newcastle United. They all looked in various states of disrepair after a long night on the lash, but accepted the footy challenge within seconds. I joined in and a 5-a-side broke out in this, one of the largest medieval squares in Europe.

It was hot and the boys were suffering. Gallons of Guinness were pouring out of them as the game lurched into life like a rusty steam engine. We were ten-minutes in with still no breakthrough, when Mark burst forward to finish off a swift passing move. 1-0 to us. The game was livening up. We soon made it two and it would have been much more if it wasn't for Big Sean, the wall in the opposition goal. This human shield was blocking and setting up attacks with his mammoth throws, but even he couldn't stop us taking a 3-1 lead before the lads finally ran out of steam. A brilliant, quickfire game with these friendly footy loving chaps, and a great way to kick off this leg of the journey. Just the ticket.

I walked for many hours on the second day, in and out of every nook and cranny of Krakow's lovely streets. All I got to show for it were big bleeding blisters on each heel. The closest I came to a game was when a dog ran off with my ball. Sunburnt and crippled, I arrived back at my hostel to find a new chap had moved into the dorm. Another Polish Robert was in the bed next to mine. I slumped on my bunk knackered, but Robert was full of beans. It was the first day of his holidays and I was his new best friend. He started chunnering away to me excitedly in Polish. We both waded through thick mental porridge trying to communicate. It was all waving arms, nodding heads and mad stares. After a good twenty minutes of this, we were both none the wiser about each other. From what I could gather, he made plastic miniature chip-shops for the Klingons.

GAME 50: CZECH REPUBLIC

Date: August 6th 2019, 7.30pm
Ground: Minoricka Street, Brno

THREE-DAY-WOBBLE

From Krakow, I travelled five hours by bus through the beautiful rolling fields of Moravia, one of the historical lands of the Czech Republic, listening to Ben Howard's hypnotic *Nica Libres at Dusk* on repeat as we went.

Arriving in the country's second largest city of Brno, I thought I'd got lost trying to find my hostel, so asked the first person I saw for help. This turned out to be the one and only Kleber Buriolla, a splendid looking Brazilian chap, heavily tattooed with marvellously stretched and decorated ears. He gave me a big wide smile with his gold teeth and pierced lips. Kleber said he was staying at the same hostel as me and that I was actually stood right outside it. He unlocked the main door and showed me where to go before disappearing into town.

Reaching my room, I sat on my bunk and had to have a word with myself. Something hadn't felt right since I started this leg of the journey. Usually I feel very free and ready for whatever comes next, but this trip had felt like one big effort so far. Before setting off, I'd been working ridiculously long hours and I'd lost my mojo...but it wasn't just that. I'd arrived as an observer, not an instigator, and I'd felt alien to the thousands of young, vibrant, shiny people who'd flooded past me in Krakow. Then it dawned on me. For the first time in my life I felt old. Turning 50 in January was having more of an impact than I thought. I was plagued with self-doubt. Would people take me seriously at my age? Had I lost all relevance? Should I just go home? Life was for the young after all... What!? Where was all this fear and negativity coming from?

Salvation came partly from the unlikeliest of sources. I remembered a radio interview I'd heard with that expert life-coach and renowned philosopher Liam Gallagher from Oasis. The presenter asked Liam if he ever thought about death and growing old. He gave the best response I've ever heard about this subject... *I'll think about that when I take my last breath. Let's ave it!* With that, and the neon sign flashing in my mind *'don't regret growing older, it's a privilege denied to many'*, my three-day-wobble was over. Thanks Liam.

After a right good cup of tea, I grabbed my ball and headed out into the warm air and cool vibe of this medieval, gothic and modern mixture of a city. After an hour or so, I spotted the walking art form that was Kleber the Brazilian again sat outside a bar. Considering how I'd been feeling earlier, this ultra-laid-back cat from Sao Paolo turned out to be the perfect footy companion over the next two days. He helped me rediscover my fire and focus without even knowing it. I joined him for a pint before explaining my mission. He jumped at the chance of a game.

THE GAME....

Kleber (known in true Brazilian style as Klebinho back home) was a market trader from Sao Paolo and absolutely full of mischief. We headed out into the heart of the city before plonking the jumpers down in Minoricka Street, close to the central bar area. After a few passing grumps with very serious faces had declined to play, we managed to convince four young random locals to join us. They were partners Martin Vynazal (28) and Lucie Vachoua (27); Jolana Kantorova (21) on her way to work, and Natalia Felinity (25) who was out for a stroll. A 3 v 3 with Natalia and Lucie on Kleber's side. Natalia kicked off her flip-flops and Klebinho did the same. Lucie was worried her shoes would get ruined and didn't want to play at first. Ten minutes later she'd transformed into a bare footed starving lioness chasing blood!

Martin and Jolana were combining well for our side and we took a quick two goal lead. That's when Klebinho came out of his nets and started to show off his samba skills, dancing in and out of tackles, laughing all the while. They pulled a goal back through Captain Lucie, but we replied almost immediately. They hit back to make it 2-3 but we sealed victory when the all action Jolana nipped in to put away Martin's cross. A bright and breezy, joyful game of footy with some lovely young souls from Brno, and the irrepressible Klebinho. As for me, I was back in the game.

GAME 51: CZECH REPUBLIC

Date: August 7th 2019, 6.30pm
Ground: Jacob's Square, Brno

DOCTOR EVIL

In the steaming hot mid-morning, Klebinho and I headed out of the city in search of a game. We wondered on through Brno's largest park, Lužánky, then on to Masarykova University, but it was a sleepy day and we hardly saw a sausage. In fact, a sausage would have been an improvement. Kleber and I got along famously, considering his bitty English and my non-existent Portuguese. The little Spanish I know seemed to do the trick. He showed me photos of him back in Sao Paolo, taking his mum shopping in his kayak, like you do, and told me about the Bola de Neve (Snowball) Church that his brother attends. The church had originally been started on a beach in Sao Paolo by Apostle Rina, a pastor and a surfer. Only in Brazil could a church have a surfboard as it's altar. Bola de Neve appeals to younger generations with its absence of dogma, tradition and expected dress-code. I think JC would approve.

Our search for a game had proved fruitless so we headed back into the city. Klebhino was the star attraction, especially amongst the young women. With his head-to-toe tattoos and beach-chilled demeaner, he was lapping up all the smiles and giggles as we strolled through old town's picturesque streets. He was great company; a cross between Hong Kong Fooey and The Fonz. We eventually found ourselves in Jakubské Square. By night, this is one of the liveliest spots in Brno, surrounded as it is by restaurants, bars and the huge gothic St James Church. The paved area at the centre of the square was perfect for footy. It felt gladiatorial as we placed the jumpers down. All eyes were upon us. I imagined that those staring on from the bars, and sat on the church steps, were expecting fire-eating or sword swallowing, not two plonkers kicking a ball to each other.

THE GAME....

We called out for players and were soon graced by Doctor Ondrej Zizlavsky, a James Bond baddy and evil genius masquerading as a tourist. Hana Fridrichova stepped up next. She was a former student of the doctor's and now his insidious moll. Gabriela Popezkova and Andrea Vitova came next. They were Polish commercial shipping managers, who no doubt turned a blind eye as the doctor's deadly green nerve gas was loaded at Gdansk for world-wide distribution.

What a great game. The doctor, Hana and I took on the rest. Andrea for them was crackers. She picked up the ball at one point, ran the length of the pitch, chucked it in the net, then romantically whispered in my ear "I used to play volleyball for Brno you know ". No-one had ever said that to me before and one of my little toes tingled. We took a deserved 2-0 lead through the determined Hana, who was definitely out to please the doctor. If she were a cat, she would have licked him repeatedly on the thumb (ignore that). As yesterday, Klebhino turned on the samba skills when the chips were down, bringing it back to 2-2. Hana was having none of it. Responding to an icy stare from the doctor, she bludgeoned us to an unassailable 4-2 lead as if her life depended on it (It probably did). A great laugh in a brilliant space, in a fantastic, intriguing city. The doctor looked very pleased with his night's work. He now had a perfect alibi, as he reached into his man-bag and casually pressed the button to start the missile launch on Washington.

GAME 52: AUSTRIA

Date: August 9th 2019, 12.30pm
Ground: Karlskirche, Vienna

THE WANDERER

Apart from 10 bollocks in China, the only people I've fallen out with on this journey are taxi-drivers. What is it with these bastards? £22.00 he wanted for a five-minute ride to my hostel from the train station? I said I wasn't paying that and he started to raise his voice and mention the police. I said 'Don't come the hard man with me big balls" He replied "Don't call me big balls" I said "Ok. Don't come the hard man with me small balls" before giving him £12 and walking off. Tosser.

Vienna is grand. Once the residence of Mozart, Beethoven and Freud, the city is packed with majestic imperial palaces, historical buildings and monuments. A lot of them look like giant coffee and cream gateaux. The finest big cake for me is the Karlskirche (St. Charles Church) in Karlsplatz, a baroque church resplendent with a huge water filled oval in front of it.

I'd come across this place by accident the night before, after being moved on by security from in front of the Presidential Palace. I'd attempted to get a game going there with some punks who were sat nearby drinking. They looked a rum bunch of pirates, with four out of the six of them sporting black eyes. Their leader from Germany, who introduced himself as Paranoia, was first to get up and play. How looks can be deceiving. With his mohican, ripped jeans and torn 'Slime 1979' T-shirt, he looked like he was gonna kick someone's head in. Probably mine. Paranoia turned out to be a lovely, polite and engaging chap, if a little worse for wear off the drink. We were happily chatting, passing the ball to each other when a big burly security tag-team showed up and moved us on. Gutted. With his mates either not willing or incapable of moving on to play somewhere else, we said our goodbye's and I headed back to the metro station. Emerging at Karlsplatz, I walked through a small park and there it was, this lovely church all lit up in the beautiful warm evening. I vowed to return the next day for a game.

THE GAME….

It was already pretty hot when I headed down to Karlskirche in mid-morning. There were queues at the water fountains and kids were dancing in and out the sprinklers. I put my jumpers down in the paved area between the church and the huge oval water feature, then called to folk sitting in the shade of the church steps to play.

I was soon joined by Can, a friendly curly haired chap and Fenerbace fan from Turkey. His mate Kris also played. He was a wired, jittery sort of fella from Poland who spent the whole game saying" I've got to go now, this better be quick". I said he could go anytime he liked but on he played. I had a feeling that "I've got to go now, this better be quick" will be carved on his gravestone. Carsten from Germany was pushed into action by his mates and it was game on. A 2-2 in front of this splendid church.

Carsten was on my side and was struggling in the heat, especially after his quick spurt to try and stop the ball going in the water. He kept shaking his head at me saying "Why?". Curly man Can could play a bit and Kris was scarpering around like a caffeined meerkat. Can side-footed in the opener as my partner in crime Carsten struggled to get back. It really was hellish for the big German, his miserable day complete when he scored an own goal. We never got near their nets in the whole game and, with it being far too hot to continue, we ended the game with a 2-0 defeat. I gathered the lads in for a photo at the end and Kris predictably said" I've got to go now, this better be quick". Bet he's great in bed.

As I gathered in the jumpers, young Juan from Spain came to join me and we had a game of keepy-ups. Juan was from Bilbao and fiercely proud of being from the Basque region. In the ten minutes we played, he gave me an articulate potted history of his beloved Athletic Bilbao, explaining how, to this day, they only sign Basque players, unless an outsider has come through the youth ranks. I asked him if this policy had held the club back at all. He replied that sticking to this tradition was more important than their final league position. Juan said the Basques were like the Catalans. They don't see themselves as Spanish. To him, Real Madrid were the spawn of the antichrist.

I returned to Karlskirche later that day. What a stunning sight it was, all lit up in the lovely warm evening. There were people sat all around the edge of the large oval pool in front of the church, some bathing their feet in the water. I sat on a bench between a musician and a wanderer. The musician was an elderly Turkish fellow, who's virtuoso violin and oboe playing filled the still, peaceful night with beautiful ancient folk music. The wanderer was a man called Sascović from Monte Negro, and was as rugged as its mountains. He was wearing a battered black baseball cap, which he lifted occasionally to pick at scabs on his scalp. His soft white beard and piercing blue eyes brought light to his weathered leather face. The loose, worn and dirty bottle green t-shirt covering his slender frame, and his torn, light blue three-quarter length pants, made him look strangely youthful. He wore no shoes and his tough feet were powered by strong calf muscles that had walked many a mile.

As that intoxicating music filled the air, we shared my last bit of chocolate and gazed at the splendid sight before us. Sascović told me that he had been wandering for years, and had lived in fifteen countries across Europe, sometimes employed and sometimes homeless. He had learnt the languages of every country he'd been to, and to prove it he gave me a quick burst of words from Strasbourg to Serbia. To Sascović, most jobs are a trap and amount to nothing but slavery. When he felt the walls closing in, he'd down tools and head off back into the world, money or no money. He said he would always be free. Being near him, his sense of freedom was tangible; a clear, strong omnipotent energy. We said our goodbye's and, not for the first time, I'd felt elevated by someone who had nothing but had everything.

GAME 53: AUSTRIA

Date: August 10th 2019, 12.30pm
Ground: Ressel Park, Vienna

AN EXCITING KIND OF AVERAGE

After yesterday's game, I'd spotted some skate-boarders grinding around a statue in Ressel Park next to Karlskirche. I'd wandered back there this day to see if they were still around and fancied a game. I found street-skaters Egon Wiesinger and Nils Tavmann (Austrian) and Lukas Gorab (Brazilian), bombing about, mounting steps and pushing their boards to the limit. Egon was particularly determined, his t-shirt drenched in sweat as he furiously sought air and flip-tricks. (Did you like that? As if I know what I'm talking about).

THE GAME....

I chatted to Nils and pretty quickly we had a 2 v 2 going in the park by the statue. For skateboarders, they couldn't half kick a footy. Nils and I took on the other two. He was fiercely competitive, banging in two quick-fire goals before removing his t-shirt in the sweltering midday. The wiry, cool Egon, playing with a fag in his hand, was having none of it, slotting in a couple of belting assists from Brazilian Lukas to draw them level.

It was a tight game. I got on the score-sheet a couple of times, then Lukas slid in to make it 3-4. They broke away again and Lukas belted the ball right in my peculiars. Filming was temporarily halted. I heard giggles from behind me as I bent double, waiting for that special kind of pain to subside. Magdolena Derzko and Patrycia Josefek from Poland had been watching on and wanted to play. Magdolena joined our side and Patrycia joined Lukas and Egon. Magdolena is a sports coach who had played footy for years back in Poland. She was very skilful and a great passer of the ball. Patrycia was very strong and direct, rushing for goal every time the ball landed at her feet. She had a powerful shot on her too. There was a great ebb and flow to the game and a keen edge written on serious faces. Egon stole in at the back post to draw the teams' level at 4-4. A few moments later, Patrycia picked the ball up on the right and surged towards goal. I thought I had it covered but she walloped it between my legs to for the winner.

Afterwards, we sat talking on the steps of the Joseph Ressel statue (he was the inventor of the ships propeller back in the 1820's). What great young folk they turned out to be. The boys explained the mind-set of the urban skater. Lukas is a hip-hop artist from Sao Poalo, Brazil, going by the name of 'An Exciting Kind of Average' on his own label, Bearstew Records. It's very chilled out stuff. (You can check him out on YouTube). He'd been living in Vienna for just over two years:

"Just as much as the obstacles and boards you skate can influence you, the people you skate with can influence you too because everyone's got a different style and perspective on how to do tricks. The space where we are today can be skated a thousand different ways. When I was skating alone, I didn't feel the kind of progress as I do now when I'm skating with the crew. Everyone pushes each other…that community hype…we had it yesterday…I skated a rail and landed it. Nils was then hyped to do it too and did it, then the other guys went for it. I used to skate simple tricks like a Nollie or a 50-50 which is a basic grind, but now I try to be more creative and I don't skate big gaps or big stairs like I used to. It all depends of the mood…sometime I will skate some ledges or a flat-rail. It always changes"

Nils is studying mechanical engineering in Vienna. I told him that I had been surprised to see so many locals openly drinking cans of beer in the parks and streets (This was the case across all the countries I visited in Europe, in contrast to the ban we have at home.) I just didn't expect to see this in a grand place like Vienna. Was there a drinking culture amongst the skaters?:

"Vienna is a very laid back, safe city. You can wander around here at midnight and never be in fear. There is hardly any crime. There are some skaters who go to the park at noon and pop like six cans of beer and smoke joints. I like drinking but I don't need to drink at this time. There are hundreds of places to skate all over the city and hundreds of crews too. Some do drugs, some don't. We just love skating and have fun with it and there are some seriously skilled and dedicated skaters in the city. You can't skate too well if you're too far gone so what's the point?"

Once again, that round thing had worked its magic. I would never have had this conversation in a million years, or had the slightest idea about skating culture without having a kick-about today. We said our goodbye's and I sat on the steps of the statue writing a few notes. Something made me look up at precisely the point my mate's son Elliot from home walked by. An unbelievable coincidence that topped off a magical hour with magical young people in this beautiful city.

GAME 54: AUSTRIA

Date: August 11th 2019, 4.00pm
Ground: St. Stephen's Cathedral, Vienna

RAIN STARTS PLAY

My last afternoon in Vienna was spent whizzing around for hours on the metro looking for places to play. I must have got off at all the wrong stops. Everywhere I wandered seemed pretty vibe-less and the clock was ticking. It looked for all the world like a lost cause. Checking the metro map again, I decided to take one last punt. It was around 3.30pm when I emerged from the underground to be met by the towering St. Stephens Cathedral, the seat of the Archbishop of Vienna no less. Now I get that it's good to gather to worship, but I can never get my head around the size, extravagance and expense of such houses of God. There's no way Jesus would have approved of spending all that money on these buildings, however magnificent some of them look. He'd have fed significantly more than the 5000 with all that dosh, and, being a proper chap, would have probably chucked the hungry pigeons a loaf or two. Feeling knackered, I wandered through the crowds and sat on a bench to the right of the cathedral. I was listening to the brilliant Piledriver Waltz by The Arctic Monkeys, and thinking how good Caitlan Rose's version of the song was, when a mighty rain storm came. People scattered everywhere for cover but, being a daft northerner, I stood up and showered under the warm revitalising downpour. Lovely.

Soaking wet, but happy as a teenage otter, I was fully back in the day and ready to play. There was a perfect paved area in front of me and so down went the jumpers. The patrolling cops and cathedral security had clocked me but didn't approach. The rain began to subside and folk began to appear from their temporary shelters in shop door-ways and the like. It would take me a while to persuade people to join in as they hurried to finish their shopping and get home.

THE GAME...

Thankfully, George Ablin and Luke Pettican from Essex and their friend Romi Hudakova from Slovakia did join in. They were swiftly followed by Antanas Budnys from Lithuania, who had something of the Andy Kaufman's about him. Roman from Ukraine completed the line-up and joined me and Antanas against the others. Luke was a fibber. He said he couldn't play but was a total monster, battering his team into a 2-0 lead with his big shoulders. We struck back when the slim and nimble Antanas stole in at the back post to put away a slide-rule pass from Roman. Game on. Romi threw the ball out to George to re-start the game. I ran out of my nets to close him down, but before I could reach him, he turned and slotted home. George was a lovely, well-mannered, stand-up chap; the kind a parent would want their child to grow up and marry. He was still feeling the pain from Tottenham's Champions League Final defeat to Liverpool earlier in the year.

3-1 quickly became 4-1. Things went from bad to worse when Roman stubbed his toe and limped off with a pained expression. There was more than a hint of his injury being related to not wanting to get his pristine white trainers dirty. Whatever the reason, Roman's questionable departure proved to be the turning point of the whole game, when on came the mighty Andrzej Staniszewski from Poland for us. He'd been watching on from the side-lines and jumped at the chance to play. What a player! Strong, intelligent, quick and with a great hunger to win. Just what we needed. His introduction triggered Antanas back to life. Little Mubarak from Saudi Arabia then joined our team as we set about reducing the deficit. A sizeable crowd had gathered by this time and the game was electric; end to end on a warm, muggy night.

Luke had run out of steam for the opposition, and every shot the busy George struck was cannoning off me and out of play. Our luck had turned and Andrzej was proving unplayable. Miraculously, we fought back to win 5-4, with Andrzej scoring four. Cracking game. Half an hour earlier I'd been sat on that bench feeling tired, contemplating going back to the hostel. Then the rain came and now here we were, people from six different nations united by footy, feeling alive and exhilarated. Marvellous.

GAME 55: SLOVAKIA

Date: August 12th 2019, 2.30pm
Ground: Bratislava Old Town, Slovakia

MESMERIC MALLETS

Welcome to the Hostel Bratislava. Such a lovely place…not. It was rougher than a witch's hairy chin wart. With 1970's brown throughout, this gloomy, dirty and dank hostel had all the appeal of a gone-off poached egg. Once in my bare room, I carefully charged my phone using the socket hanging off the wall, before opening the door on to the balcony. This was strewn with rubbish and the battered and burnt chair at the far end sort of symbolised the whole place. Ah well, it was only for a couple of nights and I was sure I'd get on great with all the spiders and termites. Grabbing my ball, I risked again the slim sarcophagus lift down to reception and escaped back onto the streets.

The local accent in Slovakia's capital city of Bratislava is incredibly sexy, so much so that when a lass in a coffee shop asked me if I wanted milk in my brew, I went mute, blushed and stared down at the table. Old town Bratislava is a beautiful wee place set along the Danube River, and only a ten-minute tram ride from my death hostel. It reminded me of Brno a bit, with its gothic cathedral and medieval square, conjuring up images once more of a Bond or Bourne movie; our hero caught up in a high-speed bike chase through its narrow streets, or throttling a few henchmen before making love with a beautiful but deadly foe in the bed chamber of its ancient castle.

Wandering down Panska Street, I came across the famous bronze statue of Cumil the sewer cleaner, popping up out of a man-hole with his cheeky smile. Some think if you rub his head, you'll have good luck. Others think of him as pervert looking up women's skirts. Wandering further, I became spell-bound by a young woman playing xylophone in the centre of a beautifully cobbled boulevard. How did she hit all the right notes at such high speed? A world champion fly-swatter.

THE GAME...

It was just a few yards up from her mesmeric mallets that I decided to try and get a game going. The boulevard was a perfect, urban playing surface; flat and wide enough to not disturb pedestrians too much. The problem was the heat. It was boiling and passers-by were reluctant to play.

Just when it started to feel like pulling teeth, young Alex Schütz from Stuttgart, Germany came bounding down this splendid thoroughfare with his partner. They were on their way to join a city tour and were running late. The pull of a game of footy was too great for Alex though, and he managed to persuade his partner that the tour wouldn't leave without them. That's commitment for you. I then tried to persuade a Spanish family to play. They were eating ice-cream under the shade of some nearby trees. Eventually, the father and daughter duo of José Martin and Alexandra from Barcelona cracked and agreed to join us. Alex and I took them on; England and Germany on the same side for once. (I'd let him take the penalties if it came to it).

The diminutive José was a cracking player; bags of natural ability, with that in-born Barca ability to look after the ball as if it was his only child. He was loving it and was competitive from the start. Alex and I were combining well. We were on the same wavelength; little one twos and unspoken moves. We took the lead when I back-heeled one in that was meant as a pass. The lively Alex took it to 2-0 for us before Alexandria chipped in a beauty at the back post.

José pressed for an equaliser, the ball and his foot now happily married, but our defensive wall proved impenetrable. Both he and Alexandria did hit the post though before Alex broke away for us to clinch it 3-1. What a marvellously enjoyable pop-up game this had been, played in a great spirit from the start. I sat down on a bench next to an elderly local chap after the game. He must have been in his 80's. He told me he would have played if it wasn't for his dodgy knee. He meant it too. Brilliant

GAME 56: SLOVAKIA

Date: August 13th 2019, 7.00pm
Ground: Kollárovo Námestie, Bratislava Old Town

EXPLODING HALIBUT

They have some peculiar sayings in Slovakia. For example, we say *drinking like a fish*, they say *drinking like a rainbow*; we say *that place looked like the end of the world*, they say *the dog died there*. They also say *party like a halibut* according to Jan Pan and Martin Sunik, the two rascals who plied me with the local brew all night. I don't know the collective noun for halibut, but we partied like three of those deliriously happy flat-fish, slapping each other on the back and supping in a sea of ale 'til we were hauled to our beds. This was only the third time I'd been plastered on the whole trip, and again, of course, it was not my fault.

It was my last evening in Bratislava. I'd set off walking from my hostel at 6.00pm, determined to play footy with Slovakians. I came across a little Italian restaurant and had a quick bolognese before wondering for a while through the grounds of a nearby university. It was quiet and there was rain in the air. "Not much chance of a game tonight" thought I, before turning a corner and seeing the vision that was the Kollarko Pub and Beer Garden. The place was bouncing with twenty-somethings drinking and acting their age. I introduced myself to everyone sat around the packed tables outside, before placing my jumpers down on a nearby patch of grass and calling folk to play.

THE GAME...

I was quickly joined by Chris Vevoda from Kremnica, Slovakia, and two other local chaps, plus Jano Litavsky from Serbia, Peter Barrer from New Zealand and Tobias from Southern Germany.

After less than five minutes, with the game at 0-0, the ball deflected off the knee of Tobias and wedged under a bus waiting at the lights. Tobias felt very responsible for this and sprinted over to ask the driver if he could retrieve the ball. The driver was having none of it and, with a pantomime smirk, he revved his engines and rolled over our precious sphere. Bang! The explosion brought 25 gasps, 3 screams and 2 little scared underpant wee's from the young folk outside the bar. Apparently someone had fired a gun near this spot a few weeks ago and nerves were still fraught.

Sorrowfully, I gathered up my deceased ball and, with no spare in tow, had to abandon the game. Returning to the bar, loads of folk offered me a drink in sympathy for my loss. I sat down with Jan and Martin and staggered to my feet some hours later. This comedy double act wouldn't let me pay for a drink, taking great delight in getting me well and truly halibutted. Martin was a big, broad rugby player type of chap in a cowboy hat. He was the Eric Morecambe to Jan's Ernie Wise. Jan, who had something of the Mr. Tumnus about him (upper half), was happy to play the straight man as Martin laughed and bellowed his way through a stream of anecdotes and one-liners. What brilliant craic and just what I needed.

After closing, we all walked back towards my hostel and the conversation turned to romance and lovers. Martin said he'd never told his partner of five years that he loved her, but he had told her that of all the people he had met he hated her the least. Funny chap.

GAME 57: HUNGARY

Date: August 14th 2019, 11.00am
Ground: Hősök tere (Heroes Square), Budapest

MUCKY LUVDUST

My mate Mickey Loveder was built in 1968 and is a most impressive monument to cheeky rascality. He flew out especially to join me for a few days, and it was brilliant to have my old pal's company after travelling alone for a while.

Mickey, who has been known to introduce himself as Mucky Luvdust, is one of the best singer/songwriters I've ever heard and one of the most unique and funny chaps I've ever met (but don't tell him that). He can converse on anything from string theory to string vests and even looks great in a dress. We are from the same small town, Stacksteads in East Lancashire, and were in a band together for ten years called *The Mighty Asylum*. Those debauched years were very very special, playing gigs in and around Manchester and London, convinced we were going to make it. Maybe we would have done if the craic hadn't overtaken the creativity. We'll never know now, but I wouldn't swap the music we made and the special bond that us six lads still have for anything in the world.

Me and the Luvdust decided to spend some time hopping on and off the hop on hop off bus around the city, realizing later that we'd got away with eventually hopping off without paying. They'd be hopping mad if they knew (*ok..that's enough of that- Ed*). Whilst sight-seeing, we'd passed by an impressive square which we returned to around 10.30am. With our sunless Lancashire legs cutting through the grey day like fog lights, we strode into the largest square in Budapest, Hősök tere (Heroes Square), which had been built to mark the thousandth anniversary of Hungary in 1896.

THE GAME...

It didn't take us long to get a game going. A family from Belgium joined us (the first Belgians to play on the whole trip so far). They were Riet Scheurweghs and Mattias de Winter, both teachers from Antwerp, travelling the world with their children Jack (3) and Josephine (4).

Here's Mickey's take on proceedings:

"We alighted upon a huge stone flagged square. Two massive museums yawned elegantly opposite each other, to our left and right, while some couple of hundred yards ahead, great chunks of granite gave rise to huge bronze statues of remembrance, waving their swords and spears towards us and the pavement on which we stood. "Perfect" gleamed McCluskie. We coiled our way through patches of touristic photographers, the jumpers went down and the hawking began. "Would you like a game of football?"

The polite bemusement of the closest likely victims hit home. I was way out of my comfort zone. I thought we were going for one of them European holiday morning beers, get warmed up for the day, just maybe pass the football about to unknown but equally merry folk…no! Here I was, replete with beer belly and hiking boots, trying to do keepy-ups and losing."What the fuck am I doing?" I mumbled.

"Would you like a game of football?". I could hear McCluskie somewhere behind me, as I managed to tackle myself and the ball span away towards the ever-busying "Holy Square of Heroes". I jogged Johnny Vegas style for the ball and gestured towards a couple of very smart, black suited fellows, hoping they would kick it back. The closest of them stared at me aggressively, tapping the rather large sub-machine gun at his side, "Security!" his badge shouted, "Sheepish" I smiled and picked up the ball.

Meanwhile a child called McCluskie was unwrapping his latest Christmas presents, namely some Belgians touring the world. "Halo" they said like twins, and we shook hands; their amazingly well-behaved children sat astride their tiny bikes and looked on. "This won't take long little ones" father ventured as his deft touches kept the ball aloft. On and on, the ball danced above the ground as his serious looking wife stretched like a ballerina then sprinted on the spot. Me and Ste looked silently towards each other with raised eye-brows, like a pair of Mr. Spocks.

He kneed it to her, she headed it to me and I tapped it through their goalposts. 1-0! For some reason the goal didn't stand (You were still warming up -Ed). Very soon we were 3-0 down, both of us panting like chased-out-cheetahs. They were taking the piss, dribbling about and jumping to high-five, and people were beginning to notice."F'fucks sake" I mumbled, sulking off for the ball that had once again found its way through our, now contentiously narrow, jumpers for goalposts."I didn't sign up for this" I mumbled on, with visions of the guards gunning down our super-fit and talented opponents.

I kicked the ball back into play and Ste's eyes met mine…we nodded…."Right! That's it!" I took the ball wide but she was at me again….laughing…laughing! I backed towards her and a completely innocent elbow jabbed her in the ribs. She knelt wounded. Ste feigned a soft run towards me, fooling his marker, then he was at the back post all of a sudden, and somehow through my fumbling hobnail hobbit boots I managed a fantastic floating chip. Time stopped…the world watched…and with all the grace of Swan Lake, Ste rose and rose and headed in our goal ! "Yes! Yes! Get in!" We'd scored! My first assist in thirty years! In a flash I was transported back to being a kid, playing football on any flat bit with whoever was about. The simplest most inclusive game in the world, surrounded by friends in heroes shirts.

The crowd gathered and held us aloft. The guards fist-pumped and shot their guns to the sun. "Hooray! They've scored! The fuck-wits have scored!", screamed a toothless old lady, as the crowd, crying and laughing, carried us away to that golden beer keller in the sky. I couldn't help but think "Yes Ste! Now I understand…jumpers for goalposts!" We let the Belgians win of course. This began an uplifting and liberating series of simple, giddy and sometimes sobering little games of football, making friends throughout Budapest and maybe, I think, even winning a game. Big kids never grow old. Cheers Ste."

GAME 58: HUNGARY

Date: August 14th 2019, 2.00pm
Ground: Deàk Ferenc tèr, Budapest

PESTS

Budapest is split into Buda on one side of the Danube River and Pest on the other. We were drawn to the Pest side for some reason. Mickey and I had a wander and found a square of shallow water in the city centre. Young tourists were sat drinking there and dangling their feet in the lovely cooling pool. Off came our socks and shoes and there we sat, laughing at all the young poseurs and how we used to be just like them. After an hour or so we tried to have a game by the water. Rory and Mickey from Holland were willing players but after a minute the ball bounced off my knee, flew over a balcony and landed below in someone's dinner. Proper pests. Security were quick on the scene and the game was over almost before it started.

THE GAME...

We then moved on to Deàk Ferenc tèr, a grassy area with the huge Budapest eye circling around in the background. Plonking the jumpers down, we asked a few people on the benches nearby to join us. Within ten minutes, Hungarians Adrienn Horuàth (Doctor), Simon Szabó (Lawyer), Gergo Jòuàs (a young drifter) and Ferenc Vàrallyai (a homeless guy asking around for money in the park) joined us for a game.

Simon, Ferenc and myself took on the others. Mickey was playing well for the opposition, with his strong tackles and blocks. Adrienn looked a bit worried and tentative in the nets for Mickey's team, but had a right go nonetheless. Completing their line-up was young Gergo. He was everywhere and absolutely loved the game. It was his appetite for playing that ignited the games competitive edge. He played in skins and had "Carpe Ediem" (Seize the day) tattooed across his back. I asked him what this meant to him, to which he replied "Marijuana and music".

Simon struck first for us. For a chap who said he hadn't played much football he had great skill and vision. Doing a Bergkamp, he picked a high ball out of the air with ease before slotting it away. He went on to make it 3-0 to us before Gergo began the fight back, scoring two quick goals past the laughing, toothless Ferenc in our nets. The game had a good ebb and flow to it and the tension was turned up a notch when Gergo made it 3-3. Simon poked us back in the lead but Mickey made it 4-4. Next goal's the winner! Simon collected the ball on the right and played a precise through ball. I couldn't miss. I'd actually scored my first winning goal of the whole trip, at the 58th attempt! Brilliant game, played in a great spirit with a real diverse bunch of folk. Mickey and I said our goodbyes and went off exploring, but not before Ferenc tapped us up for a few bob.

GAME 59: HUNGARY

Date: August 15th 2019, 3.00pm
Ground: Klauzál tér, Budapest

BUDAPEST!

It was Mickey's last morning in Budapest. We headed up to the famous Széchenyi Spa to soak our bones. What a place! Thermal baths of varying temperatures and budgie smugglers of all nationalities. The blokes on the continent have no shame do they? The tighter the trunks the better, whatever their age, belly or bird size. There wasn't so much as a beak left protruding in the cold pool I can tell you.

We said our goodbyes after lunch. It had been fantastic having Mickey with me, but now it was back to flying solo once more….well almost. We'd met a young couple from England the night before, policeman Dan and teacher Nicki from Coventry, whom Mickey had destroyed with tequila. I met up with them and their still banging heads later this day, and we wondered through the city looking for a suitable place to play.

THE GAME…

This game could have been a scene from a musical. We came across Klauzál tér, which was the largest square in the former Jewish quarter of Budapest. There were friends dotted about chatting on benches, lovers entwined on the grass and one or two sat alone, listening to music or chatting on phones. Imagine now a slow rumba building as Dan, Nicki and I split off to different parts of the square to convince people to play. Congas and claves, shakers and scrapers and a little piano are cooking as we begin our verbal dance of seduction. The rumba then turns to cha-cha as we quick-step our willing players in perfect symmetry over to the basketball court to the sound of raised Latin percussion and double bass. We are all smiling insanely now about nowt, as they do in musicals. We reach the court and throw our collective arms in the air and our heads back, singing with great gusto and dramatic eyebrows "BUDAPEST ! BUDAPEST!". The game begins and for the next thirty minutes we swing dance around the pitch as the trumpets and saxophones work us into a big sweaty mess, stopping only to cry out "BUDAPEST! BUDAPEST!' every five minutes with our perfect teeth and yearning teary eyes.

...or something like that. The cast was made up of Brits, Dutch, Germans and Indians. Nicki lured Sophia, a student from Amsterdam and I prattled on to an inebriated Bodhisattwa (Bodi) and Avhirup, car designers from Delhi. Dan badgered Lewis and Samira, students from Berlin, until they too caved in and agreed to play. Me, Dan, Samira and Sophia took on the rest. After a cool spell, the sun popped out and the temperature soared as both teams ripped into each other.

Nicki scored the first past my despairing dive (well offside). The two dominant stags, Dan and Lewis, seemed locked in mortal combat, not giving an inch, determined to prevent each other from scoring. Dan did manage to squeeze in a deflected shot to make it 1-1. Sophia, tough and trained in self-defence, was battling hard for us and shooting from anywhere. She too was having a running battle with Nicki. Samira stuck to the wing and spent most of the game trying to get past the rapidly sobering Bodi. Avirhup, a classical musician who could speak four languages, was a big hairy honey monster in their goals and hard to beat.

All square at 1-1 we changed ends. The match remained competitive. Dan won the battle of the stags, scoring our first four goals. Nicki and Lewis scored a brace each and, with the match balanced on a knife-edge at 4-4, we won it when a lucky ricochet fell to Sophia who belted if through the legs of Avirhup, much to her joy and amazement.

Brilliant game out of absolutely nowhere. We all went to the bar across the road together afterwards and everyone got on superbly. The camera drew away from us, out of the bar and up above the buildings, panning across the city as thousands of people raised their arms to the skies and sang out "BUDEPEST!" one last time before going about their daily business.

GAME 60: SLOVENIA

Date: August 17th 2019, 12.30pm
Ground: Kralji Ulice Day Centre, Ljubljana

KINGS OF THE STREET

My phone had died on the train to Ljubljana and I needed it to find my hostel. From the station, I walked across town until I found a café where I could charge it. That's when I heard him. "Kralji Ulice!" (Kings of the Street) he bellowed repeatedly out there on the pavement. Exiting the café, I was headed off by this tall bloke with thick black hair, a wide grin and wild eyes. "You want to buy a paper sir?!" he shouted, not two feet away from my strawberry shaped nose. Edin was selling the equivalent of The Big Issue and made Brian Blessed sound like a brownie. He'd clearly been through some hard times for a young chap, but, as the great bard wrote, *A Man's a Man for a'that*. Not for him to be a *coward slave*, but a brave and honest fellow was he. We chatted for a while about the services for homeless people in Ljubljana and agreed to meet the next morning.

Arriving at my hostel, I met the very lovely Wan Ying from Malaysia. She was curious about my ball (my football that is) and I explained my mission. The following morning as I was leaving to meet Edin, Wan Ying asked if she could tag along. I love the confidence and freedom of young travellers. Over twenty years my younger, she was phased not one bit about strolling around town with a stranger old enough to be her Dad. Wan Ying turned out to be the perfect companion; interesting, wise, funny and up for a bit of risk taking. I salute you mighty one!

We met Edin as arranged at 11.00am and visited the homeless day centre he uses, also named Kralji Ulice. The very lovely and hardworking Andrea and Kata were on duty that day. Andrea is a resettlement worker for homeless folk in the area and Kata a volunteer. Approximately fifty people use the centre each week, mostly men. It's a lifeline for many, offering a safe space, a hot drink and company. Kralji Ulice also offer one-to-one support on the street to people who do not want to access the centre. During the time we were there, many men dropped in to pick up their magazines to sell. They paid 50 cents for each copy, which they could then sell for a euro. We chatted to Andrea and Kata for half an hour then went outside, where a few blokes had congregated for a smoke and a beer.

THE GAME...

I spoke with Edin and we decided to have a game right there in the paved area in front of the centre. Frankie and Wan Ying joined me. Edin was joined by Denis and Miha. It was a rough and tough game from the start, aided and abetted by alcohol and some brutal tackles. Miha in particular was putting it about a bit, but Frankie for us was his match. Tall, rangy and agile for his size, Frankie managed to snuff out many of Miha's forceful attacks. Denis played with a can in his hand and a smile on his face. Edin hung back for the opposition and blasted the ball goalwards at every opportunity. Despite our best efforts, we were 4-0 down after ten minutes.

The reluctant Wan Ying finally agreed to go in goal for us. She looked in a state of shock at first as these grizzled guys raced towards her with the ball, stepping aside at times to avoid being crushed. *This wasn't in her itinerary.* She grew in confidence though as the game went on and got stuck right in. We called for reinforcements from the watching crowd. Matteo joined us and we began the fight back, remarkably getting it back to 5-5 at one point.

The game didn't let up. Miha continued his belligerent form and almost single-handedly secured victory for his side, 10-5. The lads seemed to have really enjoyed the game, particularly the big smiling Frankie.

What a really enjoyable game at such an inspiring centre, providing essential services for some of the city's most needy. We chatted to these warm, friendly chaps for a while afterwards and they all welcomed us and wished us a great time in their city. Is that not the true worth of a person? To not be defined by wealth or possessions but by the kindness shown to others? Wan Ying and I said our goodbye's, gave Edin a big thankyou hug then headed off into town.

GAME 61: SLOVENIA

Date: August 17th 2019, 4.00pm
Ground: Šuštarski Most (Shoe Makers Bridge), Ljubljana

GOOD VIBRATIONS

Ljubljana was my biggest surprise on this European leg of the trip. It's a stunning, fairy-tale city with the River Ljubljanica running through the heart of it. Seventeen bridges span it's waters, each unique and adding to the storybook feel of this atmospheric and special place. The city is made all the more romantic by its association with dragons. They are everywhere you look. Legend has it that the city was founded by Jason (he of the Argonauts) who, on his way back to Greece with the golden fleece, had slayed a dragon near the source of the Ljubljanica. The dragon was latterly seen not as a monster but as a protector, dominant now on the city's coat of arms. Dragons Bridge is protected by four of Ljubljana's most famous dragon statues, and has sixteen smaller ones decorating its span. Go visit if you can. It's great. Strolling through the medieval streets, past its cool cafes, bars and shops, Wan Ying and I were crossing Šuštarski Most (Shoe Makers Bridge) when we spotted some musicians sat to one side having a break between sets.

THE GAME…

A quick chat and soon Uros Jezdie (accordion) and Klemen Braćko (violin) had joined us for a game. Eva Jurgel (oboe) and her friend Manca Biber watched on. I was a bit wary of plonking the jumpers down on a bridge in such a popular tourist spot, but I needn't have worried. When the ball ran to a pedestrian, they would add to the vibrancy of the game by showing off their own skills, before passing the ball back into play to the sound of "Olay!" from the musicians. At one point, the ball dropped to a sprightly elderly bloke, who curled one in with his left. He looked well chuffed with his effort. His wife reached into her purse and showed me a beautiful, classic photo of the young proud Italian Pietro, lined up in his strip with his mates from his village footy team. The bridge was bouncing with positive vibrations.

On the pitch, Uros and Klemen were having a running battle, literally wrestling with each other at times and loving the craic. I was on Uros's side, but had little to do as he took us into an early 3-0 lead. The determined Klemen brought the scores level before Uris powered home a couple more past the hapless Wan Ying. Fantastic game! When it was over, Eva remarked about how happy and childlike the game had seemed to make people feel as they passed by, or had a touch of the ball. The band, known as *Autento*-The Folk Embassy Band, then played a beautiful rendition of a Slovenian folk-song to cap off a wonderful experience.

Here's Wan Ying's take on events in Ljubljana:

"I first met Steve in the Ljubljana hostel and was impressed by his idea of connecting with the locals though football. I didn't have anything planned for

the next day, so I decided to just tag along and participate in one of the 80 games. I'm very grateful for that spontaneous decision as it turned out to be one of the best days during my two months solo trip to Europe.

Steve was connected by chance with the homeless organisation in Ljubljana and we stopped by there to have a chat with the managers. Before we left, we managed to have a small game with the guys who use the centre. At first, I was sceptical with Steve's suggestion to play with the guys, but he went ahead to set up his two mini goals with just the four t-shirts and the football he brought along with him. Soon more people were joining us and in no time it became a really friendly and exciting game where everyone was just genuinely having fun laughing and cheering as their teammates scored goals. The fun didn't end there! When I thought I was just going to be play in one game, Steve walked up to the musicians who were getting ready to perform on the Shoemaker Bridge to strike up a conversation with them. I was delighted when the guys were up for some fun!

Playing football on a bridge! How cool is that?? This has shown me how even though people may not be able to communicate with each other very well due to the language barrier, football can do the job in connecting people who love the sport. It is always intimidating to have to talk to strangers, more so when one doesn't speak the local language. Nevertheless, Steve's passion and enthusiasm for football was contagious and I'm sure the people on the streets could feel it as I did. It was a great experience connecting with people from all walks of life in such a unique way while travelling. I am very grateful for this very positive and memorable experience".

GAME 62: AUSTRIA

Date: August 19th 2019, 3.00pm
Ground: Residenzplatz, Salzburg

THE HANDYMAN CAN

Salzburg, in the west of Austria, is worth visiting by train from the east because of the glorious alpine mountains and valleys you go through to get to it. Apart from that, it's a bit boring, or at least that was my first impression. This is Mozart's birthplace and don't we know it. The maestros little red cheeks and wig are stamped on everything from chocolate violins to lettuce. Salzburg is a very conservative place, with more than a touch of tweed thrown in. There's a whiff of wealth everywhere you go and too many blazers with leather elbow pads for my liking. It felt so well-mannered and status led that I wanted to blast The Sex Pistols *Never Mind the Bollocks* across the city from 80 foot speakers.

I stayed at a hostel just around the corner from the train station. It was there that I was propositioned by a handy man from Switzerland. I got talking to this tall, skinny bloke from Lausanne in my dorm. He reminded me of Slugworth, Wonka's enigmatic whisperer in the original Charlie and the Chocolate Factory film. All was fine until day two when he came out of the shower naked, save for his glasses, sat on his bed and, with only me in the room, asked me to accompany him on the nine hour drive back home that night "We could have some fun, if you know what I mean. I am a handy man in many ways". He then cackled a wide-eyed insane cackle; that of on an in-mate on *Shutter Island*, crouched in the corner of his dank cell with the small bones of unknown creatures scattered all around. He composed himself and cleared his throat. "I am leaving in an hour. Come." "Er, no mate. Gotto go. See ya!", and with that I bolted for the door with my ball. I was in the lift, through the lobby and out into the street before you could say "pass me the nut-tighteners baby". Each to their own but this guy was creepy.

THE GAME...

I made my way through the pretty Salzburg streets and over the bridge to Residenzplatz, a very large square in old town. The square has the Residenzbrunnen at its centre, considered the largest baroque fountain in Central Europe (I was feeling pretty baroque myself after shelling out a king's ransom for a cheese butty). It features dramatic limestone horses and a statue of Triton, and is the very fountain that Julie Andrew stopped at to flick water in the Sound of Music. This was the scene where she was skipping away from the convent to join the Von Trapp asylum, singing "I have confidence". After thirty minutes of trying, I had no confidence at all of starting a game this day; the locals scoffed down their all- knowing snouts at me, fobbing me off with silken gloves and rolling eyes. Even the dogs looked away ashamed.

Finally, three great fellows from Munich agreed to a game in front of the fountain. Luis, studying psychology in the city, said that trying to get a game going with Austrians this way in Salzburg would take a miracle. It went against all cultural norms. See, told you it was boring here. These lads were far from boring. Three great mates, Luis, Lorenz and Robin put everything into the game. Poor Lorenz, who looked like Shakespeare, spent a lot of time slipping and sliding and landing on his bum on this gravelly surface. I was on his side but to be fair to him, he worked ten times as hard as I did. (*He's got years on me guv*).

Robin was technically excellent; great close control and really hard to get the ball off. Luis had a bad habit of sticking out one of his big feet when it looked all the world like a goal for us. The game ebbed and flowed brilliantly, but still no participation from the local tweedies. The match was frenetic, the score quickly reaching 4-4. It's a wonder Lorenz had any arse left in his trousers by this point with all his falling over. Luis sealed it for the opposition with a neat finish.

We spoke for a while after. These easy-going chaps, all heading for masters degrees, had loved the game. There were all incredulous about Brexit and wondered what lessons from the two world wars we'd missed. They thought it was a hoax at first. Robin and Lorenz had wanted to study in England but the situation was too precarious. However, they all agreed that the one consolation of Brexit was that our national embarrassment, Nigel Farage, might finally shut his cake-hole. Great game in a neutered world.

GAME 63: SWITZERLAND

Date: August 22nd 2019, 11.00am
Ground: ETH University, Zurich

NED AND THE EINSTEINS

True magic can be found where your vision, your soul and the earth come together. The stunning train journey through the Alps from Salzburg to Zurich is one I will never forget. How lucky are those people to wake up to those scenes every morning? Even the goats looked smug.

Arriving in Zurich in the late afternoon, I wheeled my case over one of the many bridges spanning the Limmat River, which is an outfall of the splendid Lake Zurich to the south-east of the city. This took me to old town where all the buildings are made from crackers and cheese, chocolate biscuits, wafers, double cream and Battenburg Cakes. Fairy tales echo around every cobbled street corner and out from quaint, wooden shop doorways. Reaching my hostel, I lugged my case up several flights of stairs to my room before slumping in a sweaty heap on my bunk. I was feeling dizzy and sucking on my inhaler for dear life, when in walked Ned Flanders and started talking my head off. This American dude, sat on the bunk across from me, just wouldn't shut up. Could he not see that I was the colour of a particularly radiant radish and was wheezing like a 126-year-old? He was a friendly enough chap, but about as tactful as a washing machine being chucked through your window when a knock on the door would do. Regaining full consciousness, I agreed to go out for a pint with him just to shut him up.

"That will be 25 francs please?" "Sorry, I think you've made a mistake. I only ordered two pints of Guinness? That can't be £20 quid!?", "Welcome to Zurich". Welcome to Zurich indeed. Here I was, twenty quid down, listening to Flanders rabbit on for a whole hour until I zoned out, his voice sounding like a radio had been left on somewhere. I'd long since stopped listening to him because he hadn't shown much interest in listening to me. I was just watching his lips move, nodding in all the right places until I'd finally had enough. I told him I was tired and needed my bed. It was a better move I thought than giving into my rising urge to frisbee beer mats at his babbling mouth. The next day I set out early to avoid being trapped by Ned again.

THE GAME...

ETH Zurich in the most prestigious university in Switzerland, the best in continental Europe and in the top six universities in the world. No less than twenty-one Nobel Prizes have been awarded to graduates of the ETH. Einstein himself studied mathematics and natural sciences there in the late nineteenth century when it was a polytechnic.

The ETH is perched atop a steep hill overlooking the city. It was a nightmare getting up there. As my fellow lung gasperers will testify, any steep hill can feel like Everest to us. Crowds of hairy young students strode confidently past me with their long, skinny legs stuck in sprayed on jeans. I snailed my way up, reckoning to check my phone every two minutes just to have a breather and maintain my cool. Eventually I arrived at the terrace in front of the university. This is one of the finest vantage points in Zurich from which to gaze out over the Aldstadt, the city's historic heart. Stunning.

It was time to engage with some of the world's brightest young minds. I placed my jumpers down on the terrace; a perfectly flat, wide and lengthy place to play. Moritz Fontboté and Midori Pittini were first to join in. They were both physics students and lovely engaging folk. Moritz reminded me a bit of R.E.M. guitarist Mike Mills. He was a very enthusiastic chap with a constantly enquiring mind; the kind of mind that would view sleep as an unnecessary distraction. Next to join us were Francesco Gotti from Ancona, Italy, about to finish his final year in mechanical engineering, and Samuel Pflaum from Germany. Game on!

Midori, Francesco and I took on the others and a fellow in yellow whose name I didn't get. Francesco had all the Italian flair and skill but it was Midori who stole the show. She ended up with a hat-trick for us, the last one a perfect little chip at the back post to cap a 5-3 win. Moritz worked hard for the opposition and was very competitive, and Sam crunched into the tackles throughout, but we were always ahead by the odd goal. A really enjoyable, energetic game and a great laugh throughout.

Talking to the troops afterwards, it was clear that their workload was very heavy, and the pressure from their fee-paying parents to succeed was immense. Nevertheless, these vibrant and engaging young Einstein's loved university life and didn't want it to end. It had been a real pleasure to be in their company and can only hope that their great gifts will be used to benefit the world. On my way back down the hill I noticed the bleedin' cable car I could have taken to get up it! Oh well. I needed the exercise.

GAME 64: SWITZERLAND

Date: August 24th 2019, 5.00pm
Ground: Musik Pavillon, Bürkliplatz, Zurich

BANDSTANDS AND A BRUSH WITH FIFA

You can tell a lot from a bandstand in an urban area. This one had no graffiti, no pee stains and no litter. Despite being accessible to the public at all times, it had only been abused by the elements. This was symbolic of Zurich; clean, well ordered and safe. I'd visited the lovely city of Lucerne earlier this day and found the same comfortable, safe vibe, and even more buildings made from ice-cream, chocolate and fudge.

THE GAME...

Returning from Lucerne in the late afternoon, I spotted three wee rascals having a sneaky fag in the bandstand in Bürkliplatz. College lads Alec and Sergio from Rüschilkon and Shervin from Kilchberg were well up for a game. The bandstand was a perfect size for a 2 v 2. Sergio and I took on the others and a great, lively competitive game ensued. I actually found some energy from somewhere and ran around like a middle aged wart-hog fleeing a shotgun. I scored a couple as did Sergio but little Alec was super competitive. He was the Keegan to the tall, rangy Shervin's Toshack and between them they fought back to level at 4-4. Shervin blasted the winner through my legs soon after - cheeky git! Cracking little game in this pristine bandstand.

Talking afterwards, the lads acknowledged that things were very expensive in the city, but that high taxes meant a good, respected police force, a feeling of safety and security, a good health service and a peaceful way of life. They told me that there wasn't a huge drug problem amongst young people in Zurich. Since 2011, the sale of cannabis products containing up to one percent THC has been legal in Switzerland. The lads believed that making it accessible in this way, particularly in regards to young people, had lessened their desire to crave more. They also felt that, culturally, Swiss youth do not like to live in an extreme way. No place can be this perfect can it? It certainly felt that way.

Later that evening, I was invited, through my Ugandan mate who knew someone in Zurich, to meet Fatma Samba Diouf Samoura, FIFA's Senegalese Secretary General, at some mad concert/carnival on the shores of Lake Zurich. Apparently, she was very interested in my journey, excited to meet me and wanted to discuss 'possibilities'. Three hours I waited with her pa, watching the parade of acrobats, fire-eaters and full Swiss-cheese Euro-pop singers do their stuff. True to form, FIFA didn't show up.

My European tour was over. A whirlwind 7 countries, 16 games in 19 days featuring people from 32 nations. Some incredible memories, lucky escapes and fantastic kick-a-bouts with my beautiful brothers and sisters across these stunning lands. The more I travel, the more I know for sure that this world is not all dark, dangerous and miserable as the media would have us believe. Its full of good folk who just want to get on with each other.

*"Maybe you were the ocean
When I was just a stone"*

Ben Howard

GILMA'S GAME

GAMES 65

MEXICO

GAME 65: MEXICO

Date: January 25th 2020, 6.30pm
Ground: Playa Norte, Islas Mujeres

WOMEN ISLAND

The Isle of Women (Isla Mujeres) is off the coast of Cancun. According to folk-lore, the island served as the sanctuary for the goddess Ixchel, the Maya goddess of the moon, fertility, medicine and happiness. When the Spanish arrived in the 16th Century, they named this tiny jewel in the Caribbean Sea *Isla Mujeres* because of the many images of goddesses they found there.

It seemed very fitting that the next game on this journey would be played on Women Island. The passing of Natasha, my son's mum, and my former partner of twenty years, had thrown light once-more on the fact that all my life I had been surrounded by strong women. I would be nothing without them. From my grandma who worked in the cotton factory at 14 and brought up five children, to my mother who worked all her life in the shoe factories and brought me and my brother up against the odds, to Natasha who had cared for vulnerable children and hated lies and injustice, I have been blessed to have been inspired by such incredible fighters and such strong, beautiful souls.

These were the darkest days of my life. Losing Natasha had been absolutely devastating for both myself and our son. The trip to Mexico had been planned for a while and so I decided to go. Maybe it would help, but I certainly had no intention of having a game of footy. However, another incredible woman met me in Cancun and convinced me otherwise. Remember Gilma whom I met in Medellin, Colombia? Well, we'd not only kept in touch after that first encounter, but had met several times since and were now engaged. Gilma's upbringing had been very tough. She was one of four sisters and four brothers who had moved to Medellin from the countryside to work their way out of poverty. She'd lived through the Escobar years and is a very tough, determined woman who knows the true meaning of survival against the odds.

THE GAME......

We'd sailed across to Isla Mujeres from Cancun at 1.30pm and spent the afternoon, bizarrely, trundling along the bumpy island roads in a golf cart (the preferred mode of tourist transport here) and had the bruised bums to prove it. Some of the views from the cliff-tops at different spots around the island were incredible. We finally wound up at the stunning Playa Norte beach as the light was beginning to fade. Hiring a couple of beach beds, we laid back and thought of burritos.

It was then that we heard the fun and frivolity behind us. A group of folk were sparring with a giant beach ball. Gilma said I should ask them for a game (she'd convinced me to buy a footy earlier). I really didn't want to but she insisted and marched over to one of the women to explain my mission. Not two minutes later it was game on.

What brilliant people! Eber and Isabel, Alma and Flavio and their families from Mexico City gave it everything. It was Women v Men and us blokes didn't stand a chance, especially as our keeper, big Flavio, was trolleyed off the tequila. Fittingly on Women Island, the women came out easy winners, 4-1. Paulina, Martha and the gang were much too young and energetic for us even though Juan, the Zorro 'tashed orange flash, did everything he could to keep us in the game. The beach staff joined in at one point but we needed more help than that against our hungry opponents. A great laugh throughout with these lovely, kind folk. A little light in a bleak time. Gracias Gilma.

Covid-19 was first reported in Wuhan, China on the 31st December 2019. In the ensuing 22 months, the virus has accounted for 4.95 million lives world-wide*, and left us recycling a new, forbidding apocalyptic language......

Lock down, Crisis, ventilators, social distance, bubbles, PPE, PCR, lateral flow, track and trace, green-amber-red, long-covid, isolate, CLOSURE, masks, vaccines, deteriorating MENTAL HEALTH, mutation, wash your hands avoid contact, stop the spread, stay alert, at risk group, DELTA variant, warning, breathless, don't hug, don't kiss, don't VISIT YOUR LOVED ONES, control the virus, hands>face>space, ANXIETY, order oF priority, R number, infection rates, deaths within 28 days of a positive test, Shield, transmission, don't mix, conspiracy, SPIKE, shortages, high temperature, A NEW continuous cough, stay home loss/change to your sense of smell or taste, DEADLY STRAIN, INVISIBLE THREAT, QUARANTINE, DON'T TRAVEL, the new normal

*(Data from JHU CSSE COVID-19 Data and Our World in Data: 23rd October 2021)

GAME 66: ENGLAND

Date: October 23rd 2021, 2.30pm
Ground: York Minster, Dean's Park

THANKYOU

After twenty-two long pandemic months, it felt important to restart this journey in a respectful way. Game 66 was a tribute to all those essential workers up and down the land who had worked tirelessly and fiercely against great odds. To the bus-drivers, nurses, doctors, teachers, recovery workers, bin-men and women, posties, service sector workers, supermarket staff, lorry drivers, care workers, trades people, cleaners, police and ambulance services, fire fighters and funeral directors, to name but a few, THANKYOU!

York seemed the perfect place to get the ball rolling again. According to legend, the first ever purpose built almshouse in England was established in the city. Over a thousand years later, we continue to be an incredibly charitable nation*, never more evident than in recent times.

THE GAME......

For this trip, I was fittingly accompanied by three essential workers; two of my oldest friends Simon Kilshaw (nurse) and Tracy Seal (SEN worker), and my big cousin Jim Hill (young adults support worker). It was just after 1.00pm when we headed out into the teeming Saturday afternoon streets of York. We made our way across to York Minster, the second largest gothic cathedral in northern Europe, and close to the site where the first almshouse once stood. On her first trip to England, I took Gilma to visit the cathedral thinking she'd love it (she's well into God). However, she took one look inside, pulled her face and said the millions spent to build it should have gone on feeding the poor instead. She then gave out a little involuntary fart which echoed around the cavernous nave.

We circled the Minster before placing the jumpers down on a paved area to the right of the main entrance. It was a busy spot and we were quickly joined by three eager beavers, but then the cops showed up and moved us on. We continued to ask people to play and the brilliantly named Prince Atubrah from Ghana and Jim Kamarudin from Malaysia joined us. They were both studying for MSc's in Structural Geology with GeoPhysics at Leeds University. (Think that's something to do with rocks).

318

We walked around to the other side of the building and found Dean's Park, where the playing surface was tremendous - flat lush green grass with a colourful sprinkling of fallen autumn leaves. It all felt a bit Brideshead Revisited. We were just short of cravats and plumbs in our mouths. It wasn't long before Marcus joined us with his little daughter Emmy. Marcus was a logistics expert from South London whose company had been distributing vital PPE throughout the pandemic.

What a cracking game this turned out to be. Cousin Jim, Tracy and Simon took on the rest of us. After a five-minute stalemate, Tracy shot her team into the lead with a carefully placed strike. The lively Prince struck back for us and the game ebbed and flowed this way until half-time. We swapped ends with our team in the lead, 6-5. Cousin Jim was putting in a great shift and having a stormer. He dinked one over my flailing carcass to make it 6-6, before little Emmy scored a penalty to take his team into a 7-6 lead. Prince was having none of it, scoring two quick-fire goals to help us regain our advantage. Malaysian Jim took us to the brink of victory (first to ten), but then Tracy completed a brilliant hat-trick to bring the scores level at 9-9. Next goal's the winner! Cue Prince Atubrah. Moving at pace, and with a body swerve Thierry Henry would have been proud of, he left the hapless Simon chewing grass and slotted home the winner.

---

*According to statista.com, there are approximately 169,000 registered charities in England and Wales as of 2021

Player Profile: Tracy Seal

ATW80G

Have you ever played football before?
No

Favourite food?
Italian

Favourite music?
Paul Weller and The Jam

Team you support?
Burnley (because of my mum)

Where do you work and what do you do?
I work at Waterfoot Primary School, Rossendale Lancashire, where I am a Special Educational Needs Teaching Assistant and an Emotional Literacy Support Assistant

Have you worked through the pandemic?
Yes

What has the experience been like?
Initially it was very stressful. The added responsibilities brought a lot of anxiety-trying to follow all the protocol whilst caring for the children

Was it difficult trying to keep the children socially distanced?
Kids naturally gravitate towards each other, but they were better at following the rules than we were. Once we were in bubbles it was easier.

What impact has working under these conditions had on you personally?
Trying to look after myself and my family and support children at school took its toll. I was waking up with anxiety every day, having to put others before myself.

What impact do you feel the pandemic has had on the children you support?
I think it has been good in some ways. Before Covid everything was driven by targets to get kids to a certain level. This experience gave the opportunity for them to develop different skills such as building resilience and socialization, without the pressure of them working towards set standards. They could just be kids.

How did you enjoy today's footy experience?
Way more than I ever thought I would. I thought I would struggle. It helped to have a livener beforehand! It just shows that you don't need to know people to quickly become connected to them.

Lastly, you say you have never played football before but today you scored a hat-trick? Are you a liar?
No!

PRE-SEASON FRIENDLIES

GAMES 67-70

ICELAND-WALES-PANAMA

GAME 67: ICELAND

Date: Saturday 6th November 2021, 1.30pm
Ground: Center Hotels Plaza, Reykyavik

After such a long delay in proceedings, and before my final push to complete the 80, I decided I needed to play a few pre-season friendlies to get the old mojo working again. But where? On reflection, it seemed that most places I'd visited so far had been scorching hot. It was time to head to the frozen north.

SMOKY BAY

A freezing blast of air slapped my face and filled my lungs as I exited Keflavik Airport. It was midday and minus one, but with the wind chill I could have cut glass with my nipples.

My taxi driver was young Huginn. He was named after one of Odin's ravens whom he sent around the world to gather knowledge. Huginn (meaning 'thought' in Old Norse) was aptly named, offering his muse on everything from Scandinavian linguistics to the price of fish. He was a great chap and at last (cue the trumpets) a taxi driver who had a genuine interest in me and didn't want to rip me off. In fact no tip was required. This would prove to be the way of every Icelander I met- smart and convivial.

We cut through the eerie moss-covered lava fields on our way to *Smoky Bay* – the literal meaning of Reykyavik. There were no trees in sight on this inhospitable plateau, only clouds of steam emitting from the fumarole earth. The country sits on the boundary of two divergent tectonic plates, whose movement and separation causes lava to move closer to the surface. This has resulted in Iceland having more than two hundred volcanoes and a geothermal underbelly which provides the country with an abundance of subterranean hot water. Iceland has harnessed its natural resources and become a world leader in the use of clean, renewable energy to heat homes and power businesses.

Arriving at my guesthouse, I was greeted by Ingi, the jovial elderly owner who sounded just like Goldmember, the title character from one of the Austin Powers movies. Have you seen the film? Beyond funny. Goldmember is a crazy Dutch guy who has a gold penis as the result of an 'unfortunate shhmelting acshhident'. He loves 'gooooold', offers a 'shhmoke and a pan-cake' to his guests and fends off attacks with a boot from his gold clogs. Ingi appeared to have none of these traits or physical oddities. However, he did give me a map of the city and pointed out that the "shhhwimming poolshh were definitely worth a vishit".

I dropped my bags in my room and went for a wander around Reykyavik, the world's northernmost capital city. I found it packed with cool coffee houses, art shops, quirky eateries and hand-made woolly jumper shops, but it was far from busy. In fact, I never walked down a crowded street all the

323

time I was there. There was no need to rush and push and the people were kind. In that respect, it reminded me a lot of New Zealand.

Reykyavik seemed to me like a city of good intentions. *Rainbow Street* sums up the city's ambiance. This is one of the popular shopping streets leading out of the city to its main reference point, the huge 73 metre-high Hallgrimskirkja church up on the hill. The street was painted in rainbow colours for the Pride Festival in 2015. Popular mayor, Dagur Eggertsson, picked up a roller and joined in the painting, later describing the work as *'more powerful and beautiful'* than he could have imagined. *"This is one way to make our city more lively, more human and simply a better place for collaboration and beautiful thinking'* (*from his Facebook page*).

THE GAME......

FREEZING! This was the coldest game I'd played in since winter 1979, kicking uphill in a blizzard for my primary school. It was 1pm when I set off into town with Magdalena Golon; a painter, sculptor, writer and film maker who lives and works at Ingi's guest house. Magdalena likes to meet guests with unusual stories and make short films about them. Today she picked on me.

The streets were quiet and the odds of a game slim as we arrived at a square at the far end of town. It was sleeting and treacherous underfoot. Down went the jumpers but there was hardly anyone around to badger. The odd shivering couple hurried past with scarves covering their faces. We were about to turn for home when Justas from Lithuania rocked up, swiftly followed by Markos (Greece) and his partner Blanka (Romania) and four great friends from Poland, Adrian, Rafal, Michal and Artur. Game on! Poland v The Rest of the World.

We all had a go at landing on our arses as we slid about, tearing into a lively and competitive game just to keep warm. Adrian was knocking them in for fun for Poland, scoring 8 in the end with his rocket of a right foot. They'd taken a 9-3 lead when the fight back began, led by the Frank Ribery-esque Markos. The Greek was skilful, elusive and deadly from close range.

9-4, 9-5, 9-6, 9-7...could we do it? The big Poles looked knackered, but then a jammy deflected shot was tapped in at the far jumper to seal it for them. What a mighty effort from the boys in sub-zero temperatures. I'd loved this experience once again for the comradery, banter and instant connection it brought, and the fact that these maniacs ignored the weather and skated around risking broken bones, just for the love of the game. I said my thanks and goodbye's and went for a brew with Magdalena. She had been amazed by the spectacle. For her it had been *something strange and mysterious...a new social situation full of energy and fun...created out of nothing....like an art performance*".

GAME 68: ICELAND

Date: Sunday 7th November 2021, 3.00pm
Ground: Austurbæjarskóli, Reykjavik

AT THE END OF THE WORLD

Magdalena suggested we go for a Sunday swim at the nearby outside baths. What? In these temperatures? What a brilliant hour it turned out to be. With the geothermals keeping the water nice and toasty, we dipped in and out of the different pools at our leisure. The baths are a popular place for locals to meet for a natter and blow happy little fart bubbles. What a strange feeling it was to be bathing in the sub-zero open air. We left feeling cleansed and totally invigorated.

I did other touristy things in Iceland, though despite three attempts I never got to see the aurora borealis. I did however take a dip in the famous Blue Lagoon geothermal pools, with its 35-degree water welled from 2000 metres below ground. This was a special experience, especially when it started to snow. The visit to the south shore topped the lot though. Walking fully around the Seljalandsfoss waterfall, witnessing a rainbow at the Skogafoss falls, gazing in awe at the Sólheimajökull glacier and treading the spectacular Reynisfjara 'black sand' beach. Wow! Standing there staring out at the Atlantic, I felt like I'd reached the end of the world. With the towering headland behind me, with its striking rock pillars and caves, it felt every bit as epic as when Charlton Heston rode along the shoreline at the end of Planet of the Apes (1968) and found the remains of the Statue of Liberty on the sands.

THE GAME......

I'd popped into a local hostelry a few evenings prior, and happened upon a load of Icelandic Liverpool fans watching a champions league game. I got talking to a few of these fellows and we exchanged numbers, though with beer at an average £12.00 a pint we didn't exchange rounds. I arranged to meet some of them again on the all-weather pitch at Austurbæjarskóli, a centrally located primary school. The huge Askell Hardarsen and Tömas Joensen and their friends Ôlafur Ásgeirsson (Oli), Robin Möberg from Sweden and Vikram Pradhan from India joined us, as did brothers Stefan and Ben Hermannsson.

Askell, Oli, Ben and I took on the rest. What a game! Full blooded and ferocious from the start, with not an inch or second given for free. Stefan was brilliant for them. A red flame lighting up the pitch, scoring a few past the old dodderer in the nets. His younger brother Ben was totally unphased by the giants all around him. He played a blinder, nipping into great spaces and scoring a couple too. It was a tight game but we had Oli. He was most definitely at the wheel, scoring 7 for us as the game reached a nail-biting 9-9. The very technical Vikram, prop forward Tömas and the cool and composed Robin pushed us all the way, but Oli smashed home the winner in the end. 10-9. We had a cracking penalty competition afterwards, and I must say I did ok in the nets and was secretly pleased to leave the pitch with bruised hands. What brilliant lads. Their English was incredible and they took the piss relentlessly. The biggest compliment that I can pay them is that I felt like I'd know them all my life. Thank you so much for your friendship.

Chatting with man mountain Askell afterwards, he proved to be much more than just a loveable grizzly bear. He was brought up by musicians and studied classical music and jazz, and is a sound engineer at a local production company (101 Production) and radio station (101 Radio), mixing sound for tv series, commercials and podcasts. His obsession with music led him to becoming a DJ and starting up his own record label, BORG Ltd. Not only does he produce electronic music, house and techno, but you can find his own tunes under 'Askell' on Spotify. Check him out…he's right good.

Askell *"Its cool to be part of a small nation. You get to know a lot of people and the community is small and intimate, though it's hard to go incognito as people tend to know everything about everybody. Overall it's a good place to grow up and hopefully grow old. Iceland has many beautiful destinations. I'm a big fan of the Westfjords for its serenity and tremendous beauty. Tourism has created many jobs and has been good for the economy and infrastructure. Maybe the biggest downside is when culturally important venues in downtown Reykjavik have been torn down for new hotels. In most ways though the tourism explosion has been very positive".*

GAME 69: WALES

Date: Wednesday 2nd February 2022, 12.20pm
Ground: Newbridge Road Industrial Estate, Blackwood

PRIDE AND PORRIDGE

Coed Duon (Blackwood) is a former coal mining town on the Sirhowy River in the South Wales Valleys, and the birthplace of the boys from the The Manic Street Preachers. I was down there this week delivering training for one of the UK's leading infection prevention companies. They have played a major role in the fight to combat Covid-19, seeing their productivity rise by 60% during the pandemic.

I met some brilliant people at the site; salt of the earth folk who exuded hard work, fairness, warmth, dignity and respect, despite being stretched to their absolute limits. Anthony Gregory epitomised this - a lovely chap who, although nursing a serious knee injury, refused to give up playing the game he loved: *"Footy for me is about purpose, friendship, banter and lastly fitness, or these days fatness! Injuries are secondary. I've literally just about been able to walk over the last three months, and I'd happily be one of your jumpers if it meant I got onto the pitch! We've got one guy who plays, we call him Robo-cop, he's got that many straps and plasters on every week, but he turns up regardless."*

He feels that switching from playing 11 to 6 a side recently *'certainly helps'* with regards to wear and tear on the body. Anthony is still inhabited by the football spirits which possessed him as a kid. Growing up an avid Cardiff City fan, he fondly remembers attending games at their old Ninian Park ground: *"The anticipation, jumping on the free bus on a Saturday morning, or latterly the train. The walk up from Grangetown station, with what seemed like a million people when you're a small lad, fans singing, Bovril and a pie to warm the hands at half-time."*

Being in Coed Duon reminded me of my own roots in the Rossendale Valley, East Lancashire. For decades we were known for shoe manufacturing and most of us, myself included, left school and started work in one of the many factories up and down the valley. The people had pride in their valley. However, like with so many other working class areas, there was no plan B when manufacturing declined. Cheap foreign imports led to mass factory closures, draining the valley's economy and vibrancy and fracturing its sense of community.

Coed Duon, and many other mining towns in the region, went through similar changes with the decline of the coal industry. However, Anthony believes that the people of the Welsh Valleys have retained a strong sense of community and are a *'special breed"*. Cymraeg (The Welsh language) is not spoken much locally, though it has enjoyed more of a renaissance in recent years. It's now compulsory learning in schools up to GCSE level. Wales of course is famous for rugby and singing. Anthony had to hang his rugby boots up as too many injuries meant too much time off work. *"On the singing side, I've been known to carry a tune on occasion, not quite in the league of James Dean Bradfield, but certainly proficient enough not to embarrass myself."*

THE GAME......

...and so it was that me and Anthony, with his work-mates Doug Bradbury, Mark Nolan, Jason Window and Holly Williams, headed down to a patch of grass within the industrial estate for a kick-about one lunch-time.

The pitch was lumpy porridge but we still managed a cracking game on it. Me, Doug and Anthony (proudly wearing his Wales shirt for the occasion) took on the others. The lovely smiling Holly was an all action player for them. She's a goalkeeper by trade who plays in the second highest league of women's football in Wales. Mark, whose daughter Kylie has represented Wales at international level, was a big presence in their goals. Jason proved to be a real live wire throughout the game, but for all their energy and focus, they couldn't prevent us racing into a four goal lead.

Doug, the young man mountain, was surprisingly agile for such a big chap, especially considering he was playing in his work boots on a clumpy sur-face. He and Anthony were combining brilliantly. Anthony criss-crossed the field like a deliriously happy teenage whippet. His appetite for the game was marvellous to witness. Despite a hat-trick for the hardworking Holly, we ended the game 8-3 winners. Our last goal was poetry in motion - a beautiful cross from the left from Anthony on the run, for big Doug to nod it home at the back jumper. Superb! Brilliant folk who took time out of their incredibly busy working day to play. Diolch pawb!

GAME 70: PANAMA

Date: Sunday 10th April, 2022, 9.00am
Ground: Bijao Beach Resort, Santa Clara

FAMILY

Panama is the only place in the world where you can watch the sun rise on the Pacific Ocean and set on the Atlantic Ocean from the same spot. It could also be the reason that people walk upright.

The Isthmus of Panama is the narrow strip of land that extends from the border of Costa Rica to the border of Colombia, connecting North America and South America and separating the Caribbean Sea (Atlantic Ocean) from the Gulf of Panama (Pacific Ocean).

The formation and closure of this land bridge re-routed ocean currents in both the Atlantic and Pacific Oceans. Scientists believe that one of the effects of this was to cause North Africa to become drier. Savannahs and open grasslands developed which the former tree living primates colonized. The more smarty pant primate groups used their front limbs for tool making and evolved to walk upright (Much better for the back they reckoned).

Fast forward a few million years, and this wretched little homo sapien could barely stand up when he arrived in Panama. The long dark English winter had done for my lungs again and I was pretty poorly, having also fallen back into the trap of working too much, eating out of a microwave and struggling to exercise. I'd have been better off living up a tree. If it wasn't for the fact that I was meeting up with Gilma, I'd have stayed in bed for three weeks instead.

I hadn't seen Gilma in the flesh for two years and two months. Colombia had remained on the Covid travel red list forever and the wait had been agonizing. We decided to celebrate our reunion in style with a week in Panama and then two weeks at her home in Medellin, Colombia. Gilma was the picture of perfect health. She's a great believer in healthy eating, and over the next three weeks she brought me back to life on a diet of polite bollockings, papaya, chicken, fresh vegetables and gallons of water.

We were staying at the very lovely Bijao Beach Resort on Panama's Playa Blanca. Our first night at the hotel was interrupted by the karaoke being blasted out by the side of one of the pools. A pissed woman was trying to sing Celine Dion. I can only describe her voice as that of a wolf with tooth ache being dragged forcibly by the balls through a house fire. Thankfully, this torturous practice was only rolled out once a week.

THE GAME......

After eight wonderful days reunited with my Gilma, thoughts turned once again to the footy. It was fitting that this game involved a family as this part of the world is so family orientated. Many extended families were staying at the hotel, and it was beautiful to see so many of the younger generation fussing over their grandparents.

On what was our last morning in Panama, we found a grassy space near the beach and invited a family splashing about in the pool to play. Gilma did all the interpreting and within a minute we had a 4 v 4 going, first to three. Ariel Mojica and his family and friends from the Azuero region of Panama couldn't wait to play. Ariel Junior, little Daniel and I joined Ariel senior's side. Artur, Yatzhii, Juan Carlos and Edwin made up the opposition.

Artur helped to run activities at the resort and was Mr Energy for them; rapid across the ground with great close control. It had been drummed into me as a kid not be intimidated by a player's size or skill. Afterall, it was the football I was after not a photograph. With this in mind, I managed to keep Arthur at bay by ignoring his mesmeric step-overs, and concentrating on stealing that round thing between his swift feet.

Ariel Junior was hilarious for us, spluttering like a struggling engine when things didn't go his way. No words, just splutters. To the sound of holiday beats blasting out from Artur's beach shack, we played out a cracking family game of footy in the sea breeze. We must have had a hundred shots, but try as we might, we couldn't beat Juan Carlos "The Wall" Carvajal in their nets. In contrast, the opposition had three shots and they all went in. Just one of those games.

COMING HOME

GAMES 71-79

SCOTLAND-ISLE OF MAN- REPUBLIC OF IRELAND- ENGLAND

GAME 71: SCOTLAND

Date: Thursday 2nd June, 2022, 6.00pm
Ground: Port Street, Stirling

JUBIFREE

My dad was Scottish and my mum was English. They met on the Isle of Man and someone once told me that the McCluskie's had ancestral roots in Ireland. It seemed natural to visit all of these places before completing my journey, as I wouldn't be here without them.

My father was born in the west of Scotland, in a town called Hurlford in Ayrshire. Being a half Scot, I've always felt at home when venturing north of the border. We'd been granted an extra day's holiday in June this year because of the Queen's Platinum Jubilee, so I thought I'd use the time to play some footy in the land of the square sausage. On the morning of departure, I carried my duvet and pillows out to make up the blow up bed I'd squashed into the back of the car the night before. All done, I turned back towards my house to see that it was dressed in Union Jack bunting! This could only have been the work of one dastardly fellow. Remember Mickey Luvdust (Games 57 & 58: Hungary)? He knows full well that I'm not a monarchist. I could hardly take it all down for laughing, the cheeky chimp.

There is a widespread misconception that if you think the monarchy should be consigned to history, then clearly you hate your country. This is absolute nonsense. In fact the opposite is true. Britain is a fantastic place to live. The people, the music, the literature, the humour, the warmth, the towns and villages, the cities, the countryside, the resilience.... there's so much to love about this unique, green and pleasant home of ours. For me, the institution of the monarchy harks back to a time of conquest, subjugation and empire, and has little relevance in today's world. It should be phased out...castle by castle...yacht by yacht. In a democracy, shouldn't we at least be having a serious debate about this? When a man blindly follows a regime whose very origins lie in the theft of that man's land, then the journey to serfdom and servitude is complete. The perfect illusion is to give the lie oxygen even when you yourself are choking in the fight to survive.

Now I'm sure the Queen herself and some members of her family are lovely people, but there are millions of lovely people. They just happened to be born into a different reality. Does that make them any less important? Of course not. I think we should celebrate the true Queens of England; the daughters, mums and grandmums that have worked their socks off in our communities for generations. They have been the absolute glue that have held families and this country together, with their resilience, sense of justice, compassion and care. I'd wave my flag and have a street party for them any day of the week.

My fears of heavy bank holiday traffic proved unfounded. I had a straight run up to beautiful historic Stirling in central Scotland. My mate Tracey described Stirling as a "mini-Edinburgh ", and now I know what she meant. It has a famous castle, an old town, statues and monuments and a history of resistance. It was also a former capital city of Scotland. It's just not on the grand scale of Edinburgh. In 1297, the Battle of Stirling Bridge took place in the city, when old brave heart himself William Wallace defeated the English. Bannockburn is a stone's throw from here too. I remember going watching Scotland v England as a kid at Hampden Park and seeing a "REMEMBER

BANNOCKBURN" flag being waved in the crowd. This referred to another famous defeat of the English by the Scots in 1314. Maybe the remembrance of these battles, and general salty feelings towards the auld enemy, fed into the scarcity of Jubilee bunting in Stirling? I couldn't say, but the city felt very Jubifree.

THE GAME......

After a couple of hours of walking around and gawping at stuff, I set up for a game at the far end of Port Street, one of the main shopping areas. It was 5.30pm and all the shops were closing. Most folk had gone home and it took me a good half hour to gather some players. Local lads and friends Keith Cooper, Kieran Cowper and Brandon Thomson-Hoare were the first to join in. They were all in their early twenties and doing shop work. They enjoyed living in the city and having tourists around too. What a great set of friendly and chatty blokes they were.

A few minutes later, Ashok (Ash) Kumar and Nirmal Balley, from Bilston in the West Midlands, joined us. They were more than twice the age of the Stirling boys. Ash, Kieran and I took on the others and what a cracking little game we had. Brandon was brilliant! Super skilful, twisting and turning with all the skill of a seasoned politician avoiding a straight answer. He struck first for them, chipping me as I sprawled on the ground expecting a shot into the corner. Clever sausage. I pulled one back with a hopeful shot but then Brandon struck again with a darting run and shot across the hapless Ash, who by this time was knackered and breathing through his ears. Keith was into his skateboarding and was not a footy fan, but nevertheless he had a right good go in the nets for them. Nirmal played in little spurts. It was just fantastic to see him and Ash turning back the clock, running after the ball and tackling each other. Just for a moment they were teenagers again. Everyone played with a big smile on their face. This quick, enjoyable game ended 2-2 after Kieran struck the equalizer. Football for the hell of it, briefly uniting people across cultures and generations. Marvellous stuff.

GAME 72: SCOTLAND

Date: Friday 3rd June, 2022, 11.10am
Ground: Helix Park, Falkirk

THE KELPIES

As previously mentioned, I'd decided to kip in the car on this trip, though my car isn't really built for it. I wedged a blow-up bed in there and set about making it as comfy as possible. The back seats don't fully recline, so there was a bit of a slope type thing to contend with, and it was only suitable for a 5ft 5" person and I'm 5ft 10". Over the next few days, I'd be living off bananas, bran-flakes and Paul Weller and Simon and Garfunkel albums

My mate Tim suggested I visit the Kelpies on this journey, so I'd driven down from Stirling to Falkirk the previous evening. I pulled up in a spot in Helex Park, just around the corner from the sculptures. I was parked between proper mobile homes like the runt of the litter. Climbing into bed through the side door, I felt as excited as a teenager on his first adventure away from home, but the excitement didn't last. The bed deflated during the night and I awoke with a sore back, a numb leg, a crick in my neck and a headache. I caught site of my face in the rear view mirror and it looked like a bleached scrotum after a long bath. Making pained noises, I forced myself head first out of the door into the cold morning air. From the outside it must have looked like a polar bear giving birth, as I hit the floor and scrambled around blindly on the wet ground trying to stand up. I managed in the end and sneaked off for a pee in the bushes.

After some brekkie, I wrapped up warm, packed my ball, jumpers and camera into my rucksack and walked the half mile to see the Kelpies. What an incredible site they are. These 30-metre-high horse-head sculptures are truly breath-taking. Each sculpture is made from 300 tonnes of steel and are a monument to the horse power that once drove Scottish industry forward. (In folklore, a kelpie is a malevolent shape shifting water spirit that entices children to climb on its back, before plunging back into the loch, thus taking the children to a watery grave). I felt a great reverence when near them, and was sure that aliens would have to ask their permission if they wanted to land.

THE GAME......

Staring upwards opened mouthed, I circled around these giants until I found myself at a coffee van. I grabbed a brew and took a seat at one of the benches in front of the sculptures. By this time a few more tourists had started to arrive. I had to have a game here. There was a field to my left, so I guzzled down the coffee and threw down the jumpers. Within ten minutes I'd been joined by Ivan, Bertan, Moses, Kevin, Elden, Ayan, Naveen, Neil and Dominic; a real cultural mix of people from Rwanda, the Philippines and India. They were all members of the Seventh-day Adventist Church in Harlow, Essex. The church is of Adventist Protestant Christian denomination, though Naveen told me that they learn from all religious traditions, but believe that there is only one true God. They also believe in the second coming of Jesus, and in having a great game of footy!

I joined Moses, Ayan, Bertan and cool little Neil wearing sunglasses to play the rest. This turned out to be a keenly fought game in front of the Kelpies. Ivan from Rwanda was doing some shape shifting of his own, wriggling in and out of tackles and chipping his side into the lead. I was absolutely rubbish in the nets throughout the game, playing like I had two oversized wellies on. It was my worst display on the journey by far. I couldn't pass straight or save a shot to save my life. Of course, my devout religious brothers forgave my many errors. Moses was funny, playing almost the entire game with his hands in his pockets. He just stood on the ball when it came to him, then started to laugh until he was tackled. Ayan was playing well for us and scored our equalizer with a neat finish. It stayed 1-1 for a while, largely down to young Kevin from the Philippines in their nets. Unlike his opposite number, he was having a stormer. He didn't drop a thing and anticipated every shot.

The boys were putting loads of effort in on this nippy, overcast day. Little Neil was cracking me up. He was the son of Moses (*was he? – Ed*), and like his Dad, he was wearing cool American highway police sunglasses. This little fellow patrolled the pitch like an unstoppable pac-man, eating up the grass and determined to score.

A five minute stalemate was followed by a flurry of goals 2-1, 2-2, 3-2, 3-3 and all the way to 4-4. Next goal's the winner! The impressive Kevin strode out from his nets and banged one in low to my right to win it for them. It had been a brilliant, competitive game with some genuinely friendly folk. There seemed to be a real unity and happy brotherhood amongst the group. Gathering up the jumpers, I looked up and noticed that one of the Kelpies was looking down on us approvingly, whilst the other was looking away in disgust. Can't please everyone.

GAME 73: SCOTLAND

Date: Saturday 4th June, 2022, 11.10am
Ground: Millport Beach, Isle of Cumbrae

CROCODILE ROCK

Leaving the Kelpies, I drove into Stenhousemuir just so that I could say that I'd been to Stenhousemuir. It was only five minutes up the road. As a kid, I remember hearing the name of this unusual sounding football team being read out on final score every Saturday. I'd picture their ground being in a rainy, windswept, desolate place where the sky was always black. The one wooden stand would be creaking and falling to pieces, and they'd only have four spectators every home game, all aged ninety-six. I'm happy to report that none of this is true.

Stenhousemuir FC, 'The Warriors", have a tidy little ground, Ochilview Park, and a proud 125 year history. They've spent much of their time in the lower leagues, but did taste success in 1996 when they beat Dundee United on penalties in the Scottish Challenge Cup. Stenhousemuir FC are a proper club with immense resilience, surviving through sheer pride and good will. The Warriors Supporters Trust has the largest share percentage in the club, which ensures that no one individual could wrestle the club away from the fans. They work closely with the board and supporters club, giving time, money and labour to ensure that the club develops and is safeguarded e.g. contributing towards new floodlights and financing and labouring on the roof which now covers the terracing. Community in action. Superb.

From Stenhousemuir, I travelled west to the coast. My cousin Jim had suggested I visit Millport on the Isle of Cumbrae. To get there I would have to catch the ferry from Largs, a popular seaside resort on the Firth of Clyde in North Ayrshire. I drove the hour to Largs and parked by the sea just out of town. After an afternoon stroll, I spent a beautiful evening watching dolphins playing just out to sea. At night, I hung t-shirts around my car windows and hoped I wouldn't be harangued by youths as I slept there at the side of the road.

The next morning, after an undisturbed sleep, I took the ten minute ferry ride over to the Isle of Cumbrae. I then hopped on a bus into Millport, the island's main town, and made my way to the beach. With only a few distant dog walkers about, I stripped off and ran into the sea with gay abandon. Fffff Flippin eck! How cold was the Fffff Firth of Clyde!? After a few seconds of wading out I couldn't feel below my knees. Sod it. I decided to dive in. Oh dear. My peculiars shot inside behind my belly button and my brain screamed for help. Some folk do this every morning ….in December!

Thankfully it was a hot day and my cuticles returned to normal pretty quickly. I roamed around the town a bit and met the famous *Croc Rock*. As the story goes, in the early 1900's, a local man named Robert Brown was heading home from the pub when he noticed a rock which resembled a crocodile. Full of hops and barley, he grabbed his paints and brushes and returned to create what is known today as Crocodile Rock. Legend has it that every Spring, a mermaid comes up from the sea to give the crocodile its annual paint job.

THE GAME……

I wandered back onto the beach again in the early afternoon. It was now full of families with little cherubs building sandcastles, collecting shells and living in their beautiful, innocent magical worlds. I set out my jumpers and called on folk to play. First up was Colin from Erskine in Renfrewshire. He wandered over with his son James and his nephew Juan Cruz. Juan's mum is Argentinian and Dad Scottish. Next to join in, with their parents' permission, were identical twins Amber and Jade, plus brother Lewis and friend Rachel.

Lewis, James and Rachel joined my side. Juan Cruz' feet were definitely South American. What a player! Fast, technical and a clever finisher too. He went on to score one like Owen's against Argentina in the World Cup, surging to the right then unleashing a cracker across my flailing carcass. James and Lewis were both incredibly enthusiastic and competitive throughout for us. The twins and Rachel stuck mostly to the middle of the pitch, blissfully unaware of just how many chances they set up by accident with the odd flick and kick here and there. They were just having fun, totally unphased by the serious boys scarpering all around them.

Colin was brilliant craic. At one point he surged forwards and nutmegged me to score, then two minutes later blasted one into my already delicate peculiars. This was getting personal.

We got to half time leading 5-4 then changed ends. First to 10. Concentration levels were high and the tackles were flying in. We battled it out for forty minutes in the blazing sun until the scores were level at a nail-biting 9-9. I think I'm right in saying Lewis scored nine of our goals and the brilliant Juan Cruz about seven of theirs. Next goal's the winner. Colin shot just as two tiny wee tots appeared, pulling little buckets of sand across my goal line. I moved across to protect them and the ball flew in. VAR decision – no goal. I retrieved the ball and punted it forward to James who swung a leg and deflected it past Colin for the winner. What a game at the seaside with brilliant Colin and the super cherubs! I sailed back to Largs after the game and decided to head home, but not before visiting Glenbuck.

The brilliant football documentary "The Three Kings – The makers of modern football", directed by Jonny Owen, tells the tale of three Scottish working class men who changed the game forever. Bill Shankly (Ayrshire), Matt Busby (Glasgow) and Jock Stein (Lanarkshire) were born within a half hour of each other. They were all coal miners before going on to leave their indelible marks on the game.

These three formidable leaders of men set standards, raised expectations and made dreams come true. They transformed the very soul of their respective clubs, and their legacies live on to this day. Ferocious Anfield is Shankly's 'bastion of invincibility', Old Trafford's "Theatre of Dreams" conserves Busby's edict that the club had a "duty to entertain" and Stein's electric Celtic Park forever proves his mantra that 'football is nothing without fans'. Thanks to these remarkable men, Liverpool, Manchester United and Celtic now have a collective estimated global fanbase of over two billion people.

I arrived at Bill Shankly's birthplace, Glenbuck, in the late afternoon. This small mining village in East Ayrshire is now uninhabited and most of the buildings are gone. Shankly was one of five brothers who all went on to play professional football. The town's remarkable Glenbuck Cherrypickers team spawned no less than fifty professional players between the 1870's and their demise in 1931. An incredible accomplishment for a village of just over a thousand people. Glenbuck's heritage site has information boards dotted about telling tales of its history and of the Shankly family. In addition, there are memorial tablets to the illustrious Glenbuck Cherrypicker's and to the great man himself.

It was around 5.30pm and all the other visitors had gone home. I walked down the path to the Shankly memorial, which is sited where his home once stood, and took a seat on a bench there. My eyes welled up and my whole body flooded with emotion as I gazed at the beautiful tribute before me, and imagined how the old mining town must have looked. Everything I've ever loved about football and thought important about life was encapsulated in this moment. This magical game was driven on for a century by men and women with unwavering working class values of hard work, honesty, loyalty, integrity and unity; the very foundations on which our beautiful game stands, and the very qualities that make this world a better place.

I wonder what Shankly. Busby and Stein would have thought about the recent Super League debacle? That clandestine intention of the so called *dirty dozen*, including Liverpool and Manchester United, to form an elitist break-away league, was the ultimate expression of greed. The very idea of a super league encapsulates everything that's sickening about the modern game. Its ugliness and gluttony reminded me again of why I am on this particular journey. The game is ours. It's a love affair and money can't buy me love. Another absolute football legend, Bobby Robson, put it this way:

"What is a club in any case? Not the buildings or the directors or the people who are paid to represent it. Its not the television contracts, get-out clauses, marketing departments or executive boxes. Its the noise, the passion, the feeling of belonging, the pride in your city. It's a small boy clambering up stadium steps for the very first time, gripping his father's hand, gawping at that hallowed stretch of turf beneath him and, without being able to do a thing about it, falling in love".

GAME 74: ISLE OF MAN

Date: Saturday 9th July, 2022, 7.00pm
Ground: A field in Ballaugh

WALLABIES AND WONDER

It only takes half an hour to fly from Liverpool to Ellan Vannin, or the Isle of Man as we know it in English. I landed on a lovely warm summers morning, with songs from Sam Fender's two magnificent albums running through my head. Arriving at my hotel in Douglas, the island's capital city, I climbed the stairs to my third floor room, then lifted up the old wooden window to let some air in. Peering out over the promenade, I was bewitched by the sunlight dancing out there on the water. I just knew this was going be a great adventure.

Although so close to home, my knowledge of the Isle of Man was very limited. I knew it was in the Irish Sea. I also knew that the people were referred to as Manx, that Manx cats had no tails and that the Manx flag displayed an unusual three-legged symbol. Lastly, I knew that the world famous TT motor bike races are held there every year. So not much really. What a wonderful surprise it turned out to be.

I was due to meet up with my old school friend and islander Bev Armitage, but she was 'across' when I arrived, meaning she was in England. Manx people don't refer to England or Britain as the mainland. They feel proudly independent of all those countries that ring around the isle i.e. Northern Ireland to the west, England to the east and Wales to the South. You can also see the west coast of Scotland from the north of the island. I was to learn that the Isle of Man is in fact a crown dependency and not actually part of the United Kingdom. It has its own parliament, government and laws, though it works with the UK on matters of defence and foreign policy. Just to confuse matters more, Manx people are British citizens. Quirky.

Here are some other quirks and claims to fame that I discovered. There are no foxes, badgers or otters on the island, but there are wild wallabies! The story goes that a couple of wallabies (passionately in love), escaped paw in paw from a wildlife park in the 1960's, and now there are over a hundred of them bouncing around. On the roads there are no fixed speed cameras and no national speed limit. MOT tests are also not required. The island has the world's oldest continuous parliament, Tynwald, and the world's largest working water wheel, Laxey Wheel, known locally as Lady Isabella. It has its own bank notes, coins and stamps and is a tax haven, with the standard rate of income tax being just 10% and the higher rate just 20%. Loaghton sheep can boast up to six horns and brilliant sprint cyclist Mark Cavendish is from the island, as are the The Bee Gees. There is a statue of the Bee Gees on Douglas prom, but it had been removed to be cleaned when I visited. Tragedy (*dear me-Ed*).

The latin motto for the famous Triskelion, or three-legged symbol of the Isle of Man, is Quocunque Jeceris Stabit – *whichever way you throw it, it will stand*. This seems to symbolize perfectly the island's historic quest for self-determination. The Manx language, closely related to the Irish and Scottish Gaelic, almost died out with the death of the last native speaker, Ned Maddrell, in 1974. However, there have been recent efforts to revive the language as an integral part of the islands identity.

As I mentioned, my friend Bev was 'across' when I arrived on the Friday and, due to her return flight being delayed, we didn't meet up until the following morning. She'd been a regular visitor to the Isle of Man for as long as I'd known her, before finally deciding to settle in Douglas in 2021. It was clear to see why. The Manx saying "Traa-dy-Liooar", meaning 'Time enough', is the islands 'mañana' and expresses their relaxed approach to life. Everyone I met seemed genuinely friendly and had time for a chat.

Bev is brilliant. We have known each other for over forty years and she hasn't changed a bit - always funny, kind, generous and full of laughter and adventure. She also turned out to be the best tour guide a chap could ever wish for. Bev works for Rentakill pest control and is one of only two of their responders on the island. When I asked about rats she nearly choked *"Rats! You can't say that word on the Isle of Man! If you do, you'll have to turn around three times and spit! It's considered bad luck, so much so that when the The Boomtown Rats (famous Irish band) came to play on the island, they changed their name to the Boomtown Longtails for the night"*. For the next two days we would bomb about this brilliant island in her Rentakill van, risking our own extermination at some very high speeds. "Vroom! Vroom!" she roared and laughed as we tore along those limitless highways. "Shit! Shit!" I screeched in reply.

We met up on a hot Saturday morning and toured the south of the island. From lovely Port Erin to the south west, past the living museum village of Cregneash, and on through stunning scenery to view the Calf of Man, an island located a half mile from the mainland, across the Calf Sound. Here, at the southern tip of the island, a few tourists had gathered to watch the sunbathing and splashing seals lapping up all the attention. We then went on to the former Manx capital Castletown. The island's quirkiness was on full view here in the shape of the pink police station, with rainbow trimming, that had paintings of dogs pulling the pants off burglars on the side walls.

Passing street names such as Lerghy Chripperty and Boilley Spittal only served to add to my growing suspicion that I was playing a part in the Manx version of Camberwick Green, the iconic British children's animated series set in a fictional, picturesque village. Honouring the tradition of saying hello to the fairies as we crossed over Fairy Bridge further compounded this notion. Later we visited Tynwald Hill at St. John's. This four-tiered hill is said to contain soil from each of the islands seventeen parishes. It is from here, in an annual open air ceremony held each July 5th, that the thousand year old parliament sets out its plans for the year, and islanders can lobby lawmakers by submitting petitions. The day is marked by a national bank holiday.

THE GAME......

After viewing the stunning coastal headland at Eary Cushlin, we had a paddle in the crystal clear sea water at Niarbyl Bay. This lovely little spot, with aged and protected whitewashed cottages, has been a location for scenes in many a movie. We then nipped through Peel, then on through the brilliantly named Cronky-Voddy, before reaching Kirk Michael and then onto Ballaugh, our final destination of the day.

Bev's friends, Emma and Barry were celebrating their 100th birthday (She was 40 and he was 60) with a huge bash in a field in Ballaugh, to the west of the island. We drove out into the countryside for ages, before turning off a narrow lane and finding this mini festival in the middle of nowhere. There was a huge bouncy castle, axe throwing, clay pigeon shooting, a free bar, a double decker food bus, a huge marquee and a fire pit. Marvellous! Spotting a sizeable patch of grass between the parked cars and the marquee, I placed the jumpers down and the sales pitch began. Young tall Christian was on it straight away and helped me to invite people to play. Most of the revellers had just eaten, but it wasn't long before a small army of them joined us. It was around 7pm but still pretty hot.

7 v 7 and what a belting game! We played for around an hour with a drink's break in between. Flame haired Michelle, from County Tyrone, Northern Ireland was the absolute star of the show. Before we kicked off, she came over to tell me she had bad knees and would have to go in the nets. She must have saved a least fifty shots in the first half, her flowing dress like a Venus fly trap gobbling up the ball. We only managed to squeeze one past her. Meanwhile, Grant and Lindsay's kids Noah and Harry were playing

blinders. Super quick and skilful, they were running rings around the big folk. Harry scored a quick fire hat-trick, his third a cheeky chip over my sweaty prone shape. Their fourth goal came courtesy of our own player. The ball dropped at Nicola's feet, who then turned and inexplicably blasted it past me! 4-1 at half-time and a well-deserved break.

It was a lovely late evening. The sun still shone but a little chill had entered the air. Long shadows stretched across the field and someone lit the fire pit. We resumed battle once more. For some reason known only to herself, Michelle joined our side and went up front. She was as formidable as Millie Bright. This outwardly cool, respectable woman single-handedly smashed the opposition to bits- flying into tackles, going up for headers, shoulder charging and bludgeoning her way towards goal. If this is what she played like with bad knees, it's frightening what she could do when fully fit. A brilliant performance that left everyone in stitches.

Michelle was entirely responsible for bringing us back level at 4-4. Next goal's the winner! The opposition pressed and pressed. Paddy was surging forward, Noah and Harry were having shot after shot. Lindsay thought she'd won it but she'd kicked the ball out of my hands to score. This was serious. I urged our team to camp in front of their goals, then chucked the ball high into the air towards them. Michelle was on to it. There were bodies flying everywhere, until the only person left standing was the warrior queen herself, who blasted the ball home. Victory was hers and ours. What a fantastic night of footy.

I got chatting with Manxman Grant after the game. He played for the Isle of Man until he tore his cruciate ligament when he was twenty six. He told me that FC Isle of Man now play in the North West Counties Football League against English sides, and they can get up to 2000 spectators at their national sports centre for home games. He felt that cycling was beginning to impact the game on the island, as many young people were taking that up instead. When I asked him if he ever spent time thinking about life off the island or what was happening in Westminster, he replied that he couldn't care less. This seemed to sum the day up perfectly. The people on this wonderful island had no reason to get caught up with all that stuff *across* there. Traa-dy-Liooar indeed.

GAME 75: ISLE OF MAN

Date: Sunday 10th July, 2022, 11.30am
Ground: Douglas Promenade

WALKIN' AND TALKIN'

The Isle of Man brings out the child in you. Feelings of wonderment and possibility are rekindled by its beaches, bays and bikes, fairies, woods and warmth. On my last day I met a group of people who epitomized this spirit.

Bev asked me along to the Douglas Walk 'n' Talk group on Sunday morning. The group was set up by Gary Christian. Gary was going through a very low time in his own life, when he noticed that many people, day to day, were walking along the promenade alone - *"I thought how nice it would be to bring strangers together and walk and talk with people they didn't know. To find out a little more about their lives and trials & tribulations.... for people to meet new people and form lifelong friendships. So from that thought I formed Douglas Walk "n" Talk group".*

The group is now entering its third year and has over four hundred members. It helped Gary to heal, and many others to connect and form life changing bonds and friendships. Bev has attended the group for a while, and it really helped her to settle in to her new life on the island - *"I knew nobody when I moved to the island. Finding the walk and talk group means everything to me. The people I met have become firm friends. We meet up at other times too. I've also joined some of the girls in the group to go sea swimming 'The Manx Blue Tits", which has widened my circle of friends even more".* The walk 'n' talk group meet every Sunday, with people dipping in and out throughout the year. Their usual route is along Douglas promenade, starting at the electric railway station, then arcing around 'til they reach the sea terminal building (which looks like a giant lemon squeezer), before having a brew and returning to the start. It's a good walk, around three and a half miles in total.

Meeting up with the group, I was warmly welcomed and hugged by all. What lovely folk. We walked and talked our way down to the 'lemon squeezer', past the rows of tall Edwardian-era guesthouses to our right, and the ornate façade of the Gaiety Theatre and Opera House, built in 1900. These buildings are part of the wider Villa Marina and Geity Theatre complex, which hosts contemporary bands and comedians from 'across'. (*Even you're at it now- Ed).*

THE GAME......

After a walk and a brew we had a game of footy on the prom. Bev, Gwen, Graham, Gary, Rebecca, Chris, Gill, Jane, Hassan, Caron, and my sunburnt self, had a brilliant laugh in the mid-morning sun. There were a few slips, trips and falls and much hilarity. At one point, Gary and Hassan were sent crashing to the floor after colliding with some metal barriers, and Gill went skidding on her back across the prom. Thankfully no-one was hurt. Holiday makers stopped to watch the spectacle as the troops tared around like teenagers. Our team - Caron, Hassan, Graham, Jane and myself- lost 1-0 in the end but no-one cared about the result. As we walked back up the prom to our starting point, all you could hear was the magical sound of conversation. Walking, talking, connecting, living.

Caron: *"From that first Sunday two years ago ......wonderful connections, support & hugs. Smiles from people who are positively pleased to see you, genuine interest in who you are, fantastic advice if needed, diversifying debates, kindness and care, tears and celebrations all shared, fun, silliness & laughter too!! And as the group grows, some friends made for life. I no longer feel lonely, I feel a part of an awesome tribe who, after finally coming out of my shell, have accepted me just as I am!! Thank you so much guys"*

GAME 76: ISLE OF MAN

Date: Sunday 10th July, 2022, 2.30pm
Ground: The Creg-ny-Baa, Onchan

MODS v ROCKERS

An Irish folktale attributes the formation of the Isle of Man to Ireland's legendary hero Finn McCool (Fionn mac Cumhaill). In pursuit of a Scottish giant, Finn scooped up a huge mass of Irish clay and rock and hurled it at the fleeing beast. However, he missed his target and the chunk of earth landed in the Irish Sea, thus creating the Isle of Man. The hole he gauged out became Northern Irelands' Lough Neagh.

However it came to be formed (and I believe the Finn McCool version), the island was left blessed with the topograghy to host the world's most famous motorcycle racing festival, the Isle of Man TT. Described on its official website as 'the ultimate test of man and machine' (*https://www. iomtt.com/),* the festival attracts over 40,000 visitors per year, almost half of the island's population. Since the inaugural race in 1907, the course itself has undergone many changes, as bikes have become more powerful and roads more accessible. It was once the case that the mountain circuit was no more than a horse and cart track. The first rider out would have to open all the gates along the way, and the last rider shut them. A far cry for the full-throttle tarmac and leather blur of today. It's a risky business though. A total of 265 riders have died at the Isle of Man TT since 1911, but still they come. As my friend Mickey says, you've got to die of something, and as one of my favourite poets, Charles Bukowski put it *'find what you love and let it kill you'.* Better to die doing something you love?

I know next to nowt about bikes and racing, but Bev does and so does my mate Russ Brookes who, by happy coincidence, was touring the island on his bike with his Dad and his pals when I was there. I arranged to meet him at the famous Creg-ny-Baa pub. The "Creg" is probably the most famous pub in motorsport. Greats such as Mike Hailwood, Agostine and Joey Dunlop have had their photos taken in front of it - taking the right hander, breaking heavily, before whizzing on down towards the grandstand.

All this was new to me. I grew up a mod, into sixties soul and motown, The Small Faces and The Jam. We dressed smartly at all times and mods drove around on vespas and lambrettas to preserve their cool. Leather clad hairy rockers and greasy motorbikes were our antithesis, as was the rock music they were in to. It's pretty amazing that me and rocker Bev became friends at all. We'd rib each other constantly at school about music and hair length, but always got along famously. Of course, she was now in her absolute element living on bike island.

THE GAME......

We met up with Russ, his Dad Glenn and his biking pals from St. Helen's at the "Creg" at 2pm. It was scorching hot. Russ introduced us to his old army buddy Stuart, who lives on the island, and his partner Roz. We managed to persuade these crazy bikers to have a kick about in the long grass behind the pub in their motorbike boots.

Stuart, Andy and I took on Russ, Barry and Bev. It was tough going. Long grass, big boots and Tahiti temperatures. Between deep gasps for air and hands on knees, the game somehow got to 4-4. Russ and Stu, veterans from the Queens Lancashire Regiment, were fiercely competitive and scored three each. Russ was throwing everything at it to get the winner, but the ball finally spilt kindly to Stu, who tucked it away past Roz inside the far jumper. We all walked back towards the pub, collapsed on a grass verge and hydrated. Fantastic game with brilliant people at an iconic racing location. Even for a mod like me, being surrounded by bikes and leather hadn't turned out so badly after all.

Bev and I said our goodbye's to Russ and the gang, and headed out to see some more of the island. Firstly, we called at the Laxey Wheel but it was under repair so we couldn't really see it. We then met up with Bev's friend Ken and his two children who were going kayaking at Port Lewaigue. After a little swim there, and a spot of tea in Ramsey, we made our way to the Point of Ayre, the northernmost point of the island and just a short hop from Scotland. The tour was complete. North to south, East to West, Bev had come up trumps, and then some. The Isle of Man had been a big surprise to me. With its sandy beaches, crystal clear waters, coastal and mountain glen's, wallabies and general quirkiness, it really is the gift that keeps on giving. More importantly, its where my old friend has found her happy place.

GAME 77: THE REPUBLIC OF IRELAND

Date: Friday 15th July, 2022, 1.00pm
Ground: Straide and Foxford United AFC soccer ground, Foxford, County Mayo

MARTHA AND THE BRODERICKS

Thirty years we'd been talking about it. One of my oldest mates, Niall Broderick, has roots in Foxford, County Mayo. He and his family had visited regularly for years, and we'd often talk about going over for a weekend. Well, we finally made it. Together with my son's Uncle Paul, we landed at Knock Airport on a summer's morning and proceeded to laugh for the next 48 hours.

Over to you Niall:

"Foxford County Mayo. It's unlikely that you will have heard of this small town in the West of Ireland. Perhaps you may not have even heard of the county itself? Not surprising, as despite being the third largest county in Ireland, Mayo is often overshadowed by more well-known counties that so readily slip off the tongue in music and poetry, such as Dublin, Galway, Kerry or Cork. As for Foxford, there are countless similar towns scattered across Ireland which remain known only to those who reside there. Yet, Foxford remains a popular destination for the tourist. Some are drawn to visit its famous woollen mills, others to fish for salmon on the banks of the beautiful River Moy, while others may visit to explore the curious origins of the Argentinian Navy. Yes, believe it or not, Argentina owes its Navy to one of the sons of Foxford - a certain Admiral William Brown.

For me, Foxford is inextricably woven through my family. My grandfather was born there in 1913 and, like millions of other young Irish men, emigrated to England. He married my grandmother, also a Foxford native, in 1937 and like the Moy salmon, they retuned every year during the summer holidays, bringing along their children and later their grandchildren. It is this connection which brought three friends to Foxford in the summer of 2022, to continue with Ste's epic journey around the world. Game 77, and the first in Ireland, could only have been in Foxford. For years, I have bored the pants off Ste with tales of Foxford, how my grandfather would take me, his eldest grandchild, to sit at the bar in Clarke's, McEnroe's or The Friendly Tavern, listening eagerly to news of the past year with a glass of Guinness nestled in his hand. How I often listened to my Dad sing traditional Irish songs to a packed function room at Jones' Hotel. I caught fish longer than an arm and even fell into the river once and nearly drowned. Yes, game 77 had to be in Foxford.

THE GAME......

We arrived in town just before midday. It was quiet, with few cars around and even fewer people. Indeed, the possibility of Ste being able to work his magic, and in his words, *'get a game going,"* were slim. A quick tour of the town followed, the origins of the Broderick family were highlighted before we promptly withdrew to Guiry's Bar to re-group and sample a Guinness. Martha, the landlady, greeted us warmly and began to pull what is widely regarded as the finest pint of Guinness in Ireland. As the three pints settled on the bar and the reason for our visit was shared, the wonderful Martha was on the phone and before the final pull of the pints was administered, a team was rallied and the game was on.

Ian Clarke, his wife Helen and their son Jamie, together with the Flatley siblings Kiera, Mark and Jack, plus young Dylan and Darragh, led us past the woollen mill and onto Straid and Foxford AFC's impressive pitch. Fighting the rising bravado of Guiry's marvellous Guinness, and the echoes of my youthful footballing prowess, I wisely retreated to the safety of the goal. A prudent decision given the youth, fitness and enthusiasm of our hosts, along with the fact that Darragh, Dylan and Jamie for the opposition currently play for Straid and Foxford. They proudly wore their team shirts this day. The other goal lay empty until Ste, with his blue Scottish skin, already reddening in the July sunshine, quickly retreated into it. This left Paul to impose his experience onto the game, which, to his credit he did ... for a full two minutes. A loose ball, an over stretch, a yelp of pain and Paul slumped to the ground in agony holding his hamstring. The game continued, the skill levels rose, the first goal was conceded, and Paul hobbled into the distance with Helen in search of ice. A steady flow of goals ensued, aided by some poor goal keeping and clinical finishing by Dylan and Kiera, which brought the scores even at 4-4 at half time. We swapped ends, exposing fresh areas of skin to the increasing heat of the afternoon. Youthful enthusiasm kept the second half tempo high in the sapping heat. The game finally ended, much to the relief of two old frazzled keepers, in a 10-7 victory for Ste's team.

During the game, I began to think about what it was like to grow up in quiet Foxford in 2022. Would there be a sense of isolation, a feeling of the world racing past and a longing for the lights of the bigger towns and cities? As we sat down and Ste began his now familiar post-game interview, it became quickly apparent that our hosts felt a sense of belonging, pride and self-awareness so often missing in many other young adults. Far from a feeling of isolation, they loved the feeling of living in a small town, citing the fact that everyone knew each other as the primary reason. As Ste delved deeper, there was a shared appreciation of the importance of sport in their lives. Not the billion-pound world of the Premier League, but the traditional amateur sports of Gaelic Football and hurling.

Despite Mayo not winning Gaelic Football's All-Ireland Final since 1951, there was a deep rooted pride in the fact that to play for Mayo, you have to come from Mayo. The idea of bringing players from other counties to win the championship was abhorrent. Mayo have reached the final a total of eleven times since their last championship and lost every time, earning the unwanted title of Ireland's unluckiest team. Yet, was it just bad luck that has kept them from winning ? Apparently not. Maybe the answer lies in Foxford. After their triumph of 1951, and still clutching the Sam Maguire Cup, the team paraded through the town of Foxford and passed a funeral. Reportedly. the players did not stop to pay their respects, which prompted an enraged priest to utter the fateful words: "For as long as you all live, Mayo won't win another All-Ireland." The wait continues.

And what of hamstrung Paul, you may wonder? With no sign of the stricken maestro, we walked back into town, passing Helen on the way. "He's on our roof terrace." She said, "the door's open, let yourselves in and I'll be back in a minute." And there, laid out a sunbed, with a glass of iced water and an ice pack on his leg, was Foxford's Maradona. Helen returned with Ian and, with the incredible hospitality and friendship that symbolises this wonderful county, we sat in view of the green and red colours of Mayo, and chatted about their boys, their town and our own lives and families. An hour later, we retreated once more to Guiry's and with Martha's steady hand at the pump, sampled a few more of Ireland's finest pints of Guinness. And now, perhaps more than ever, I am proud to say that I am a Mayo man and a son of Foxford."

What a day it had been. As we stood on the corner waiting for our taxi to Ballina, it seemed like the whole town was out tooting their horns and waving goodbye to us. We'd only been in Foxford a few hours, but we'd been enveloped in the effortless, magical west of Ireland welcome, giddy with Guinness and friendship. Long live the Broderick's of Foxford!

GAME 78: THE REPUBLIC OF IRELAND

Date: Saturday 16th July, 2022, 2.45pm
Ground: Eyre Square, Galway City, County Galway

LATIN SATIN

What a craic we'd had in Broderick country. The following day we headed south towards Galway on the bus, stopping at Clairemorris on the way. Paul valiantly hobbled along as we sought a suitable place to play. However, the town was quiet and sleepy. Our best efforts to get a game going by the lovely Clare Lake were all in vain. The gathering geese looked up for it though. In fact they looked like they were going to eat us, so we waddled out of there sharpish. We hopped back on the bus and landed in Galway around 2.30pm. The Galway International Arts Festival was on, and the atmosphere was electric as we entered Eyre Square in the heart of the city centre. Hundreds of people lazed on the grass in the lovely afternoon sun, as buskers busked and street performers strutted their stuff.

THE GAME......

I placed the jumpers down on the grass and went about asking folk to play. Little did I know that five minutes later we'd be a having a fantastic game of football with five Brazilians, two Mexicans, a Guatemalan, a Salvadoran, a Turk, an American and an Irishman! Apart from Dan the Irishman, they were all English language students at the Galway Cultural Institute. Deidre, from Virginia USA, was their teacher.

Niall and I went in our respective nets and poor hamstrung Paul patrolled with his camera. Karla (El Salvador), Gustavo (Mexico), Gabrielli (Brazil) Juan Pablo (Guatemala) Luis (Brazil) Dan (Ireland) and I took on the rest... or should I say, we tried to stop the incredible Pedro Dias from Brazil. What a player! A samba star with a satin touch, Pedro was unplayable at times. The ball was tied to his foot as he weaved incredulously around the lunging bodies trying to stop him. He was quick too, with instant control, and he made us all look daft. Big, tough Dan chased after him all afternoon but couldn't catch him. At one point Pedro took a high ball down with such a touch that we all let out a gasp. He'd played at a high standard in Brazil before tragically taring both ACL's in his early twenties. He said he was never the same player after that. On today's evidence, a fully fit Pedro would have been something to see.

It was all Pedro for the first ten minutes, ably assisted by the tricky Ricardo (Brazil) and the tough tackling of Deidre (USA) and Mehmet (Turkey). Luis (Brazil) and Cristhian (Mexico) were loving the game so much that they were smiling us to death. They took a 3-1 lead, with the cheeky Ricardo putting one through my legs. Smarty pants. If it wasn't for Juan Pablo, the long haired yellow flash from Guatemala, we'd have been in deep trouble. On the rare occasions that we had the ball he made it count, miraculously bringing us into the half-time break at 3-3.

The heat was starting to take its toll and the game slowed down. Big Gustavo kept signalling for me to throw it up to his big chest. He controlled it every time and always got a shot away, though he couldn't beat the Broderick in the nets. Pedro blasted a few into my big belly but the goals had dried up for both sides. We decided to play next goal's the winner. The pace instantly picked up. Deidre in particular was showing a strong will to win. After a five minute stalemate, the ball fell to Juan Pablo. He caught it all wrong, but still the ball floated up and towards goal. Time froze. We all stared open mouthed as the orb continued its slow motion journey towards glory. Surely Niall had it covered. He stretched and he stretched those long limbs of his and …missed it. Goal! We all cruelly mocked Niall's attempted save, and rightly so. What a belting game.

We sat and chatted for a while afterwards. All the troops were in Galway to study for six months and were loving life. They were smart, engaging. exuberant young people with their lives in front of them. We found out it was star man Pedro's birthday, so we gave him a rendition of happy birth-day in Spanish, Portuguese, Turkish and English all at the same time, which sounded like a feral cat with the shits. We said our goodbye's to these lovely folk then headed to the pub.

We spent the next four hours in Garavan's bar drinking Guinness and laughing our heads off with the locals. What a fantastic couple of days we'd had. To finally make it to Niall's family town of Foxford and get the reception we did, then on to Galway for such a magical connection with people from the other side of the world. The west of this emerald isle is a very special place. A conversation, a story and laughter are only ever just a few moments away.

GAME 79: ENGLAND

Date: Saturday 20th August, 2022, 7.30pm
Ground: Pendleton Village Hall, Clitheroe, Lancashire

TAKING THE LEAP

I've supported people in recovery from alcohol and drug addiction for most of my working life, and they have humbled and inspired me. They are some of the most remarkable and misunderstood people in society. I'm not going to white wash over the devastating effects that addiction can have on individuals, their loved ones, our public services and society in general. I'm just making the point that, in my experience, there is usually a deep underlying explanation, not excuse, as to why life turned out the way it did. Our prisons and rehabs are packed full of neglected children and victims of trauma; trauma that will echo through a person's life until it's acknowledged, challenged and worked through. For many, this is too tough to contemplate, and so substances become a buffer, a way to block out feelings. However, the past is always there snapping at the heels.

Year after year I have witnessed the remarkable transformation of people who were seemingly lost to addiction. However, the road to recovery is long and very tough. To get well, recovering addicts and alcoholics have to excavate their heart and soul, sinking deep into the guilt and despair that comes with acknowledging the hurt and pain they have caused. They then go through the harrowing examination of their own trauma and neglect, often experienced through adverse childhood experiences, before going on to try to make amends to the people they have hurt. All this, whilst studying a virtual master's degree is how to stay clean and sober, despite their addict brain urging them to relapse. The brilliant Jurgen Klopp talks about his Liverpool team being 'mentality monsters'. He needs to pop in to a rehab sometime.

To witness so many of these beaten and deeply scarred human beings becoming strong, healthy, spiritual and responsible individuals has been a great privilege of my life. Many re-build connections with their loved ones and go on to work in recovery services themselves, dedicating their lives to helping others. So next time you meet someone in recovery, please know that they haven't just put the drink and drugs down, they have been on a long, courageous and redemptive journey of self-discovery, fighting an incredibly powerful and insidious foe on a daily basis. Zoe, and her husband to be Mark, took the leap into recovery many years ago. Today they were to take a leap of different kind.

THE GAME......

"Why don't you have a kick-about at our wedding?" said the bride to be. "Are you crackers?" said me. "You know I am" said she.

On a lovely August afternoon in Lancashire, we gathered for the handfasting of my beautiful friend Zoe to one of the loveliest chaps in the world Mark. Handfasting is an ancient Celtic ritual in which the hands are tied together to symbolize the binding of two lives. Each cord used to bind has a different colour and blessed meaning. At the end of the ceremony the cords are pulled together into an infinity knot (tying the knot) and given to the couple to symbolize their union. There are many variations of the handfasting ceremony. For Zoe and Mark, they asked their guests to form a circle out in the field next to the village hall. The four elements were then called into their marriage circle before the handfasting began. They then exchanged rings and made a commitment to be together "as long as love shall last." It was a very beautiful and spiritual ceremony to witness. Finally, the newly-weds jumped over the broom to symbolize their leap into a new life together, leaving the past behind. This was a wonderful moment considering the battle they had both fought for years to re-build their lives. Now here they were, happy, healthy and in love, surrounded by people who loved their true selves. The power of recovery indeed. Zoe and Mark invited us all to *jump the besom* before we retreated to the village hall for fun and frolics. In between being entertained by a fantastic gypsy jazz band, a storming set from DJ T. Montana and chip butties, we managed to squeeze a game in.

THE GAME......

With the happy couple's permission, I took the ball and jumpers out onto the grass at 7.30pm, followed by a big crowd of revellers. A wild game of 10 v 10 broke out. The ball shot about like a pinball and the poor apple tree took a right walloping, shedding all but two of its fruit. In amongst the smart shirts and lovely dresses, it was the lime green haired Chimmy who stole the show. Bare footed and barnstorming, this pagan warrior won every header and tore around the pitch in a blur. The bride and groom were getting stuck in too. At one point, Zoe hilariously captured the ball under her dress. She wasn't for letting us have it back. Big Mark was an immovable force at the back for the opposition. Big Lee for us went flying at one point, but soldiered on with his injured shoulder. Shots reigned in from everywhere. Tony in our nets stood firm. It must have been a good ten minutes before the deadlock was broken. There then followed a quick flurry of goals and, with score standing at 2-2, we decided to play next goals the winner. Fittingly, Zoe and Mark's team took the victory and on we revelled into the sweet sober night. Wishing Zoe and Mark all the love in the world for a long and happy life together.

GAME 80: ENGLAND

Date: Saturday 3rd September 2022, 2.00pm
Ground: Stacksteads Recreation Ground, Lancashire

FULL CIRCLE

THE SUMMERS OF MY YOUTH

In the summers of my youth
I jumped the garage roofs
Crossed the river fully clothed
Played with worms, slugs, frogs and toads

Risked my life upon high walls
Lost at least a thousand balls
And at least a million truths
To the summers of my youth

Swung through trees in monkey boots
Watched older boys with air-rifles shoot
Watched the coal fire with my Dad
Whose blue eyes were always sad

I'd stare down the empty street
Bathed in sunlight in bare feet
And my life just seemed so long
In the summer's morning song

All was new and I alive
Before the coming of the tide
And what tomorrow did replace
Seems now impossible to chase

But those summers live in me
Bright and burning, wild and free
The magic everlasting truth
Of the summers of my youth

I was born in the front room of our council house in January 1969. My home town of Stacksteads is one of several small mill towns which are dotted about the Rossendale Valley in East Lancashire. My mum was a machinist in a shoe factory and my Dad worked on the building sites. Back then, the valley was a mecca for shoe manufacturing. Most school leavers', including myself, filtered straight into the factories. My first job aged 16 was in a machine room with around eighty women. They were ferocious. I did a lot of growing up in there! I remember on my last day wearing two pairs of jeans and three belts, but they still manged to get me down to my undies and pelt me with eggs and flour. Back then Rossendale was vibrant. Full-employment meant people spent money in their towns and villages. Local shops did well and there was a strong community spirit. Of course we didn't have much technology back then. No play stations or mobile phones. No double glazing and no duvets! We only had three tv channels, and watching Top of the Pops on Thursday's and Match of the Day with Jimmy Hill on Saturdays was as important as life itself.

I first kicked a ball on Stacksteads Recreation Ground, ' Stacky Rec', when I was four. The rec is flanked by the River Irwell on one side and the old steam railway embankment on the other. I remember the Irwell always being bright orange due to the dye factory deposits upstream. My Dad would take me and my brother Jim down there every week for a kick about. As we got older, a gang of us little warriors would head down to do battle with other lads and lasses from our town. It's no exaggeration that some nights there were so many mini games being played that it was hard to find space to play.

Stacky Rec was our primary school's home pitch too. Ray Clemence was my hero back then and I started life as a goalkeeper, which was hard work as a tiny ten year old in full-sized nets. These days matches are called off when it starts spitting, but we played in all weathers. I remember breaking my finger once playing on the frozen ground, and playing with an orange ball in snow drifts. The pitch itself was dangerous; an uneven, muddy and sandy trap full of dog shit, bricks and cinders from the old railway depot, but on we played.

Stacky Rec was also home to the legendary Frank Lord. Frank was our mate Kev's Dad, and he'd bring his wickets, pads, bat and ball down most nights of the week. What a brilliant bloke. The cry would go up "Mr Lord's here!'

and we'd all head over and join in those legendary games of cricket. Stacky Rec was also where I almost lost the fingers of my right hand when I was nine. The ball had sailed over into the rubble of the old changing rooms at the far end. As I bent to pick it up I slipped and sliced my hand open on the jagged edge of an old broken sink. I looked down to see a gaping wound across my palm and my fingers flapping around beneath it. Luckily my brother was there. He held my hand together and we made our way to the ambulance station which, fortunately for me, was just over the railway embankment. My hand was sewn back together and I got five packets of Panini football stickers to cheer me up. Result.

THE GAME......

The last game. The Stacky Rec we played on this day was very different. Gone were the bricks, cinders and sand. The pitch has been developed over the years and was now level and lush green. I found out later that my friend's husband had popped down the night before to mow and prepare the pitch for our game. Thankyou Stephen Ashworth.

It's hard to put into words just how incredible this day turned out to be. Over fifty people came down to take part or spectate. They travelled from far and wide...London, Newcastle, Wolverhampton, Cheshire, The Wirral, Chester, Leeds. Old school friends, lads I'd grown up with, mates from my student days and several family members too. There were people there from the recovery homes I'd worked in and people who had followed the story and supported my travels on social media. Remember my mate Neil from America? Well he promised to make the last match and he did. A woman called Janet showed up and presented me with a family tree she'd been researching. Apparently we were cousins on my mums side. There was a wonderful energy and it was all very humbling.

The game itself was fantastic. It was brilliant seeing my big brother Jim back in action and my son Danny getting stuck in. Stacky lads were out in force too. Peter Murray, John Sweeney, Chris Duerden and Mark Walsh, all original Stacky Rec kids. Thirty of us took to the field in the end and the game was competitive from the start. No quarter was given. It would take a full ten minutes for the breakthrough to come. A wicked cross came in from the right and I put away the header. I couldn't miss. It was my first headed goal of the whole trip and only my third ever.

The tackles were ferocious and mostly illegal. There were some brilliant performances too. Samo, Dipak and Richard grafting hard in midfield, Sam and Arron dazzling out on the wings and our kid and Raj blocking everything for the opposition. We went 2-0 up but were pegged back to 2-1 by half-time. I swapped sides for the second half, but that didn't stop Walshy making it 3-1.

It was time for the fight back. The ball broke to Chris who calmly stroked it past the keeper to make it 3-2. Then a handball brought the chance for little Himani to bring us level from the spot. She was super cool. In front of the watching crowd, she strode up and belted it between the keeper's legs. The crowd went crazy! 3-3! Next goals the winner! …and what a goal it was too. After a frantic five minutes the ball squirmed out to the right wing. We couldn't stop the cross, and there was Clinton to power home a spectacular diving header - the very last goal of the 80 games was an absolute cracker.

The perfect way to end the journey. The circle was complete.

We said our goodbyes and everyone drifted away, some to home and others to join us in the pub. I took one last look back at the now deserted Stacky rec, and there, staring back at me, were the ghosts of my Dad, Frank Lord and us.

Game 41: India – *Keep your eye on the ball Raman! Up on the roof in Jaipur*

Game 42: India – *Amber Fort's and trips to Mars as people starve, Jaipur*

Game 43: River dance – *by the Ganges, street children in Varanasi*

Game 44: *Put your back into it son! Danny launches us back across the Ganges from Blackpool*

Game 45: India – *Hormonally hilarious – the dance of the mating birds, Darjeeling*

Game 46: India – *Phew! That was close! Avinav saves the ball from oblivion- half way down a mountain in Darjeeling*

Game 47: Nepal – *Jay R Dhamala was our star man – in student-ville, Kathmandu*

Game 48: Nepal – *How can you play so well in sliders? Little Buddha ran the show*

Game 49: Poland – *Geordie stags to the rescue-Krakow*

Game 50: Czech Republic – *Jolana and Natalia get stuck in on the streets of Brno*

Game 51: Czech Republic – *3-day wobble over. Where to next? Brno Station*

Game 52: Austria – *Paranoia was a lovely, polite, engaging chap. Vienna*

Game 53: Austria – *The skilful Magdolena weighs up her options. Ressel Park, Vienna*

Game 54: Austria – *an Englishman, a Slovakian a Pole and a Saudi Arabian walked into a square. Football unites again - St. Stephens, Vienna*

Game 55: Slovakia – *the perfect urban playing surface. On the boulevard with Jose, Alexandria and Alex – Old town Bratislava*

Game 56: Slovakia – *A game threatened to break out before that pesky red bus popped our joy - Old Town Bratislava*

Game 57: Hungary – *The Luvdust in full flight "I didn't sign up for this" - Budapest*

Game 58: Hungary – *"Keep it away from me!" Doctor Adrienne prescribes no shots- Budapest*

Game 59: Hungary – *"Quick! Sing a song about a floating ball" Budapest! The musical*

Game 60: Slovenia – *King of the Streets! Edin made Brian Blessed sound like a brownie*

Game 61: Slovenia – *The amazing Wan Ying takes it to the bridge - Ljubljana*

Game 62: Salzburg – *The only living boys in town. Luis, Lorenz and Robin cut through the tweed*

Game 64: Switzerland – *Goal! Playing second fiddle to Sergio in the bandstand- Zurich*

Game 63: Switzerland – *Our future in their hands? Some of Europe's brightest put their books down for an hour -ETH University, Zurich*

GAME 65: MEXICO – *Fittingly, the women gave the men a good pasting on Women Island-Playa Norte, Islas Mujeres*

GAME 66: ENGLAND – *Cousin Jim has a stormer at lush York Minster*

GAME 67: ICELAND – *FFFREEZING! Trying to stay upright on the Reykyavic ice-rink*

GAME 68: ICELAND – *Warming up for a cracking game with a cracking set of lads*

GAME 69: WALES – Big Doug and Holly playing rugby football on a porridge of a pitch

GAME 70: PANAMA – *Focus in the flora. Slumming it at Bijao Beach Resort.*

GAME 71: SCOTLAND – *Just for a moment they were teenagers again. Ash and Nirmal bring another battle to Stirling.*

GAME 72: SCOTLAND – *Kelpie approval and disapproval in Helix Park, Falkirk*

GAME 73: SCOTLAND – *"You're going the wrong way!" The kids head for the sea on the Isle of Cumbrae*

GAME 74: ISLE OF MAN – *Long Shadows and bouncy castles - Michelle* tares into another tackle in Ballaugh

GAME 75: ISLE OF MAN – *wrapped up in the game and in friendship- Caron, Douglas Promenade*

GAME 76: ISLE OF MAN – *Long grass, heat and biker boots. Thirsty work at the Creg-ny-baa*

GAME76: IRELAND – *Martha and the Puffins. Enjoying a pint of the black stuff with our 'fixer' Martha at the splendid Guiry's Bar- Foxford, County Mayo*

GAME 78: IRELAND – *Brazilian magic. The amazing Pedro reels away after belting one into my poor belly. Eyra Square, Galway*

GAME 79: ENGLAND – *Shooted and booted. Zoe's son Ben goes for goal. Clitheroe, Lancashire*

GAME 80: ENGLAND – *The Stacky Rec Massive, Lancashire*

...beyond my wildest dreams

THE LAST BIT

Nelson Mandela once said that 'everything seems impossible until its done". I followed his wise words and tried never to look too far ahead. It's like staring at a wall with a paint brush in your hand. The wall won't paint itself. Just get your head down, make a start and keep going. Sooner or later it will be done….and now it is done. 80 amazing games, across 97,000 miles, 35 countries and 6 continents…in the blink of any eye.

What started off as a reaction to the gluttony of modern football transfigured into an incredible dream. Not only did this journey help me rediscover my love of the beautiful game, but it confirmed what I had always suspected - that this world is packed full of loving, caring, friendly souls. People like Izrael in Uganda, Nelson in Costa Rica, Genna in Japan, Sine in New Zealand, Santosh in Darjeeling, Davy in Cambodia, Askell in Iceland and Sylvie in France. Yes, there is a powerful evil minority, but 7.9 billion people aren't at war or hurting one another, though you'd think so watching the news sometimes. The great majority of us are getting along just fine. Report that.

I'm often asked what my favourite game was, and I can honestly say all of them. From grumpy cat in Zanzibar, to the incredible Entebbe women's team; larger than life Edin in Ljubljana to the remarkable tuk-tuk drivers of Siem Reap. Every game threw up a new and wonderful story. The earth shaped ball connected people of all ages and from all walks of life right across the world. Why? Because deep down we all want the same things - friendship, family, love and belonging. The warmth and kindness I've been shown has been truly humbling, and I've been treated like a brother or a son wherever I've gone.

The game as we knew it at the top level has gone forever now. It's little more than a meat market. For the most part, player loyalty has been buried under a mountain of banknotes, whilst fans are fast becoming a silent voice in a peremptory worldwide product. I hear commentators saying the game has moved on…moved on where? Outside of improved fan safety, those in charge are standing silent as football's heart bleeds dry . Apart from the rare Leicester City anomaly, elite football is fast becoming predictable, pointless and open to the highest bidder, however sketchy they may be. Fit and proper persons tests my arse. Manchester City have just won an historic treble with an outstanding team of superstars coached by a remarkable manager, but funded to the tune of billions by a regime where flogging and stoning are still legal forms of judicial punishment. The UAE government restricts human rights to the point where, according to the Human Freedom Index 2022, it was ranked 153 worldwide in terms of allowing personal freedom i.e. close to being among the worst 10 countries in the world in this regard. It's a long way from the raucous untainted passion of Maine Road, and the glory days of Bell, Marsh and Summerbee. Of course teams need investment, and God knows those City fans have been through the ringer down the years, but how did it get to the point where such blatant human rights abusers can just waltz into our precious game and change its landscape?

Like most life-long footy supporters, I have a home cinema inside my head which I can set rolling anytime. Its there that I find those black and white images of the mesmeric poetry of the young Georgie Best, Pele and Eusabio; the majestic strength, skill and brains of Beresi, Beckenbauer and Moore; the glorious midfield mastery of Xavi, Iniesta, Gerrard, Pirlo and Modric; that goal from Van Basten, that turn from Bergkamp and the absolute genius and blessing that is Lionel Messi…and on and on and on. That's the game to me, not these parasitic sports washing scoundrels reducing it to nothing more than a commodity. This really is a serious time for football. A fight for its very soul.

All hope is not lost though. The way fans here demonstrated so vociferously against the proposed super league was heart-warming, and they were listened to. In 2021, in the wake of the super league debacle and the demise of Bury FC , Tracey Crouch MP published the 162-page fan led review of football governance in this country. It calls for a football regulator, and has the noble intentions of placing 'fans squarely at the heart of decision-making' and addressing unsustainable financial practices. Action needs to be taken quickly before more of our precious clubs go under whilst the unfettered elite sail away into the sunset.

As for us lot…well, from what I have seen, we have a choice. We can view our big, beautiful diverse world through the narrow prism of fear and suspicion, or we can free our hearts. I have been reminded, time and again on this journey, that we each have a huge reservoir of love inside us. All we have to do is turn on the tap. I've bathed in that love for the past six years and its wonderful stuff. Let it flow.

I hope you've enjoyed the journey.

Steve

THANK YOU

I want to thank all the incredible people who made this journey what it is, and that includes *ten bollocks* and taxi drivers! All those who made me feel at home in their countries, all who played the games, friends and family who have travelled with me and supported me, Brodders, Mick, Neil and Win Yang for their written contributions, those who crowd funded me to get to Africa, friends I stayed with overseas, all those who supported me through social media for the past six years, all those who came down for the last game, Neil again for '*the earth shaped ball*", Tony for his encouragement and for '*incongruent*', Matthew for his proof reading and guidance, Michael for the footballs, big Sean for helping me get this thing started, my brother Jim, Mum, Auntie Ann, Honey, my Gilma and my beautiful, strong and valiant son Daniel. Thankyou eternally Tash. I see you now in the fields I walk, with Honey 'round your feet, and I see my life within your eyes as you're looking back at me.

Printed in Great Britain
by Amazon

34379341R00235